Aesthetic Injustice

Aesthetic Injustice

DOMINIC McIVER LOPES

Great Clarendon Street, Oxford, OX2 6DP,
United Kingdom

Oxford University Press is a department of the University of Oxford.
It furthers the University's objective of excellence in research, scholarship,
and education by publishing worldwide. Oxford is a registered trade mark of
Oxford University Press in the UK and in certain other countries

© Dominic McIver Lopes 2024

The moral rights of the author have been asserted

All rights reserved. No part of this publication may be reproduced, stored in
a retrieval system, or transmitted, in any form or by any means, without the
prior permission in writing of Oxford University Press, or as expressly permitted
by law, by licence or under terms agreed with the appropriate reprographics
rights organization. Enquiries concerning reproduction outside the scope of the
above should be sent to the Rights Department, Oxford University Press, at the
address above

You must not circulate this work in any other form
and you must impose this same condition on any acquirer

Published in the United States of America by Oxford University Press
198 Madison Avenue, New York, NY 10016, United States of America

British Library Cataloguing in Publication Data

Data available

Library of Congress Control Number: 2024941186

ISBN 978-0-19-893098-3

DOI: 10.1093/oso/9780198930983.001.0001

Printed and bound by
CPI Group (UK) Ltd, Croydon, CR0 4YY

For Noël Carroll and Kendall Walton, fox and hedgehog

Contents

Preface	ix
Acknowledgements	xiii

PART I

1. From Weaponized Aesthetics to Aesthetic Injustice	3
2. Cosmopolitanism, Culture, and Aesthetic Culture	23
3. The Aesthetic Capacities	34
4. The Cosmopolitan Interests	56

PART II

5. Aesthetic Appropriation	81
6. Beauty Ideals and Ideologies	103
7. Outlier Aesthetics	125
8. Identity Aesthetics	139

Afterword	161
References	165
Index	179

Preface

Contrast the glittering palette used to decorate rickshaws on the streets of Kochi, the phlegmatic angst of Nordic noir, the taut ovoids of Kwakwaka'wakw carving, or the *kawaii* invasion of parts of Tokyo. Not all culture is aesthetic culture, but it is hard to imagine any well-established social group lacking an aesthetic. The minute outsiders detect a language, religion, manners, or politics, they are apt to look further, for an aesthetic. Meanwhile, insiders are apt to assign high value to their shared aesthetic, sometimes regarding threats to it as tantamount to genocide. UNESCO defines culture partly in aesthetic terms. International conventions and treaties protect aesthetic culture under the heading of "cultural property." In sum, cultural groups differ aesthetically, and each group's aesthetic matters to it. None of this is news to you. Stroll across any city that has drawn its population from around the globe and aesthetic diversity is plain to see.

None of this is news for philosophical aesthetics either, but the field is only beginning to contend in a studied and systematic way with the role of aesthetic diversity in theorizing (Lopes et al. 2024: 18–23). Only now are we seriously asking and answering the question, what does the fact of aesthetic diversity mean for how we conduct our inquiries as philosophers?

This book offers one response to the question—a response that is distinct from but complements three other responses.

To begin with, at the very least, the fact of aesthetic diversity should transform our diet of examples. Aesthetics has for too long subsisted on a Wonderbread diet, shunning fare from around the globe and from a range of socio-economic groups. To tell an anecdote—and exact my revenge—Referee Number 2 once gave as a reason for rejecting a paper of mine its use of Kālidāsa's *Abhijñānaśākuntalam* as one of its main examples. "Too obscure," they said. Obscure to whom? Not knowing that Shakespeare might aptly be called the English Kālidāsa is one thing; the lack of curiosity is something else. Expanding our diet of examples has at least three benefits. We acknowledge the fact of aesthetic diversity, we make up in a small way for the parochialism of past writing, and we protect ourselves from generalizing from a too small sample set.

Aesthetic diversity should also prod us to rethink what appears to be a strong impulse to vindicate a uniform standard of aesthetic evaluation. Some of the impulse arguably stems from colonialism. Matthew Arnold wrote in *Celtic Literature* that "My brother Saxons have, as is well known, a terrible way with them of wanting to improve everything but themselves off the face of the earth" (1891: 11). If "improvement" implies deprecating what is deemed unworthy, then there must be an evaluative standard that applies to products of all aesthetic cultures, and that standard presumably rates Shakespeare ahead of Kālidāsa and Yr Hengerdd.

The first step in rethinking the universalist impulse is to daylight its origins. This project is well under way, thanks to pioneering work in feminist aesthetics and, subsequently, black aesthetics (esp. Hein and Korsmeyer 1993, Brand and Korsmeyer 1995, Taylor 2016; see also Lopes et al. 2024: 10–17). This work unmasks the pretension of work in philosophy that purports to adopt a neutral perspective when it has completely insulated itself from the aesthetic and artistic endeavours of otherwise marginalized groups of people.

The next step is to craft and to consider adopting accounts of aesthetic value or evaluation on which there are plural standards of aesthetic evaluation. This project is also under way. Some recent theories of aesthetic value set out to explain why there are plural standards of aesthetic value (esp. Lopes 2018b, Matthen 2017, Matthen 2018a, Lopes et al. 2024: chs. 1–2). Some articulate what we might gain from there being a plurality of standards. Among these are, for example, the benefits of being able to explore our aesthetically diverse world and its denizens (Rings 2019, Lopes, Nanay, and Riggle 2022: ch. 3, Lopes et al. 2024: ch. 3).

We asked what philosophy should do as it takes seriously the fact of aesthetic diversity. It should expand its diet of examples, and it should confront the reactionary stances of those who recoil from aesthetic diversity, replacing them with diversity-friendly stances.

A third imperative: welcome all traditions of philosophical aesthetics—including non-Euro traditions (Higgins 2017). (In this book, "Euro" refers to European cultures and their descendants around the world.) We have just seen that philosophers should craft theories that explain aesthetic diversity—that have as much to say about Kochi rickshaws as

Nordic noir. At the same time, philosophers should attend as much to the texts in aesthetics that were written with an eye to Kochi rickshaws as to Nordic noir. Work done in aesthetics with an eye to Kochi rickshaws might—though it need not—help us to craft theories that have as much to say about Kochi rickshaws as Nordic noir. Equally, work done in aesthetics with an eye to Kochi rickshaws might shed light on Nordic noir. People do not always have an adequate understanding of their own aesthetic (Lopes 2018a: chs. 1–2). Again, dialogue between Euro and non-Euro history of aesthetics is in its early stages (e.g. on South Asia, see Higgins 2007, Chakrabarti 2016, Lopes 2019, Lawson and Lopes in press; on East Asia, see Harold 2016, Hutton and Harold 2016, Hutton 2023, Lopes and Zappulli MS).

All these are good responses to the question of what the fact of aesthetic diversity means for how we should conduct philosophical inquiry. They complement each other in the sense that, in pursuing any one of them, it is likely to be useful to pursue the others. This book offers a fourth response.

Its response builds on *Beyond Art* (Lopes 2014) and *Being for Beauty: Aesthetic Agency and Value* (Lopes 2018b). Indeed, it completes what amounts to a trilogy. The trilogy's first two instalments represent the arts and our aesthetic endeavours as inherently sites of diversity, specifically because they are social practices (see also Lopes et al. 2024: ch. 2). Very roughly put, a social practice is a pattern of behaviour in a population that is due to shared norms or policies. In the first instance, the norms or policies regulate the behaviour of members of the population in their encounters with one another. Sometimes, though, a social practice includes policies that determine how a group interacts with other groups. That is, the policies regulate contact between groups. *Beyond Art* and *Being for Beauty* provide accounts of the norms of artistic and aesthetic social practices that regulate behaviour within those practices. Neither book focuses on policies to regulate contact between groups.

A world of aesthetic diversity—a world at home to *kawaii* streetwear and Kwakwaka'wakw carving—need not, as a matter of logic, have policies to regulate intergroup contact. Groups with different aesthetics might, after all, keep their distance from one another. Obviously, though, ours happens to be a world where aesthetically diverse groups are in contact with one another. Very often the contact is close and

xii PREFACE

sustained: aesthetically diverse groups inhabit the same real or virtual spaces and compete for some of the same resources. In our world of aesthetic diversity, policies regulating intergroup relations are unavoidable.

Therefore, we face the question of what policies should regulate contact between aesthetic groups. In this book, considerations of justice include those that determine what policies should regulate contact between groups. The policies are unjust if they are ones that a group should not have. We face the question of what policies regulating contact between aesthetic groups are unjust.

The fourth response to the question of how we should conduct philosophical inquiry in light of aesthetic diversity is to seek a theory of justice with respect to the policies regulating interactions between aesthetically diverse groups.

This book offers such a theory, the cosmopolitan theory. The theory is inspired by the main lessons of *Beyond Art* and *Being for Beauty*: the arts and our aesthetic endeavours are sites of diversity because they are social practices. Building upon this starting point, the theory proposes that we have an interest in aesthetic diversity and that we have an interest in the integrity of the social practices in which we live our aesthetic lives. Policies are unjust if they undercut one or both of these interests.

That only roughly describes the cosmopolitan theory, you need the details, and they are coming in the chapters that follow. For now, the task was merely to introduce how this book responds to aesthetic diversity by building on *Beyond Art* and *Being for Beauty*. Part I below articulates the cosmopolitan theory. Part II makes a case for the theory by applying it to some scenarios of aesthetic injustice.

D. M. L.
Vancouver, Canada
January 2024

Acknowledgements

This book went to press just weeks after Peter Momtchiloff stepped down as the philosophy editor at the UK division of Oxford University Press. Starting with my first book, *Understanding Pictures*, in 1996, Peter brought out what I consider to be my five most important books. Too little do we acknowledge the good will and talent of those who work, behind the scenes, to shape our careers and indeed our vision as scholars. Without Peter's wide knowledge of the discipline, his advice about audience and impact, and his unstinting support, my work would not have developed as it did. Thank you, Peter.

A sequel to *Beyond Art* and *Being for Beauty* was hardly inevitable. I hesitated to take on a project that crosses into territory that is not well known in aesthetics. Therefore, my deepest thanks to all those who encouraged me to forge ahead.

Scott Anderson, Roberta Ballarin, Kim Brownlee, Anthony Cross, Anne Eaton, Micah Favel, Rachel Fraser, Jonathan Gingerich, Robbie Kubala, Joshua Landy, Tara Mayer, Bence Nanay, Pierre-François Noppen, Phyllis Pearson, Brian Soucek, Chris Stephens, Nathan Te Bokkel, Emily Tilton, and Ying Yao read all or some of the first draft. That draft was flawed in all kinds of ways, and I am extremely grateful to have been able to rely on the insight, good judgement, and patience of so many friends as I rewrote it. The same goes for audiences at the 2019 American Society for Aesthetics Rocky Mountain Division, the 2021 joint meeting of the Wiener Gesellschaft für Interkulturelle Philosophie and the Allgemeinen Gesellschaft für Interkulturelle Philosophie, Bilkent University, Boston University, King's College London, Nanjing University, Nankai University, Peking University, Queen's University, Sichuan University, the University of Illinois Chicago, and the University of Saskatchewan.

I can never say too much about how fortunate I have been in the feedback I have received from OUP's referees (Referee Number 2 brutalizes only my journal submissions). To this book's three anonymous

xiv ACKNOWLEDGEMENTS

referees: thank you for helping me to whip the final version into shape. A special thanks to Referee B, who shared an exceptionally acute analysis and critique of the book. The best reassurance can lie in knowing that a line of thought is provocative and fruitful, rather than merely correct.

Samantha Matherne, Mohan Matthen, and Bence Nanay spurred my thinking about aesthetic culture as we worked together on *The Geography of Taste*. Bence Nanay and Nick Riggle spurred my thinking about interests in aesthetic diversity as we worked together on *Aesthetic Life and Why It Matters*. My contributions to those books complement what I have to say here.

I owe a special debt to the late Anita Silvers. In 1997, I published a paper on blind people's tactile pictures and what they tell us about depiction, perception, and the individuation of the arts. Soon after that, Anita invited me to the Banff Centre for the Arts to speak at a workshop on disability and the arts. At the time, she was beginning to do some of the work on disability and justice that informed my thinking in Chapter 7, and I now realize that she saw my 1997 work as connecting with her interest in disability rights. She was prescient, and I was slow, but I know that she would have been pleased that I got there eventually.

My thanks to the Social Sciences and Humanities Research Council of Canada for funding in support of this project and to the University of British Columbia for a sabbatical in 2020–1, during which I wrote the initial draft of the book.

The year 2020–1 was the height of the coronavirus pandemic. Writing is hard enough without the stress and worry of a global health emergency. I am grateful to the crew of MV Nicomekl for escapes to socially distanced anchorages for bouts of intense writing, interspersed with hikes in the forest and walks on the beach.

When locked down in the West End of Vancouver, I worked with a view across the water to the site of what was the village of Senáḵw. Given the content of this book, I am especially grateful to acknowledge the privilege of being able to practice my vocation on unceded, traditional territory of the Sḵwx̱wú7mesh Úxwumixw.

As I wrote this book, it became clear to me that I should express a final debt of gratitude—a more personal one. My family hails from the *concelho* or *taluka* of Bardez, along the Konkan Coast of India, and from Na h-Eileanan Siar, off the northwest coast of Scotland. Growing up in Scotland and then Canada, I learned that I was different from most people around me and also from most brown people around me, and these differences were going to be issues for me (and them). Yet I never regarded it as a burden to have had the question "who am I?" pressed upon me. On the contrary, it has been a gift. Native speakers of a language miss something in being unable to perceive the music of their own accents. I cannot help but suspect that both the cosmopolitanism in this book and the minimal conception of culture that opens onto the conception of identity in Chapter 8 spring from what I have learned about the best way for me to think about myself as a product, indeed an embodiment, of cross-cultural contact.

Excerpt from "The Importance of Elsewhere" from *The Complete Poems of Philip Larkin*, ed. Archie Burnett. Copyright © 2012 by The Estate of Philip Larkin. Introduction copyright © 2012 by Archie Burnett. Reprinted by permission of Farrar, Straus and Giroux and Faber and Faber Ltd. All Rights Reserved.

... since it was not home,
Strangeness made sense. The salt rebuff of speech,
Insisting so on difference, made me welcome

Philip Larkin

Tìr gun teanga, tìr gun anam.

PART I

1

From Weaponized Aesthetics to Aesthetic Injustice

A just society is well ordered. Put another way, justice is goodness in relatively large-scale social arrangements. Put in terms of reasons rather than goodness, those relatively large-scale social arrangements are just that we have reason to implement. Correspondingly, injustice is badness in relatively large-scale social arrangements: they are ones that we have reason not to put in place. So articulated, concepts of justice and injustice are ancient and widespread, but some concepts of some specific varieties of injustice have taken hold only recently and only in some societies. After all, unjust social arrangements tend to persist when they make it hard for people to conceptualize what makes them unjust. For example, the concept of racial injustice is a product of a long and arduous struggle, part of which was a struggle to overcome thinking that obscured the injustice of racism. The reality of racial injustice antedates our capacity to see it, with full clarity, for the injustice that it is. We should expect that we will continue to expand the repertoire of concepts by means of which we bring existing injustices into view, and we should hope for the expansion to continue until no stone is left unturned. What is about to be dubbed "aesthetic injustice" has not been fully recognized. In order to bring it into view, this book introduces and then defends a theory of aesthetic injustice.

The Cosmopolitan Theory

According to the cosmopolitan theory of aesthetic injustice:

> a relatively large-scale social arrangement is aesthetically unjust when and only when, and because, the arrangement is part of an aesthetic

Aesthetic Injustice. Dominic McIver Lopes, Oxford University Press. © Dominic McIver Lopes 2024.
DOI: 10.1093/oso/9780198930983.003.0001

4   AESTHETIC INJUSTICE

culture that harms people with a different aesthetic culture in their capacities as aesthetic agents and thereby subverts justice-relevant interests in the value diversity and social autonomy of aesthetic cultures.

This section begins to unpack the main components of the theory, raising some questions given more detailed answers in subsequent chapters. The next section contrasts aesthetic injustice with a more familiar phenomenon that will be called "weaponized aesthetics." Some cases are then presented where we can begin to see how aesthetic injustice and weaponized aesthetics interact. Taken together, the chapter's first three sections make a start at articulating the theory, and the rest of Part I fills in necessary details. The chapter closes with an outline of the argument, given in Part II, for the cosmopolitan theory.

Start with the main components of the cosmopolitan theory.

On the left-hand side of the biconditional, we see that aesthetic injustice is a property of relatively large-scale social arrangements. These are the social structures that equip relatively large groups of people to live together. Included in them are norms and expectations, habits, policies, institutions, markets, legal regimes, representational and conceptual practices, and physical infrastructures.

These social arrangements are obviously not limited to states. In political philosophy, justice and injustice are taken to be properties of states and their doings, but the cosmopolitan theory brooks no such limitation. States do intervene in aesthetic life, and the interventions matter, as we shall see. Yet some of the most consequential sites of aesthetic injustice are non-governmental—they include arrangements of ethnic groups, educational institutions at every level, arts organizations, clubs, and businesses. An aesthetic injustice is a deficiency in social arrangements at any relatively large scale.

From this it follows that aesthetic injustice is not in the first instance a property of individual acts. An act is aesthetically unjust only derivatively, when it is part of a pattern of transactions among many agents.

On the right-hand side of the biconditional, we see first that aesthetically unjust social arrangements must impact people in some of their capacities as aesthetic agents. Agents perform acts through the exercise of various capacities that they have. Aesthetic agents perform aesthetic acts, where aesthetic acts are acts motivated by attributions of aesthetic values. Having judged that a Brìghde Chaimbeul recording is quirky yet thoughtful, I play it for a friend. Or, having judged that an old Breton tune is not what it seems, Chaimbeul gives it the quirky yet thoughtful rendition. A musical performance is an aesthetic act, and so is listening to it. The one calls upon capacities for performing music; the other calls upon appreciative capacities.

This intuitive portrait of aesthetic agency is enough to get started, but the cosmopolitan theory will require more detailed answers to the following questions. What, precisely, is an aesthetic act? How do aesthetic values figure in aesthetic acts? What capacities undergird aesthetic acts? Chapter 3 tackles these questions.

As stated above, the cosmopolitan theory implies that there are aesthetic cultures. Chaimbeul performs within the context of an aesthetic culture that is not the same as that in which Stevie Wonder performs. Other aesthetic cultures: ASL poetry, Korean television, Shetland Sheepdog breeding, new world wine making, old world wine making, image memes, some philosophical writing and scientific illustration, gardening, Go but not crazy eights, abstract expressionist painting but also house painting. Chapter 2 supplies a theory of aesthetic culture.

Agents, exercising their capacities, perform aesthetic acts in the context of aesthetic cultures. Some of the acts that agents perform in the context of an aesthetic culture have an impact on the capacity of agents to act in other aesthetic cultures. Chaimbeul's borrowing might energize the Breton traditional music scene, it might undercut it, it might send it in a new direction, or it might inhibit its taking a new turn. The impact of what is done by people with one culture on people with another culture does not happen in a vacuum, however. Relatively large-scale social arrangements shape the practices in an aesthetic culture, such as Chaimbeul's, that impact the practice of another, such as the Breton traditional music scene. Notice how some threads are pulling together. In aesthetic injustice, relatively large-scale social arrangements allow for practices in an aesthetic culture that harm those with a different aesthetic culture in some of their capacities as aesthetic agents. Aesthetic injustice is a deficiency in social arrangements: the arrangements fail to protect people with some aesthetic cultures against harm caused by the acts of people with different aesthetic cultures.

6 AESTHETIC INJUSTICE

Not all harms are unjust, and the same goes for harms to people in their capacities to act aesthetically. When Sheringham's Seaside Gin sells out at the shops, gin lovers lose opportunities to taste it, and that is a harm to them in their capacity as aesthetic appreciators, but it is hardly unjust. Likewise, the University of British Columbia's prohibition on faculty, staff, and students planting gardens on the Main Mall is not unjust, although the policy harms members of the university community by blocking their opportunities to exercise their capacities in horticultural aesthetics. To be harmed is to be made worse off, but to be made worse off is not necessarily to be put in a bad position, let alone to be wronged. More is needed for a complete theory of aesthetic injustice.

The further requirement is that harms to people in their aesthetic capacities subvert cosmopolitan interests in the value diversity and social autonomy of aesthetic cultures. Since social arrangements that harm people in their capacities as aesthetic agents are not by themselves unjust, what makes them unjust is that they subvert the two cosmopolitan interests. Chapters 3 and 4 specify the content of the interests, explaining why they are served by capacities for aesthetic agency and why they are interests of justice. For now, however, it would be good to have a rough and ready working conception of the two interests.

One cosmopolitan interest is an interest in the value diversity of aesthetic cultures. There are many aesthetic cultures—ASL poetry, Korean television, Shetland Sheepdog breeding, new world wine making, old world wine making, image memes, some philosophical writing and scientific illustration, gardening, Go but not crazy eights, abstract expressionist painting but also house painting. The cosmopolitan theory claims that we all have an interest in there being a diverse range of aesthetic cultures.

The theory also claims that we have an interest in the social autonomy of aesthetic cultures. This is not an interest in individual autonomy in a social context; rather, it is an interest in group-level autonomy. Put metaphorically, it is an interest in each aesthetic culture having its destiny in the hands of its own members. The task will be to articulate the interest literally and in enough detail that appeals to it can shed light on why some harmful social arrangements are unjust. Performing the task is going to rely on prep work done in the next three chapters.

In roughly sketching the main components of the cosmopolitan theory of aesthetic injustice, this section raised some questions that get answers in the remaining chapters of Part I. A word about what has not been done. Nothing has been said to make the case for the cosmopolitan theory: no argument has been given that we do indeed have interests in the value diversity and social autonomy of aesthetic cultures. The rough sketch is not meant to persuade anyone of the reality of aesthetic injustice; it merely begins to characterize a phenomenon for whose reality an argument might be given.

Weaponized Aesthetics

Aesthetic injustice, as it is understood on the cosmopolitan theory, contrasts with a well-studied phenomenon that is aptly called "weaponized aesthetics." The contrast is worth developing for two reasons. To begin with, drawing the contrast helps to bring out what is distinctive about aesthetic injustice. More importantly, the argument for the cosmopolitan theory will exploit interactions between aesthetic injustice and weaponized aesthetics.

In weaponized aesthetics, elements of aesthetic culture are deployed as instruments of social injustice. To make sense of the phenomenon, we first need a model of social injustice and its mechanisms, then, secondly, a rough inventory of the relevant elements of aesthetic culture, and, thirdly, an understanding of how those elements figure as instruments of social injustice.

First off, according to the standard model, social injustice consists in a social hierarchy where members of subordinated groups suffer interlocked harms, as members of those groups, with respect to multiple morally significant dimensions of well-being (e.g. Young 1990). Note that, in situations of social injustice, individuals are harmed as members of groups. That is, their membership in a group is a significant factor in an explanation of the harm. Harms to *Zainichi*—people with Korean origins living in Japan—play no part in social injustice unless they are harmed in large part because they are *Zainichi*. In addition, the harms must make them worse off with respect to multiple dimensions of their well-being— political participation, educational attainment, employment prospects,

8 AESTHETIC INJUSTICE

health, housing, and personal safety, for example. Moreover, the harms are interlocked. For example, inadequate health care might hinder educational attainment and hence employment prospects, which in turn hinders access to health care. Finally, not all dimensions of well-being are ones where there are harms that figure in social injustice: something more is needed to close the gap between harm and injustice. On the standard model, the relevant dimensions of well-being (such as those listed above) are morally significant. Moral significance is, of course, a matter of debate in philosophy. For the purpose of modelling social injustice, take morality to be what prescribes the treatment that we owe others in exchange for the right to demand the same treatment from them.

The standard model of social injustice pairs with a standard model of the mechanisms that implement it. Social injustice cuts against many immediately pressing and morally weighty interests of members of subordinated groups—and against the ultimate interests of members of all groups. Hence, it is likely to persist only through violent coercion or through a self-sustaining system in which it shapes all kinds of social practices, making it the case that they sustain it in turn. Elements of aesthetic culture are not good instruments of violent coercion, so set that mechanism aside. The self-sustaining systems that ensure the persistence of many socially unjust arrangements employ social positions. A social position is a loose, dynamic, and contextually variant agglomeration of norms for how to treat members of a group, given expectations about how members of the group think and behave. The expectations and norms comprising social positions are encoded in expressive practices: the practices shape how people think about and hence behave towards members of groups. Social positions can stem from and compound generate social injustice.

Philosophers have recently argued that epistemic and affective practices stem from and compound social injustice via social positioning (e.g. Fricker 2007, Arina, Gen, and Prinz 2024, Archer and Matheson forthcoming,). Likewise, elements of aesthetic culture can be weaponized: they stem from and compound social injustice through social positioning—through shaping how people think and hence behave towards members of groups (for a survey, see James 2013; for references, see Zheng and Stear 2023).

Task number one in making sense of weaponized aesthetics was to supply a model of social injustice and its mechanisms. The standard model helps with the second and third tasks, which were to roughly inventory the weaponized elements of aesthetic culture and to give an account of how the elements can figure in social injustice.

The weaponized elements of aesthetic culture are expressive practices. Included among them are imaging and narrative practices (e.g. Eaton 2003, Harold 2006). Also included are performance practices, such as blackface (Zheng and Stear 2023). Some are practices of borrowing cultural resources (e.g. Matthes 2019). Some are practices of making, where the way of making has a social meaning. Some are practices of proposing or imposing aesthetic ideals (e.g. Widdows 2018). Often, weaponized elements of aesthetic culture deploy stereotypes, or what Patricia Hill Collins nicely calls "controlling images." As she explains, in the subordination of black women, "images of Black womanhood take on special meaning. Because the authority to define societal values is a major instrument of power, elite groups, in exercising power, manipulate ideas about Black womanhood" (2000: 69).

Stereotypes or controlling images deployed in expressive practices that are elements of aesthetic culture stem from and compound social injustice in two ways. In the first place, they licence the behaviours that harm people as members of subordinated groups. A stereotype of *Zainichi* as prone to criminality might license acts that discriminate against *Zainichi* in housing and employment, for example. In addition, it normalizes both the acts and the resulting interlocked harms by making them appear natural, expected, rational, or justified. For instance, the stereotype about *Zainichi* represents their poverty and isolation as the desserts of criminality, hence to be expected, not unfair. In sum, certain expressive practices that are elements of aesthetic culture exist because they compound social injustice, and social injustice exists in part due to the licensing and normalizing functions of those expressive practices.

Resources are now lined up and ready for assembly into a theory of weaponized aesthetics. Since the argument of the book juxtaposes aesthetic injustice and weaponized aesthetics, it will be handy to be able to refer back to a concise statement of the theory. Given the standard model of social injustice and its mechanisms:

a relatively large-scale social arrangement weaponizes aesthetics when and only when, and because, it includes expressive practices that are

10 AESTHETIC INJUSTICE

drawn from aesthetic culture and that stem from and compound social injustice by licensing or normalizing the acts and interlocked harms that constitute social injustice.

Identical phenomena cannot be closely connected in any interesting way. Aesthetic injustice is akin to but not identical to weaponized aesthetics. Weaponized aesthetics and aesthetic injustice share this in common: both are features of relatively large-scale social arrangements. Indeed, both are bad-making features of social arrangements. We have reason to act not to put either of them in place, if not to eradicate them both. Nonetheless, they differ in four important respects.

First, recall that social arrangements that harm people in their capacities as aesthetic agents are not by themselves unjust. By the same token, not all harms to people as members of groups are unjust. Something more is needed to close the gap between harm and injustice in aesthetic injustice and also in weaponized aesthetics.

On the standard model of social injustice, what closes the gap is that members of subordinated groups face harms, as members of those groups, with respect to interlocked and morally significant dimensions of well-being. The injustice of weaponized aesthetics is partly grounded in moral considerations: they close the gap between mere harm and injustice.

By contrast, the cosmopolitan theory of aesthetic injustice makes no mention of moral considerations. What closes the gap between harms and injustice is that the harms subvert interests in the value diversity and social autonomy of aesthetic cultures. One might argue that those interests are moral, for they generate rights that individuals have against others, and they generate obligations to treat others in the same way. In effect, one might argue that the interests belong in the same bucket as interests in political participation, education, employment, health, housing, and personal safety. However, this line of argument is not mandatory, and it is not, in fact, the line of argument pursued in this book. Chapter 4 makes a non-moral case that, if they exist, the two cosmopolitan interests are matters of justice.

So, weaponized aesthetics and aesthetic injustice close the gap between harms and injustice in different ways. Put another way, they appeal to different kinds of harms. This is the first point of contrast.

The first point of contrast suggests a second. The harms of weaponized aesthetics are harms with respect to such dimensions of well-being as political participation, education, employment, health, housing, and personal safety. These are not harms to people in their capacities as aesthetic agents; they are non-aesthetic harms brought about by aesthetic means. Notice that aesthetic injustice harms people precisely in their capacities as aesthetic agents. Whereas weaponized aesthetics deploys elements of aesthetic culture as instruments to produce non-aesthetic harms, aesthetic injustice yields aesthetic harms.

A third point of contrast concerns the mechanisms of weaponized aesthetics as against aesthetic injustice. Two mechanisms are constitutive of weaponized aesthetics. In weaponized aesthetics, stereotypes or controlling images license and normalize the acts and interlocked harms that are constitutive of social injustice. By contrast, the cosmopolitan theory of aesthetic injustice leaves it open what mechanisms harm people in their capacities as aesthetic agents. Some mechanisms are in play, of course, and they might include stereotypes or controlling images, but no mechanisms are constitutive of aesthetic injustice.

The fourth and final point of contrast will not play much of a role in the main argument for the cosmopolitan theory, but it carries great political weight, in the broad sense of "political" used here. Harms to people in their capacities as aesthetic agents pale in comparison to poverty, poor education, substandard health care, and blocked participation in civic life, let alone exposure to violence and threats of violence. In the world we happen to inhabit, weaponized aesthetics, which catalyzes outrageous harms to people in morally significant dimensions of their well-being, demands more urgent attention than does aesthetic injustice. Aesthetic injustice is relatively *petite bière*. Nonetheless, harms to people in their capacities as aesthetic agents do matter, and we should attend to them. That they do matter will be instructive.

Care must be taken not to overstate the contrast between weaponized aesthetics and aesthetic injustice. They are distinct, but they are not disjoint. They intersect and interact. Moreover, they do not simply happen to overlap and interact. As we shall see, aesthetically unjust social arrangements often track and work in tandem with weaponized aesthetics. The point of the cosmopolitan theory is not to supplant research on weaponized aesthetics. On the contrary, the argument for the

12 AESTHETIC INJUSTICE

cosmopolitan theory will imply that aesthetic injustice sometimes stems from and compounds weaponized aesthetics. The whole story is the story of both and how they interact. (No doubt further phenomena relate to both—see Fraser forthcoming.)

Dandelions, *Black Canoe*, and Nat

If aesthetic injustice is real, then it is nevertheless unfamiliar. The previous sections began to bring it to light first by articulating the main components of the cosmopolitan theory and then by contrasting it with weaponized aesthetics. In order to throw a bit more light on aesthetic injustice, this section sketches three scenarios where weaponized aesthetics and aesthetic injustice might seem to interact.

Keep two caveats in mind. To begin with, we want scenarios that are rich and concrete, and rich and concrete scenarios are going to concern individuals, but individual cases should illustrate patterns of behaviour in relatively large-scale social arrangements.

More importantly, the following three scenarios are not meant to pump up intuitions that aesthetic injustice exists or that the cosmopolitan theory is correct. This section is not an argument for the theory. It merely offers of glimpse of where the theory might apply.

Dandelions

A key episode in the young life of Pecola Breedlove, the protagonist of Toni Morrison's novel, *The Bluest Eye*, is a touchstone for thinking about gendered and racialized standards of personal beauty (e.g. Taylor 1999, John 2012: 196–197, Taylor 2016: 41–42).

In the lead up to the key episode, Morrison brings the central image of the book out into the open. She writes that:

> it had occurred to Pecola some time ago that if her eyes, those eyes that held the pictures, and knew the sights—if those eyes of hers were different, that is to say, beautiful, she herself would be different.... Each night, without fail, she prayed for blue eyes. (1970: 46)

FROM WEAPONIZED AESTHETICS TO AESTHETIC INJUSTICE   13

What happens in the key moment does not teach Pecola anything she does not already know. It had already occurred to her that to be beautiful she could no longer be who she is. She could no longer be black. And what happens next does not change what she wants. She already wants to be beautiful, hence to enjoy self-esteem and the esteem of others. Therefore, she wants to escape her black body. The logic of her desires, given what she believes about beauty, is unforgiving. She is "thrown, in this way, into the binding conviction that only a miracle could relieve her" (Morrison 1970: 46).

In the very next paragraph, Pecola is on her way to buy candy. The route is one she knows well. She admires the beauty of the dandelions growing from cracks in the sidewalk, and the cracks themselves, whose contours she had often felt beneath the wheels of her skates. We anticipate what will happen when she arrives at the store. The clerk first fails to see her and then betrays his disgust at her, shrinking from taking pennies from her hand. His distaste is not new to her either: "she has seen it lurking in the eyes of all white people" (Morrison 1970: 49). What happens next is new. Leaving the store, the shame ebbs, and Pecola tries to love the dandelions, but "they do not look at her." They are now ugly. She trips over a crack. Anger replaces the shame.

The familiar point is that Pecola is caught in the intersection of a feminine beauty ideal with a beauty ideal, connected with race in the United States, that stigmatizes her body as ugly. In *Perfect Me*, Heather Widdows (2018) identifies the feminine beauty ideal—be young, firm, and slim—that has now reached most corners of the globe, and she summarizes empirical studies of its costs. In attempting to conform with the ideal, women dedicate a great deal of time to cosmetic practices; they siphon financial resources into clothing, makeup, and hairdos; and they risk damaging their health through cosmetic surgery, dieting, and eating disorders. Failing to meet the standard has been shown to put women at a disadvantage in the workplace and public life, to dampen performance in education, and to deplete self-esteem. Race-based beauty standards compound Pecola's predicament. Benjamin Franklin notoriously argued that slavery should be abolished in the United States because the presence of black bodies would mar the unspoiled beauty of the new world (Mills 1997: 67). Pecola's predicament is that, being female, she must be beautiful, but, being black, she cannot be beautiful.

14 AESTHETIC INJUSTICE

Ideals of bodily beauty are obviously elements of aesthetic culture. Some aesthetic cultures include expressive practices that encode what any body should be like if it is to count as beautiful. Images of various kinds depict ideally beautiful bodies, and the stories people tell enumerate the benefits of beauty and the costs of ugliness. Beautiful bodies belong to happy and prosperous people, for example, whereas villains are often ugly.

In Morrison's telling, ideals of bodily beauty are weaponized to harm Pecola. The shopkeeper's reaction to Pecola's body is no disinterested aesthetic verdict. It is a disgust visceral enough to pervert his interaction with a mere child. It harms her by impeding the simple act of shopping, by crushing her self-esteem, by profoundly injuring her sense of self, and ultimately by inducing her to internalize his disgust. Moreover, his reaction, rooted in a racialized beauty ideal, both stems from and compounds racial injustice. The shopkeeper, in company with others, sees her as ugly because he sees her as black. In turn, his seeing her as ugly licenses him to treat her with disgust, and it naturalizes the disgust, making it seem to be a response to ugliness rather than mere phenotypic variation. Similar reactions on behalf of others limit Pecola's access to all kinds of morally significant necessities. The key episode in *The Bluest Eye* is a textbook case of weaponized aesthetics.

Perhaps it is more than that. Recall how the episode concludes. Leaving the store, Pecola tries to love the dandelions, but she can no longer see their beauty. She is harmed in her capacity to perceive beauty in the world. What once was beautiful, hence a comfort, even something as otherwise unremarkable as cracks in the pavement, now appears hostile. The dandelions "do not look at her," and she can no longer love them.

Pecola is harmed in her capacities as an aesthetic agent, and Morrison clearly regards the harm as momentous. However, the nature of the harm is couched in evocative metaphors, and Morrison simply takes it for granted that the harm matters. The cosmopolitan theory of aesthetic injustice offers a hypothesis. The harm to Pecola in her capacities as an aesthetic agent matters as much as it does because it subverts justice-relevant interests in the value diversity or social autonomy of aesthetic cultures. Is the hypothesis correct? Does it explain the significance that Morrison places on how the key episode concludes? Chapter 6 returns to these questions.

FROM WEAPONIZED AESTHETICS TO AESTHETIC INJUSTICE   15

All that is needed to motivate the search for a theory of aesthetic injustice—especially one that can complement the theory of weaponized aesthetics—is to feel the pull of these questions strongly enough to want answers. As already noted, Pecola's story is not an argument for the cosmopolitan theory. By offering a glimpse of what aesthetic injustice might look like, it motivates further efforts to articulate and defend the theory.

Black Canoe

The symbolic heart of the Chancery of the Canadian Embassy to the United States, across Pennsylvania Avenue from the National Gallery, is Bill Reid's monumental bronze, *The Spirit of Haida Gwaii, The Black Canoe* (1991). Reid, who is of Haida and Scots ancestry, was among the cadre of artists who strove with considerable success in the 1950s to resurrect west coast Indigenous traditions that had been suppressed for decades under a state policy of assimilation. *Black Canoe's* vocabulary of ovoids, S-forms, and U-forms emblazon its Haida roots, as does its iconography. The sculpture depicts a dugout canoe, crowded with mythic creatures who populate Haida life and thought, some in conflict, nevertheless paddling together, piloted by the trickster Raven, transporting the *kilstluui*, their leader, whose gaze is intent on the horizon.

However, *Black Canoe* is more than a tribute to a thriving Haida society. The political theorist James Tully reads it as additionally insisting that Indigenous societies not be viewed through a Euro lens—that they be viewed as interacting on an equal footing with others (1995: 21). What at one level represents Haida society is also, as Tully puts it, an "ecumenical symbol for the mutual recognition and affirmation of all cultures that respect other cultures and the earth" (1995: 21). For this reason, Canadians see *The Spirit of Haida Gwaii* as representing Canada in its aspiration to multiculturalism. Tully quotes Reid:

> Here we are at last, a long way from Haida Gwaii, not too sure where
> we are or where we're going, still squabbling and vying for position
> in the boat, but somehow managing to appear to be heading in some

16 AESTHETIC INJUSTICE

direction. At least the paddles are together, and the man in the middle seems to have some vision of what's to come. (Reid 1992: 15)

Sited in the Chancery, *Black Canoe* represents Canada to its powerful southern neighbour; a second casting, *Jade Canoe*, sets the tone for Vancouver International Airport; and an engraving of the sculpture was featured on the twenty dollar bill, the most circulated denomination in the country and the only one to feature an image of the sovereign (Nieguth and Rainey 2017: 96–101).

In 2019, speaking to a group of philosophers, another Haida artist, Michael Nicoll Yahgulanaas, expressed a concern about the national adulation of *The Spirit of Haida Gwaii*. Like Reid, Yahgulanaas is committed to bringing Haida aesthetic culture into dialogue with other aesthetic cultures. He is perhaps most famous as the inventor of Haida manga, which crosses the form line vocabulary and Haida stories with manga conventions. His best-selling *Flight of the Hummingbird* (2008) retells a Quechua parable with Haida-style illustrations. Nonetheless, during a discussion of cultural contact, Yahgulanaas remarked that the adoption of *The Spirit of Haida Gwaii* as a national symbol, particularly its widespread circulation on the banknote, threatens to set Haida aesthetic culture in amber. Another metaphor is perhaps more evocative. Canada's reception of the *Black Canoe* might induce what Anthony Appiah calls the "Medusa syndrome," where "what the state recognizes, it tends to turn to stone" (2005: 105).

Aesthetics can be weaponized in large-scale social arrangements that facilitate cultural appropriation. Sometimes, cultural appropriation involves the use of elements of an aesthetic culture in expressive practices that misrepresent, disrespect, or assimilate members of the culture. Practices of misrepresentation, disrespect, and assimilation serve to licence and normalize behaviours that yield the interlocked, morally significant harms constitutive of social injustice. They are part of a larger system of dispossession and disempowerment that blocks access to education, employment prospects, health, housing, and personal safety, in particular. Chapter 5 goes into the details.

Granted that cultural appropriation is a mode of weaponized aesthetics, the concern that Yahgulanaas expresses about the reception of *Black Canoe* seems not to be a concern about weaponized cultural appropriation. Reid's commission was undertaken at a time of growing sensitivity to any appearance of appropriative intent or effect. Protocols of consultation and permission were followed to the letter. The sculpture itself celebrates a cultural revival and an ideal of intercultural respect. It is hard to see how its making, display, or reception could play a part in any practice that misrepresents, disrespects, or assimilates and thereby perpetrates morally significant harms to members of the Haida Nation or other Indigenous groups.

Maybe Yahgulanaas is concerned about an aesthetic injustice. An aesthetic injustice is, in the first instance, a harm to people in their aesthetic capacities. Can there be a more vivid metaphor of such a harm than the Medusa syndrome? Yahgulanaas is saying that the national adulation of *Black Canoe* is an aesthetic paralytic. Moreover, he clearly regards the concern as serious. The cosmopolitan theory of aesthetic injustice offers a hypothesis: the harm of the Medusa syndrome is a matter of justice because it subverts interests in the value diversity or social autonomy of aesthetic cultures. Is the hypothesis correct? Does it explain why we should share Yahgulanaas's concern about the Medusa syndrome? Chapter 5 answers these questions.

To repeat, the aim is not to argue for the cosmopolitan theory by pumping intuitions about the reception of Reid's work. The aim is far more modest, to afford a glimpse of a possible instance of aesthetic injustice, one that we can flesh out in mounting the argument for the cosmopolitan theory in Part II.

Nat

In 1993, the psychologist John M. Kennedy published *Pictures to Touch*, pulling together nearly twenty years of research into the capacity of blind people to interpret and make drawings. In these drawings, raised lines correspond with the outlines of objects in pen and ink drawings. Kennedy showed that congenitally and early blind people recognize scenes depicted in silhouette and in three-dimensional space. He also found that, without previous exposure to images or any training in drawing, blind people make outline drawings much like those produced by sighted people. Albeit crude of execution, their drawings cover the full

18 AESTHETIC INJUSTICE

range of drawing systems deployed by the sighted, up to and including the use of perspective. These drawing systems are rapidly and spontaneously learned by blind adults in the same developmental trajectory as is followed by sighted children.

Pictures to Touch is more than a treatise in the psychology of picture perception. Some of Kennedy's subjects initially resisted the invitation to draw. A dogma about the essential visuality of drawing is part of folk thinking about images, and it is deeply entangled in a great deal of standard philosophical thinking since Locke (Lopes 1997). Most everyone, including most everyone who is blind, is convinced that drawing is an essentially visual capacity. All the same, Cal, Dee, Joan, Lys, May, Pat, Pau, Ray, and their peers got into their tasks in the lab, some with growing enthusiasm, and Kennedy occasionally drops his stance of scientific neutrality. Here he speaks of Nat:

> The talent grows even when denied. Nat was told by his teachers that he could not draw and it was not worth his while to try. Yet he drew many pictures in our research program, and one was picked for the May 1980 cover of *New Scientist*. The journal, appropriately enough, gave Nat the cover artist's fee for his drawing. To my knowledge, this makes Nat the first blind man in the history of publishing to be given the cover artist's fee for a magazine—a special moment for publishing, for the psychology of pictures, for the blind, and for Nat. (1993: 179)

Competence with pictures does not imply competence in the aesthetic possibilities that pictures afford, but there is no reason to doubt the aesthetic potential of tactile pictures (Hopkins 2000, Lopes 2002).

Among the targets of weaponized aesthetics are disabled people. Practices of making images and stories about them stem from, licence, and normalize patterns of discriminatory treatment that unjustly harm them in interlocked and morally significant dimensions of well-being. Chapter 7 goes into the details of recent scholarship.

No doubt Nat and his peers have endured the harms of weaponized aesthetics. At the same time, however, they have been harmed in their capacities as aesthetic agents: they have been deprived of opportunities to learn to draw. In addition, they were harmed in this way because they are blind. However, there is a gap between harm and injustice, even when a person is harmed as a member of a subordinated group. We need to close the gap. Being able to draw is not by itself a morally significant dimension of well-being (unlike being able to communicate with others). Perhaps, instead, a case can be made that the harms to the aesthetic capacities of Nat and his peers subvert interests in the value diversity and social autonomy of aesthetic cultures. Perhaps tactile drawings by blind people will have a distinctive aesthetic, and perhaps a practice of tactile drawing is a social practice whose destiny should be in the hands of the blind people who make the practice their own?

The cosmopolitan theory of aesthetic injustice hypothesizes that the harm to Nat and his peers in their capacities for aesthetic agency is a matter of justice because it subverts interests in the value diversity or social autonomy of aesthetic cultures. Is the hypothesis correct? Does it explain why we are right to regard the educational policies that closed the "visual art" studios to blind people as an injustice? Chapter 7 answers these questions as part of an argument for the cosmopolitan theory. That argument is not yet on the table, however.

The Main Argument

The first section of this chapter sketched the principal components of the cosmopolitan theory, the second section contrasted aesthetic injustice with weaponized aesthetics, and the third section presented some scenarios where aesthetic injustice might seem to interact with weaponized aesthetics. Together, the sections sketch the outlines of the theory. Chapters 2 to 4 fill in the details of the outline, and then the main argument is given in Part II. This section previews that argument.

A theory is above all an answer to a "what is … ?" question. For example, a theory of consciousness answers the question, what is consciousness? As this example illustrates, philosophers normally provide theories of phenomena with which we have prior familiarity—often concrete, hands-on familiarity. Having experienced consciousness, grappled with what counts as evidence, or worried about what we owe future generations, we craft theories of consciousness, knowledge, and moral obligation. Likewise, having noticed the role of expressive practices in social injustice, we craft a theory of weaponized aesthetics. In as much as we

20 AESTHETIC INJUSTICE

turn to theory to make sense of a phenomenon with which we are already familiar, it makes sense to seek a reflective equilibrium between prior experience and a theoretical representation of it. The theory should be true to prior experience, on the one hand. On the other hand, a good theory can give us reason to revise how we think about our prior experience.

The project of this book is unusual. Aesthetic injustice is an admittedly unfamiliar phenomenon, and the cosmopolitan theory is an instrument for bringing it to light. Therefore, the argument for the theory must be, in broad strokes, that it exposes a phenomenon that is real. Think of it this way. The theory is a description: it labels as "aesthetic injustice" any relatively large-scale social arrangement that harms people in their capacities as aesthetic agents and thereby subverts justice-relevant interests in the value diversity and social autonomy of aesthetic cultures. This statement is on a par with "the person who killed Roger Ackroyd." Its usefulness consists in picking out a phenomenon that exists as described.

In skeleton, the main argument for the cosmopolitan theory is that the theory earns its keep if it correctly describes a real phenomenon. The phenomenon is real. Ergo, the theory earns its keep.

The key premise is the claim that the phenomenon described as "aesthetic injustice" does in fact exist. Here is a strategy for proving the key premise. Unjust social arrangements cling to each other like burrs. Discriminatory housing policy keeps company with discriminatory employment practices and unfair access to health care, for example. Aesthetic injustice is no different. It is in cahoots with the usual suspects. So, we can borrow the detective's trick of locating it by tracing its known associates. Our three scenarios hint that aesthetic injustice tends to stem from and compound weaponized aesthetics. Each is congruent with and runs in the same direction as the other.

Part II implements the strategy. Aesthetics is weaponized through cultural appropriation, bodily beauty ideals, and inaccessible infrastructures for aesthetic culture. However, no picture of these instances of weaponized aesthetics is complete until we take into account how each spawns and is compounded by aesthetic injustice. Existing treatments of weaponized aesthetics are not incorrect, but they are not the whole story, either. We wise up to what we have been missing by acknowledging how aesthetic injustice stems from and compounds weaponized aesthetics.

Some of what we have been missing is likely to be considerations to take into account in crafting policy. No doubt it is very hard to see what policies should be adopted to foster more just social arrangements. Few or no policies are going to be effective in all circumstances, especially ones that obtain across a range of scales, where a range of different policy tools are apt to be effective. This book is not and cannot be a one-stop policy manual. For now, it is enough to identify the general considerations that can serve to narrow the range of policy options in a range of contexts. Some policy considerations come into sight only once we acknowledge how aesthetic injustice stems from and compounds weaponized aesthetics.

Restating the main argument: the cosmopolitan theory earns its keep if it correctly describes a real phenomenon. The phenomenon does exist as described, since it stems from and compounds weaponized aesthetics. We must appeal to the cosmopolitan theory in order to fully explain weaponized aesthetics and the remedies it requires. That is, to fully explain weaponized aesthetics and the remedies it requires, we must acknowledge justice-relevant interests in the value diversity and social autonomy of aesthetic cultures that are put into jeopardy by harms to agents in their aesthetic capacities. Ergo, the theory earns its keep.

Backup Argument: Error Theory

A backup argument is already under way. Our failure to notice aesthetic injustice cries out for an error theory. In the words of one anonymous commentator, "in this era of robust humanistic scholarship, one would expect that aesthetic injustice … has already been noticed and theorized by others." How could we miss its presence in our lives? Two points have already been made.

One casts doubt on the proposition that injustice is always apparent to those upon whom it has an impact. Many injustices persist because they disguise themselves. Time and again, we have failed to recognize injustices, even (especially) when we are their victims. No surprise that we have missed aesthetic injustice. No surprise that one might craft a theory to bring it into view.

A second point is implicit in the admission, made above, that weaponized aesthetics is a more serious problem than aesthetic injustice. Weaponized aesthetics involves harms to people with respect to morally significant dimensions of their well-being. For this reason, weaponized aesthetics tends to eclipse aesthetic injustice. Aesthetic injustice is easy to miss when it coincides with the morally egregious injustices of weaponized aesthetics.

An error theory explains why we have been mistaken about the nature of a phenomenon or why we have overlooked its existence in the first place. Having an error theory that explains why we have overlooked aesthetic injustice adds weight to the case for the cosmopolitan theory.

The remaining chapters of Part I unpack the cosmopolitan theory of aesthetic injustice by articulating the content of our interests in the value diversity and social autonomy of aesthetic cultures, by saying why the capacities that serve them are aesthetic, and by making a case that harms to those capacities would be matters of justice. Part II then argues that, so understood, aesthetic injustice exists as described by the cosmopolitan theory.

2

Cosmopolitanism, Culture, and Aesthetic Culture

The cosmopolitan theory of aesthetic injustice appeals to interests in aesthetic cultures. Unless cosmopolitanism and culture are empty concepts that contribute nothing of substance to the theory and the argument for it, we are going to need working theories of each.

Cosmopolitanism

Right off the bat, one might question whether the adjective "cosmopolitan" adds anything that can help articulate the cosmopolitan theory. So many claims and approaches have been called "cosmopolitan." Some are inconsistent with one another, some are consistent only because they tackle different topics, and not many cohere enough that their individual plausibility is boosted by taking them together. If the worry about aesthetic justice is that it is not a thing, then the reciprocal worry about cosmopolitanism is that it is too many things. The solution is to alight on a strain of cosmopolitan thought that sets us up to foreground interests that are matters of justice in aesthetic life.

Cosmopolitanism is one among several intellectual traditions that respond to a recognition that people come into contact with others who differ from them in ways that are significant or that pose a challenge (Scheffler 1999: 113, Waldron 2000: 323). This is the common thread that unifies the Euro tradition since the Stoics (Coulmas 1995, Nussbaum 1997, Kleingeld 1999, Kleingeld and Brown 2019, Nussbaum 2019). The same recognition animates Asian cosmopolitanism (Nandy 2000, Pollock 2000, Tagore 2008, Ivanhoe 2014, Ganeri 2017 on Bhattacharyya 2011 [1954]). In a nutshell, cosmopolitan interests are ones that come

Aesthetic Injustice. Dominic McIver Lopes, Oxford University Press. © Dominic McIver Lopes 2024.
DOI: 10.1093/oso/9780198930983.003.0002

24 AESTHETIC INJUSTICE

into play in circumstances of contact with cultural difference. That said, a concern with managing contact with cultural difference is hardly unique to cosmopolitans. The same concern spurs communitarian political theory and Kantian ethics, for example (see Chapter 4). Moreover, strains of cosmopolitanism tend to respond to the concern in a variety of ways.

With this in mind, the task is to tease out a strain of cosmopolitan thought that can help to articulate the cosmopolitan theory of aesthetic injustice. That strain has come to be called "cultural cosmopolitanism" (Kleingeld 1999: 515, Scheffler 1999: 111, Waldron 2000: 230, Kleingeld and Brown 2019). We can locate it by mapping various strains of cosmopolitanism around a pair of orthogonal distinctions.

One is a matter of scale, which runs from the personal to the political.

Cosmopolitan political philosophy confronts cultural difference by questioning the assumption that the state is the sole or principal regime of justice and by prioritizing global institutions that encompass the human community as a whole (Scheffler 1999: 112, Waldron 2000: 229–230, Kymlicka 2001a). So understood, cosmopolitanism opposes communitarianism, nationalism, and national liberalism, at least to the extent that, for each of these, some local community is the principal site of political allegiance. Some political cosmopolitans, most famously Kant, go so far as to advocate a global super-state (Kant 2006 [1795], Nussbaum 1996, Nussbaum 1997).

At the opposite extreme are strains of cosmopolitanism that treat cultural difference as a personal challenge to be met by cultivating traits of character that ensure a respectful engagement with others. Thus Ulf Hannerz defines cosmopolitanism as a "personal ability to make one's way into other cultures, through listening, looking, and reflecting" (1990: 239). The challenge is to elevate personal cosmopolitanism above the caricature of the shallow cultural tourist who eats *huevos rancheros* for breakfast, wears a Kashmiri shawl with Quechua silver in the afternoon, dabbles in classical Chinese philosophy, and spends the evening watching Nordic noir (Waldron 2000: 227).

A second distinction concerns the sources of cosmopolitan claims.

Many strains of cosmopolitanism ground claims concerning contact with cultural difference entirely in a vision of moral concern as extending to all humanity. Some say that such moral concern takes priority over partial concerns for members of one's local community (e.g. Herman 1997, Nussbaum 1997, Nussbaum 2019). Some prefer the weaker claim that moral allegiance to worldwide humanity is fundamental to any cosmopolitanism (e.g. Scheffler 1999). What might be called "moral cosmopolitanism" is a foundational commitment to moral concern with universal scope.

Alternatives to moral cosmopolitanism ground claims concerning contact with difference at least partly in reasons or commitments that are "rooted" or local (Appiah 2005: ch. 6, Appiah 2007, Kymlicka and Walker 2012, Matthes 2015, Ganeri 2017 on Bhattacharyya 2011 [1954]). These reasons or commitments need not be moral, and they need not carry universal scope. Thus, Iris Marion Young (1990) embraces what is arguably a rooted cosmopolitan account of city life. City dwellers share common problems and interests, but they do not belong to communities with shared final ends. Since they are "strangers, diverse and overlapping neighbors, social justice cannot issue from the institution of an Enlightenment universal public" (Young 1990: 240). Instead, they must address their common problems and interests each from the perspective of their own local setting.

Michael Rings's aesthetic cosmopolitanism is both personal and grounded in moral concern with universal scope. He proposes that aesthetic virtue is a cluster of character traits needed to undertake the "active, morally serious project of cultivating an authoritative appreciation for artworks or other cultural artefacts that are ... culturally unfamiliar to the appreciator, and doing so in a manner that is informed by a commitment to philosophical cosmopolitanism" (2019: 161). Here "philosophical cosmopolitanism" refers to a commitment to moral concern with universal scope. This commitment distinguishes genuine aesthetic cosmopolitans from shallow cultural tourists.

In sum, strains of cosmopolitanism range from the personal to the political; some are grounded entirely in moral concerns with universal scope, and some are "rooted," or grounded at least partly in local reasons. No doubt there is much to say in favour of each strain as one that we might sometimes have reason to adopt. The question here is which strain promises to advance thinking about aesthetic injustice in particular.

26 AESTHETIC INJUSTICE

The "cosmopolitan" in the cosmopolitan theory is a cultural cosmopolitanism—one that contrasts with Rings's aesthetic cosmopolitanism. It has four characteristic marks.

First, cultural cosmopolitanism is neither personal nor is it political in the narrow sense that politics concerns the state, whether national or global. On the contrary, it addresses arrangements of social life at any scale from the local community or association to global institutions. It is political only speaking broadly, in as much as it treats the state as one among many important arrangements of social life. It is personal only derivatively, in as much as it sees patterns of transactions among individuals as a function of their personal traits. *Cultural cosmopolitanism is markedly social.*

Second, also by contrast with Rings, cultural cosmopolitans ground their claims concerning contact with difference partly in local cultural reasons (Appiah 2005: ch. 6, Appiah 2007, Kymlicka and Walker 2012, Matthes 2015). In other words, the assumption is that cosmopolitan interests, which concern interactions across cultural boundaries, are sourced at least in part within those boundaries. Appeal must be made to more than transcultural moral concerns with universal scope. *Cultural cosmopolitanism is markedly rooted.*

This second mark of cultural cosmopolitanism implies a third. Jeremy Waldron expresses it succinctly: cosmopolitans treat cultures not as costume but rather as "intelligent and intelligible structures of reasoning" (2000: 242; see also Mehta 2000, Shelby 2005: 172–174, Scheffler 2007). Put more precisely, cultures provide their members with normative reasons to act and to know, and those reasons are not reducible to the fact that they are members of those cultures. Isaiah Berlin endorsed this when he rejected the idea that:

> one of the most compelling reasons, perhaps the most compelling, for holding a particular belief, pursuing a particular policy, serving a particular end, living a particular life, is that these ends, beliefs, policies, lives are ours. This is tantamount to saying that these rules or doctrines or principles should be followed not because they lead to virtue or happiness or justice or liberty ... or are good and right in themselves ... rather they are to be followed because these values are those of my group. (1997 [1979]: 591)

At most, the fact that a culture is ours gives us gives us additional and derivative reason to act or know. *Cultural cosmopolitanism is markedly normative.*

The fourth and final mark of cultural cosmopolitanism is its generally positive attitude towards cultural difference. Appiah writes that "we neither expect nor desire that every person or every society should converge on a single mode of life" (2007: xv). This is not quite right. Every person and every society should not converge on a single mode of life. Perhaps the reason is that cultural difference is good in and of itself; perhaps there are other reasons why we should promote diversity. At any rate, *cultural cosmopolitanism is markedly pro-diversity.*

As an aside, this mark of cultural cosmopolitanism does not imply a too rosy picture that was current in the long nineteenth century. The picture is painted in a famous passage from a 1788 essay by Christoph Martin Wieland:

> cosmopolitans... regard all the peoples of the earth as so many branches of a single family, and the universe as a state, of which, they ... are citizens, promoting together under the general laws of nature the perfection of the whole, while each in his own fashion is busy about his own well-being. (quoted and trans. Appiah 2007: xv)

On this view, what is good about each culture is its unique contribution to a perfect whole. Perhaps this is true, but likely not, and we need not incur the burden of establishing its truth as one to rely upon in building a cosmopolitan theory of aesthetic injustice.

Its being social, rooted, normative, and pro-diversity sets cultural cosmopolitanism apart from other strains of cosmopolitanism but also from an ethnocentrism or relativism that isolates people from one another in cultural enclaves.

Culture

Cosmopolitan interests are cultural interests ... but what is culture? Scholars have tendered a dizzying array of answers, sometimes insisting on them stridently, and there is nothing like enough consensus to invite

28   AESTHETIC INJUSTICE

deference (e.g. Swidler 1986, Kuper 1999, Sewell 1999, Appiah 2005: ch. 4, Arniel 2006, Baldwin et al. 2006, Phillips 2006). What is needed here is a minimal theory, one that smoothly applies to aesthetic culture.

For present purposes, no model of aesthetic culture can make it a monopoly of elites (Eagleton 2000). Walt Whitman warned that with the word "culture," "we find ourselves abruptly in close quarters with the enemy" (1871: 39). In its fighting sense, culture is "high culture." Activities by means of which elites secure their status are at best a small subset of aesthetic cultures. This is not a throwaway point; it will have substantive implications for the account of specifically aesthetic cultures in the next section.

We often talk of cultures as groups of people. The statement that all cultures engage in aesthetic activity evidently uses "culture" as a noun to refer to a group of people—Haida or Aberdonians, for example. The trouble is that most members of any such group belong to or have multiple cultures. To solve this problem, let "culture" be a predicate naming a feature of a group, rather than the group itself. No group of people is an aesthetic culture, though many groups have one or more aesthetic cultures.

Some conceptions of culture are identity-constitutive. On these conceptions, it is a constitutive feature of a culture that belonging to a cultural group is, in a weighty sense, part of who one is. Members of cultural groups lose themselves when they lose their cultures (e.g. Handler 1985: 66, Turino 2008: 111). Granted, some aesthetic cultures are closely associated with identities. Chapter 8 explores the implications of this fact. Nonetheless, most aesthetic cultures are not identity-constitutive, and it is important that they are not. A phase is, by definition, not identity-constitutive, and we go through aesthetic phases. For example, as we develop from infancy onward, we pass through series of aesthetic cultures, which we leave behind, without any injury to our self-conception. Identity-constitutive conceptions of culture are too narrow to model aesthetic culture across the board.

The same goes for organic views of culture (Appiah 2018: 206–207). An example of such a view is perhaps the most widely cited theory of culture, due to E. B. Tylor. Tylor took each culture to be a "complex whole which includes knowledge, belief, arts, morals, laws, customs, and any other capabilities and habits acquired by man as a member of society"

(1871: 1). So understood, the culture of a group is the complex property of its having a bundle made up of an epistemic culture, a legal culture, an artistic culture, and the like (Kilani 2019). Each of these components of an organic culture is thought to make an essential and ineliminable contribution to the whole. The whole amounts to the group's "comprehensive way of life," with its "particular rhythms, forms of beauty and achievement, and patterns of personal interaction, and with [its] different ways of ordering human experience so as to create distinctive modes of fulfilment, of solidarity, and of consolation" (Scheffler 1999: 129; see also Williams 1961: ch. 2, Margalit and Halbertal 1994: 497–498, Young 2008: 9–10). Again, the trouble is that not all aesthetic cultures fit into organic cultural wholes. Most do not.

On adaptivist views of culture, notably associated with Georg Forster and Johann Gottfried Herder, a group's having a culture is its having an organic culture that equips its members to flourish in their physical and larger social environment (Taylor 1994: 31–32, Benhabib 2002: 3–4, Kilani 2019, Zuckert 2019). So understood, culture tends to lock onto territory as well as to group identity. Perhaps some aesthetic cultures are parts of adaptive wholes, but some are not.

Will Kymlicka argues that a distinct type of culture carries special significance for political philosophy, since it is a feature of nations. A nation is, for Kymlicka, a group that, because it occupies a territory and runs a set of educational, communication, and trade institutions, is able to maintain a societal culture (1995: 11). A societal culture is one that "provides its members with meaningful ways of life across the full range of human activities, including social, educational, religious, recreational, and economic life, encompassing both private and public spheres" (Kymlicka 1995: 76). Societal cultures are organic cultures partly constitutive of national identity. Since many aesthetic cultures fail to be components of societal cultures, the minimal theory cannot be a theory of societal culture.

Minimally conceived, a culture is a regularity of behaviour in a group that is explained by members of the group sharing formative social conditions (Richerson and Boyd 2005, Patten 2014: ch. 2; see also Feagin 1995: 311, Lopes et al. 2024: ch. 2). A group has a distinct culture just when it displays a distinct regularity of behaviour that is explained by its members sharing a set of formative social conditions that are distinct from the formative social conditions of other groups.

30 AESTHETIC INJUSTICE

The theory is minimal in several respects. Minimal culture is not necessarily identity-constitutive, and it does not imply everything-sandwich organicism. Legal, linguistic, religious, child-rearing, and aesthetic regularities of behaviour can occur independently of one another. In addition, the minimal theory carries no implication that culture is static, homogeneous, or uncontested (Scheffler 1999, Waldron 2000, Appiah 2005: 256, Matthes 2016). A group has a culture even when not every member of the group behaves exactly like every other member, and even when some members behave in ways that disrupt the behaviours of others. Regularities of behaviour change over time; they are dynamic.

As an added bonus, the theory is extensible. The United Nations defines culture as "the creative productions of human thought and craftsmanship" (quoted in Brown 1998: 197). Let a material culture be the physical products of a regularity of behaviour in a group that is explained by shared formative conditions. Similarly, we can derive concepts of affective and cognitive cultures that comprise the mental resources deployed in motivating behavioural regularities of culture.

Aesthetic Cultures

Minimally conceived, an aesthetic culture is a group-level regularity of aesthetic activities—appreciating, making, performing, editing, and the like—that is explained by members of the group sharing formative social conditions (Lopes et al. 2024: ch. 2). Examples of aesthetic cultures include those with which the book opened—Kochi rickshaw decoration, Nordic noir, Kwakwaka'wakw carving, and the Tokyo *kawaii* scene. Each of these is a regularity in activities due to members of a group sharing formative social conditions—each is a minimal culture. Thus, people who wear black and attend SoHo gallery openings belong to two overlapping groups with distinct minimal cultures, one sartorial and the other artistic.

A word about why we should take aesthetic cultures to range far beyond the arts.

To begin with, non-art items embody aesthetic value. You are struck by the graceful sway and curl of an elephant's trunk. Euler's identity is beautiful because it tightly knits together so many mathematical

COSMOPOLITANISM, CULTURE, AESTHETIC CULTURE   31

primitives—zero, one, the arithmetic operations, identity, and the constants π, i, and e. A collector lovingly restores a Kochi rickshaw. In 1974, Burton Kramer designed a new logo for the CBC/Radio Canada, in which a letter C, thickened into a circle, is repeated in a radiating pattern, aesthetic unity signifying national unity through national communication. A dash of coconut vinegar makes a *caldinho* sing (tamarind is too fruity). A breeder crosses two bloodlines to produce Shetland Sheepdog puppies with rich, mahogany coats. Visiting an unfamiliar city, you notice how it prompts you to make "interestingly textured navigational choices—of noticing and discovering a hidden passageway, of deciding to take the broad, curving street or to enter, instead, the cool, dark labyrinth of an indoor marketplace" (Nguyen 2020b: 6). The local paint shop stocks cans premixed in Pantone's colour of the year, because it expresses calm, confidence, and connection. A student's essay is full of clever arguments, but the prose is wooden, so you offer her some wording with more pizzaz. Pizzaz, confidence, rich texture and rich coats, unity, and a flavour that sings: these are aesthetic values.

The kinds of items that have these values are as diverse as the values themselves. They include bits of nature, ideas, objects of design, food, domesticated beasts, clothing, personalities and performances, decoration, and writing of all kinds. It follows that the arts do not have a monopoly on aesthetic value (Lopes 2014: ch. 7, Lopes et al. 2024: ch. 2).

In addition, a case can be (and has been) made that at least some arts are not constituted by their realizing aesthetic value (Danto 1964, Dickie 1984, Carroll 1986, Davies 1991, Lopes 2014). That works of art often do have aesthetic value is no surprise, since almost anything can have aesthetic value. Nevertheless, it does not follow that what makes something a work of art is its aesthetic value.

Setting aside these more technical points, an overemphasis on the arts can jeopardize philosophical thinking about aesthetic cultures. Ever since the eighteenth century, the arts have enjoyed a social privilege that sets them apart from the broader field of aesthetic cultures. In a condescending moment, the anthropologist Claude Lévi-Strauss predicted that "the day is surely not far away when collections from distant parts of the world will leave ethnographic museums to take up their rightful place in art museums." He meant that as a compliment to the items headed for the art museums, of course, but he unintentionally slighted the ethnographic

32 AESTHETIC INJUSTICE

museums. He intimates that, whatever they are, they are not art museums. Presumably, art museums are special.

Jennifer Lena identifies the key characteristics of fine arts institutions in her sociological history of the fine arts in the United States (2019: ch. 5; see also Shiner 2001). Arts institutions bind items into genres, schools, and traditions so as to place them in grand historical narratives. Accordingly, they highlight transformational examples. They also foreground authorship and how items express authorial origins. They privilege disinterested, contemplative regard (see also Wolterstorff 2015: chs 1–3). They insist on the importance of the personal or cultural authenticity of the items they house, and they cordon off spaces where authenticity is guaranteed. They exploit the prestige of intellectualized discourse, the publishing industry, and academic fine arts and literature departments. They legitimize their activities by professionalizing them.

Theories of aesthetic culture that centre on the arts are therefore bound to commit one of two methodological errors.

One is artification (see Saito 2008, Lopes 2014: 121–124). The everyday business of housekeeping is an aesthetic activity, but Kevin Melchionne describes it as an "art of domesticity" (1998: 192). A serious discussion of the aesthetics of wine or food almost inevitably turns into an argument for culinary or oenological art (an exception is Burnham and Skilleås 2012). The trouble with artification is that there is no reason for all aesthetic activity to fit the brief of institutions with the characteristics that Lena lists. A meal of *caldinho* in a beach shack in Goa is not the same as an event by Rirkrit Tiravanija, and we should feel no need for an intellectual discourse about housekeeping in order to take it seriously as an aesthetic enterprise.

That leaves the other error, which is to forsake vast swaths of aesthetic activity. Writing in the eighteenth century, Francis Hutcheson (1738) made mathematical beauty his central case, without a breath of apology. Nowadays, mathematical beauty rarely gets a foot in the door of the journals. Dog breeding and editing students' essays? As if. The trouble with overlooking what is not apt for artification is that the features that make mathematical theorems, dog breeding, and student essays unfit for artification might be features that an adequate account of aesthetic activity must not fail to explain.

Perhaps, one might respond, the problem lies not with the arts per se, but with a mistaken conception of art that goes hand in hand with art's institutionalization over the past three centuries. No doubt that is correct, but the remedy is to treat the arts as occupying a small, if important, part of the aesthetic field, and the way to do that is to take seriously the entire aesthetic field on its own terms.

That was the first methodological point, about the dangers of artification. A second methodological point is especially important to the project of this book.

The arts are widespread across human groups, but contemporary arts institutions are engines of social inequality. Pierre Bourdieu's principal finding in *Distinction* is that "art and cultural consumption are predisposed ... to fulfil a social function of legitimating social differences" (1984: 7). Yet Bourdieu takes care to add that those excluded from fine art are not thereby excluded from "the universe of aesthetics." He insists that there are "beautiful ways of ploughing or trimming a hedge, just as there are beautiful mathematical solutions or beautiful rugby manoeuvres" (1990: 7–8). To accept the art model of aesthetic activity is therefore to run a risk of systematically overlooking injustices that are products of the very system of social inequality of which the model is a mainstay.

For all these reasons, we should take a broad view of aesthetic culture. Aesthetic cultures are not reducible to artistic cultures.

This cannot be the last word on aesthetic culture. If just about any kind of item can focus aesthetic activity within the context of a culture, then what is the point of qualifying culture as aesthetic? Without an answer, there looms a more immediately threatening question. What is the point of having a theory of injustice qualified as aesthetic?

3

The Aesthetic Capacities

The task is not yet to argue for the cosmopolitan theory; the task is to articulate its content. A core element of the theory is the claim that aesthetic injustice involves harms to people in their capacities as aesthetic agents. Central among these are culturally acquired capacities to respond to aesthetic value. This chapter introduces a theory of aesthetic value that yields a picture, fit for present purposes, of the capacities of agents to respond to aesthetic values in their own cultures and in other cultures too.

Normativity in Aesthetic Culture

Two theories of aesthetic value have been worked out (Nguyen 2020a, Strohl 2022, Riggle 2022, and Shelley 2023b are partial). One is aesthetic hedonism, which has been the widely held theory of aesthetic value; the other is a newcomer, the network theory (Lopes 2018b). The two theories share much common ground. Both regard aesthetic values as figuring in normative reasons for agents to respond and act. As a result, both portray aesthetic agents as endowed with capacities for responding to and acting in accordance with their normative reasons. Here is their shared picture of the activities of agents acting on normative aesthetic reasons given by their aesthetic cultures.

Agents make evaluations. Evaluations are states of mind that represent values. Some aesthetic evaluations are beliefs; some are perceptions or experiences, as when you see Kramer's logo as unified; and some are affects, as when your friend suddenly feels a pang over the dad jeans (on perceptual evaluation, see Lopes 2014: ch. 9, Stokes 2014, Tappolet 2016, Lopes 2018a: ch. 8, Stokes 2018, Ransom 2020c; on affective evaluation, see Nussbaum 2001, Gorodeisky and Marcus 2018, Gorodeisky 2021). Most aesthetic evaluations are tacit, and we are unaware of the dozens

Aesthetic Injustice. Dominic McIver Lopes, Oxford University Press. © Dominic McIver Lopes 2024.
DOI: 10.1093/oso/9780198930983.003.0003

that we make over the course of an average day. When are aware of them, we might not be able to articulate them precisely and accurately (Irvin 2014, Lopes 2018a: ch. 2). Assume a capacious conception of aesthetic evaluation.

Now to aesthetic acts. Any act's motive is a mental state that explains the act. An aesthetic act is one that is motivated at least in part by an aesthetic evaluation. The paint shop manager places an order of pre-mixed Classic Blue. Why? What explains her act? Suppose she orders it partly because she sees how it expresses calm, confidence, and connection. Her act is aesthetic because an aesthetic evaluation is among its motives. She might have done otherwise, had she seen the colour differently.

Stipulate to the following theories of aesthetic acts, evaluations, and capacities:

A's act is an aesthetic act = A's act counterfactually depends on the content of A's aesthetic evaluation of an item, where A's act operates on the item,

a state is an aesthetic evaluation = the state is a mental representation of some item as having some aesthetic value,

and

a capacity is an aesthetic capacity = the capacity is a capacity for aesthetic evaluation or action.

These theories are formal rather than substantive. Replace "aesthetic" with another value modifier ("moral," "epistemic," "ludic"), and the result remains true. So, each theory is really an invitation to go deeper into the nature of aesthetic value—to more closely examine the role, in aesthetic activity, of the paint's expressing calm, confidence, and connection. Only with a theory of aesthetic value do we get substantive conceptions of aesthetic evaluation, aesthetic acts, and the capacities for both (cf. Driver 2021, Lopes 2021b, Matherne 2021).

These stipulated theories of aesthetic acts, evaluations, and capacities can be used to articulate aesthetic hedonism and the network theory. Aesthetic hedonism and the network theory also agree in their aim, namely to answer one of three questions that one might raise about aesthetic value.

One is a demarcation question. Some values are aesthetic. What makes them aesthetic? Grace in the sway and curl of the elephant's trunk is an aesthetic value, but not her courage in facing down the lions. Your richly textured exploration of Istanbul is aesthetically good, but not your knowledge of the history of the Ottoman Empire. A theory of aesthetic value might state what makes it the case that the boundary demarcating aesthetic values from other values lies where it does.

The second question might be called the "value question" (Riggle 2022b, Lopes 2023a). Set aside why the value realized by the sway and curl of the elephant's trunk counts as aesthetic. The value question asks what makes the elephant's gracefulness good. Put another way, what is it for an aesthetic feature to be a merit or a demerit in an item?

The value question is not to be confused with a third question, the normative question (Lopes 2018b, Kubala 2021, Riggle 2022b, Kubala forthcoming). Knowing what makes the movement's grace an *aesthetic* value and what makes it an aesthetic *value* leave open what makes it the case that its being graceful gives anyone reason to do anything. The normative question asks this: what makes it the case that an item's having an aesthetic value is a reason for anyone to do anything?

DOM: You should try Kris Sowersby's Untitled Sans.
BENCE: Why?
D: It's crisp and integrated, but also modest.
B: Hmm ... but why is that a reason to try it?
D: Well, those are facts about its aesthetic value.
B: Obviously. But why are facts about its aesthetic value reasons to try it?

As we see in this example, normative aesthetic reasons are facts about an item's aesthetic value. They are facts of the form $\ulcorner$x is V$\urcorner$. The fact that a typeface is modest is a fact about its aesthetic value, and it is a normative reason for someone to act. With that in mind, a good answer to Bence's closing question unpacks the "should" in Dom's opening recommendation by expanding upon what makes it the case that aesthetic value fact is a normative aesthetic reason.

How might one try to answer Bence's closing question? Assume that:

the fact that x is V is a normative aesthetic reason for A to φ in C = the fact that x is V lends weight to the proposition that A should φ in C.

To answer the normative question is to give an informative reduction of the normative "should" on the right-hand side, one that completes the schema:

the fact that x is V is a normative aesthetic reason for A to φ in C = the fact that x is V lends weight to the proposition that ....

Completing the schema informatively yields a substantive account of how aesthetic values are reason-giving.

In sum, a theory of aesthetic value might answer one or all of the demarcation, value, and normative questions. Both aesthetic hedonism and the network theory answer the normative question. Here are two reasons why, for present purposes, all we need is a theory that answers the normative question.

To begin with, contemporary versions of aesthetic hedonism shy away from demarcation (Shelley 2019; cf. Matthen 2017, Matthen 2018a, Matthen 2018b, Gorodeisky 2021, Grant 2022). The network theory follows suit (Lopes 2018b, Shelley 2021). Neither denies that aesthetic values do demarcate from other values. Nor does either deny that we have folk concepts of aesthetic value that equip us to pretty reliably recognize aesthetic values when we bump into them. There is enough consensus on paradigm aesthetic values, such as those famously listed by Frank Sibley: "unified, balanced, integrated, lifeless, serene, somber, dynamic, powerful, vivid, delicate, moving, trite, sentimental, tragic" (1959: 421; see also De Clercq 2002, De Clercq 2008). Values that are paradigms in other aesthetic cultures remain recognizably aesthetic—Yoruba *jijora* and *tutu*, Japanese *wabi-sabi*, and the beausage admired in off-road bicycles, for example (Thompson 1983, Morphy 1996, Layton 2012). We pretty reliably recognize some values as aesthetic. At any rate, the choice between aesthetic hedonism and the network theory does not hang on issues of demarcation.

38 AESTHETIC INJUSTICE

In addition, the choice between the theories cuts across the (nascent) debate about whether aesthetic values or normative reasons are fundamental. Everyone agrees that the aesthetic field is a home to value, even if they forsake the V word, and everyone agrees that there are aesthetic reasons to perform various acts, if only acts of appreciation. Meanwhile, there is (nascent) disagreement on whether values or reasons come first in the order of explanation. Tradition reduces reasons to goods: what we have reason to do is promote what is good. On reasons-first approaches, value facts reduce to normative reasons (e.g. Ewing 1939, Scanlon 1998). However, neither aesthetic hedonism nor the network theory implies a particular order of explanation. The network theory gives priority to neither, and, although most aesthetic hedonists proceed value first, some proceed reasons first. Bernard Bolzano, an aesthetic hedonist, might have proposed the first reasons-first approach: he took any good to be just what should be made actual (2007 [1834], 2023 [1843 + 1849]; see also, Rosenkoetter 2014, Lopes 2024a). Aesthetic hedonism and the network theory conflict in their answers to the normative question, not necessarily on the question of where values and reasons stand in the order of explanation.

Aesthetic Hedonism

Aesthetic acts are acts motivated by aesthetic evaluations, where aesthetic evaluations are states attributing aesthetic values. Aesthetic cultures are regularities of aesthetic acts, where shared social formative conditions equip agents with capacities to assess and act upon aesthetic value facts. What, then, are aesthetic values? The widely held view is aesthetic hedonism (for overviews and references, see Lopes 2018b: ch. 3, Van der Berg 2020).

Consider the following biconditional:

x is V if and only if x merits A's taking pleasure in x

(for any item, x, any aesthetic value, V, and any agent, A). So formulated, the biconditional echoes pronouncements spanning more than two thousand years of philosophy (De Clercq 2019: 121). For Plato, beauty is "that which is pleasing through hearing and sight" (*Greater Hippias* 298a). Hutcheson took for granted that "the ideas of beauty and harmony, like other sensible

Ideas, are necessarily pleasant to us, as well as immediately so" (1738: §14). For Bolzano, "the beautiful must be an object whose contemplation can cause pleasure in all people whose cognitive powers are duly developed" (2023 [1843]: §11). Mary Mothersill voices the contemporary consensus that "what we take to be beautiful pleases us" (1984: 342).

To accommodate different flavours of aesthetic hedonism, we must interpret the biconditional broadly. We have already seen that items bearing aesthetic value are hugely varied, as are the determinate values they bear. Works of art, bits of nature, people, cityscapes, designed objects, and intellectual contents can be graceful, unified, rich, or shocking. Over on the right-hand side of the biconditional, read "pleasure" broadly too. Pleasure is not always sensual or sensory. To mark this, some prefer talk of "finally valuable experiences." Even then, finally valuable experiences need not be perceptions or perceptual imaginings. The beauty of Euler's identity is not something perceived by the senses or their imaginative counterparts.

Meriting injects a dose of normativity: meriting A's taking pleasure is just adding weight to the proposition that A should take pleasure. The boldness of a dress merits A's taking pleasure in it even if A does not take pleasure in it. Moreover, meriting is pro tanto. The dress's boldness merits A's taking pleasure in it, so that weight is added to the proposition that A should take pleasure in it, yet maybe A should not take pleasure in it, all things considered. Maybe the dress is bold yet too garish. Or too expensive.

The biconditional does not yet state aesthetic hedonism (Lopes 2021c). After all, the biconditional is true when we plug any value in for V. The chess move is clever, the gazelle is fleet, the journalist is courageous, and this is a sturdy umbrella just when it merits our pleasure. Anything is good in any way just when it merits our pleasure. In none of these cases is the merited pleasure responsible for the goodness, however.

Aesthetic hedonism supplements the biconditional to yield a constitutive account (Watkins and Shelley 2012). In rough sketch:

aesthetic hedonism: (1) necessarily, x is V if and only if x merits A's taking pleasure in x, and (2) x is V because x merits A's taking pleasure in x.

Here, the "because" signals metaphysical explanation (or grounding), so that (2) says that what makes it the case that x is V is that x merits our pleasure.

40 AESTHETIC INJUSTICE

Aesthetic hedonism might be modified to answer the demarcation question by identifying distinctively aesthetic pleasures (e.g. Konstan 2014: 161–166, Shelley 2021; cf. Wolterstorff 2015, Riggle 2016, Lopes 2023b, Shelley 2023a). However, contemporary flavours of aesthetic hedonism only address the normative question, what makes it the case that x is V gives anyone reason to act? Aesthetic hedonism is ready with a perfect answer. That x merits pleasure implies that it yields pleasure when correctly appreciated, and we always have reason to do what it takes to get pleasure. (Sometimes, happily, our reason is decisive.) In other words, aesthetic hedonism delivers (but does not imply) a theory of aesthetic normativity:

an aesthetic value, V, is reason-giving = the fact that x is V lends weight to the proposition that it would bring A pleasure were A to φ in C.

Aesthetic normativity is hedonic normativity. (As an aside, some aesthetic hedonists arguably have non-hedonic theories of aesthetic normativity—see Zuckert 2010 and Lopes 2021a on Kant 2000 [1790], Lopes 2019 on Bhattacharyya 2011 [1930], Lopes 2024a on Bolzano 2023 [1843 + 1849]).

So stated, the hedonic theory of aesthetic normativity is consistent both with less and with more demanding conceptions of aesthetic normativity (Lopes 2018b: 58–60). Note that non-aesthetic pleasures can be merited. A warm bath might merit pleasure, as might a crossword solution or a pat on the back for a job well done. As a rule, though, most merited pleasures are subject only to a personal normative standard. Someone who likes a pat on the back might fail to be pleased by a particular offering of praise. Perhaps they are distracted or they are biased against the person praising them. Nonetheless, they should be pleased. They should take the pleasure that would be taken in suitable circumstances by a version of themselves that meets their personal standard for hedonic response. However, few philosophers are content with the proposition that aesthetic normativity is this basic form of normativity (Santayana 1896, Melchionne 2007, Melchionne 2010, Melchionne 2015, Kölbel 2016). All others wrestle with the problem of taste.

Bernard Williams once quipped, "I simply don't like staying in good hotels" (1985: 125). If aesthetic normativity is basic, then his quip is

THE AESTHETIC CAPACITIES 41

incoherent. If to be aesthetically good is just to merit Williams's pleasure, then he is saying that he fails to meet his own personal standard. But he is not saying that, for he stands by his aversion to good hotels. He is saying the hotels are good by a standard that he fails to live up to and that is not his personal standard. He recognizes an aesthetic normativity that implicates a standard external to him, and he simply confesses that he does not meet that standard.

Apparently, there is an intersubjective standard of aesthetic value. Joseph Addison's prose is better than John Bunyan's, and Untitled Sans is a better typeface than Arial. These facts are not indexed to individuals or types of individuals. Anyone, no matter who they are, should take more pleasure in Addison and Untitled Sans than Bunyan and Arial. The problem of taste is to understand how pleasures can have anything more than basic normativity. How can pleasures not be indexed to individual standards?

Tradition answers that aesthetic values are constituted by the hedonic responses of ideal responders, David Hume's "true judges" (1777). According to:

standardized aesthetic hedonism: necessarily, x is V if and only if x merits A's taking pleasure in x, and x is V because x merits A's taking pleasure in x, where A's response is calibrated to those of true judges.

In their celebrated reading of him, Mothersill (1989) and Jerrold Levinson (2002) argued that Hume makes a case for the theory of aesthetic normativity that falls out of standardized aesthetic hedonism. Hume asks, what reason does Williams have to acquire a capacity to like staying in good hotels? What reason do those who select Arial from the drop-down menu have to acquire a capacity to select Untitled Sans instead? His answer is that we get more pleasure by being more like the true judges. That is:

an aesthetic value, V, is reason-giving = the fact that x is V lends weight to the proposition that it would maximize A's pleasure were A to φ in C, were A's hedonic responses calibrated to those of true judges.

42 AESTHETIC INJUSTICE

Anyone who has reason to do what it takes to get pleasure also has reason to acquire the hedonic capacity that will maximize their pleasure. As Servaas Van der Berg describes them, "the true judges are idealized creatures whose sensibilities are perfectly calibrated for the maximization of aesthetic pleasure" (2020: 3). Aesthetic normativity is hedonic normativity subject to the standard for maximal pleasure set by the true judges.

Aesthetic Hedonism and the Problem of Diversity

Two variants of aesthetic hedonism appear to be stable. One rejects the problem of taste entirely and settles for basic aesthetic normativity; the other solves the problem of taste by standardizing. Either way, aesthetic hedonists must accept that the diversity of aesthetic cultures is contra-normative.

This is easier to see on standardized aesthetic hedonism. Suppose that I have most aesthetic reason to appreciate in a way that aligns with true judges. They provide a universal, culture-transcending standard of taste with respect to which most aesthetic cultures fall short (Lopes et al. 2014: 10–16). My belonging to a group where I learn to comply with a local hedonic standard interferes with my acting on my true aesthetic reasons—the ones that align with the verdicts of true judges. What I should do is break free of the culture's yoke and cultivate my hedonic capacities to coincide with those of true judges (Levinson 2010, Riggle 2013). Indeed, the state might have a role of ensuring that everyone is suitably trained up to appreciate the best of the fine arts (Beardsley 1970, Beardsley 1973, Smith 1975, Pankratz 1983). Standardized aesthetic hedonists dream of a world where everyone has the aesthetic capacities of the true judges. In our world, diverse aesthetic cultures would dissolve, leaving behind an aesthetic monoculture.

Suppose instead that aesthetic normativity is basic. I have most aesthetic reason to appreciate what would merit the pleasure of the best version of myself in suitable circumstances. Also suppose that I belong to a group that sets a hedonic standard of aesthetic value. There are two cases. In case one, what merits the pleasure of the best version of myself is precisely what complies with the group's standard. The coincidence need not be accidental: I might acquire my aesthetic capacities as a result of being a member of the group. In case two, what merits the pleasure of the best version of myself is not what complies with the group's standard. Someone's membership in a group does not guarantee that their aesthetic capacities comply with group standards. Indeed, basic aesthetic hedonists often see groups as stifling aesthetic individuality (e.g. Melchionne 2007, Melchionne 2010, Melchionne 2015). In this case, my acting in compliance with the group's standard interferes with my taking pleasure in what merits the pleasure of the best version of myself. What I should do is break free of the culture's yoke and act on the exercise of my idiosyncratic aesthetic capacities. Now, whether or not the first or second case obtains is contingent. Nothing rules out the second case, and it is hard to believe that it is rare in our world. Basic aesthetic hedonists declare that there would be nothing amiss were people to cultivate and act on their idiosyncratic aesthetic capacities. Many aesthetic cultures would dissolve, leaving behind a large population of aesthetic monads.

Either way, the current ecosystem of diverse aesthetic cultures is contranormative. Aesthetic hedonists must be prepared to see that ecosystem transform into an aesthetic monoculture or a population of monads. For some of them, this is a feature of aesthetic hedonism, not a bug.

One might conclude that this is sufficient reason to reject aesthetic hedonism (e.g. Nehamas 2007: 83–84). A different conclusion is pertinent here: cultural cosmopolitans cannot accept the result that a diverse ecosystem of aesthetic cultures is contra-normative. Cultural cosmopolitanism is markedly social, rooted, normative, and pro-diversity. Basic and standardized aesthetic hedonism forces a choice between normativity, on the one hand, and sociality and cultural diversity, on the other. We can have one but not both.

What is wanted is a theory of aesthetic value that explains two facts. First it explains why our aesthetic capacities produce regularities of behaviour that are apportioned out into the diverse ecosystem of aesthetic cultures with which we are familiar. In short, it explains why:

(1) aesthetic activities sort into diverse cultures.

That is not all. Aesthetic hedonists can explain (1) as a consequence of our failure to act on our normative aesthetic reasons. Since cultural

44   AESTHETIC INJUSTICE

cosmopolitanism is markedly normative, it insists that each aesthetic culture supplies agents with normative reasons to act, upon which they often enough act. Therefore, we also need a theory of aesthetic value that explains (1) by appeal to the fact that:

(2) agents often enough act on their normative aesthetic reasons.

Cultural cosmopolitans want to have their normative cake and eat their cultural diversity.

Basic and standardized aesthetic hedonism cannot explain (1) by appeal to (2); they deny that we sort into diverse aesthetic cultures because we often enough act on our reasons. If aesthetic hedonism cannot explain (1) by appeal (2), then it cannot equip us to articulate our cosmopolitan interests. It is not fit for cosmopolitan purposes.

We can now augment the backup argument for the cosmopolitan theory of aesthetic injustice. The backup argument is an error theory. It explains why we have failed to see that aesthetic injustice is a thing. To this end, Chapter 1 noted that folk thinking about injustice has been faulty and that aesthetic injustices are eclipsed by the morally egregious injustices of weaponized aesthetics. Here is a third point. Aesthetic hedonism has been the default theory of aesthetic value. Its truth is so taken for granted that its proponents have not felt any need to give arguments for it, even to the extent of replying to objections (e.g. Shelley 2010, Shelley 2011, Wolf 2011, Lopes 2018b: ch. 4, Shelley 2019; see also Van der Berg 2020). So deeply has it seeped into thinking about aesthetic value that the terms in which it is formulated have become the only terms available to pose the questions it is taken to answer. Questions about aesthetic justice must fight their way to the surface.

The Network Theory

If aesthetic hedonism has moulded folk aesthetics in its image, then resources for crafting an alternative to it are unlikely to be found by mining intuitions. What would be an intuition-independent approach? In as much as aesthetic values are values that organize acts in aesthetic cultures, alternatives to aesthetic hedonism might answer to facts about acts in social context. If we are not to examine how we think, then why not examine what we do and the competences that equip us to do what we do? The network theory of aesthetic value is a product of this method.

Being for Beauty opens with case studies of several aesthetic experts, agents whose aesthetic competences equip them to act reliably well (Lopes 2018b: ch. 1). They are a gardener and her grandson, who restored the garden to life, a photographer who promoted the work of her predecessor, a talk show host who started a book club (you can guess), a video game source code sleuth, and a dance educator. Some will be surprised by the lineup. None is a consummate appreciator or critic; none is a Bernard Berenson or an F. R. Leavis. Surprise on this point is a sign that the method is working. A sample of aesthetic experts cannot be limited to the fine arts or members of the social elites.

Six facts about these cases need explaining:

1. *Aesthetic agents hail from almost all demographic niches.* Allied to many social niches are aesthetic niches, and a theory of aesthetic value must explain why that is the case. No good theory of aesthetic value may abet attempts to reserve aesthetic culture—or serious or legitimate aesthetic culture—to those who command social privilege (Bourdieu 1984, Shiner 2001, Lena 2019). Steps must be taken both to acknowledge aesthetic agents who hail from all walks of life and also to explain how local aesthetic agency is shaped by social dependencies.

2. *Aesthetic agents jointly cover the whole aesthetic universe.* This is the converse of the first observation. Tradition singles out some regions of the aesthetic universe as homes to genuine agency and overlooks expressions of aesthetic agency elsewhere. The aesthetic universe includes popular art as well as fine art. Looking beyond the arts: the Alessi Juicy Salif by Philippe Starck but also the Dyson Big Ball, Alexander McQueen couture but also hoodies from the Gap, perennial borders but also suburban lawns, El Bulli but also The Keg Steakhouse. A theory of aesthetic value should take account of all aesthetic cultures.

3. *Aesthetic agents specialize by aesthetic culture.* A skilled critic of French cooking is not thereby a skilled critic of Tamil poetry. Someone

46 AESTHETIC INJUSTICE

competent at conserving superhero comics is unlikely to be competent at conserving video games. At the same time, competence for aesthetic performance is not entirely siloed. A skilled critic of French cooking will do better with Italian than Mexican food. A theory of aesthetic value should explain the overlapping fragmentation of aesthetic competences into aesthetic cultures.

4. *Aesthetic agents specialize by activity.* Aesthetic acts include editing, curating, collecting, conserving, exhibiting, teaching, and connecting audiences, as well as appreciating, making, and performing. Within a single culture, agents performing these different types of acts differ in their competences. Someone good at teaching Tamil poetry need not be competent at writing or editing it. Again, there can be overlap. A Tamil poet might manage as an editor but not a teacher.

5. *Specialization by activity and culture interact.* The same type of action can be performed in different aesthetic cultures, and cultural specialization means that competence in acting in one culture does not amount to competence in acting across cultures. To see the difference cultures make, hold act-types constant. To see the difference act-types make, hold culture constant. One and the same aesthetic culture sees agents busy at different tasks, and specialization by act-type means that being good at one task in a culture does not ensure competence in other tasks in the same culture. The specifics of an act are a function of both the aesthetic act-type and the aesthetic culture. All aesthetic competence is local: each agent uses a competence tailored to what they are doing and where they are doing it. The specificities give us something grippy to explain. Aesthetic values figure in the doings of agents who are specialized by aesthetic culture and act-type.

6. *Aesthetic expertise is relatively stable.* Aesthetic experts perform reliably well; they perform well time and again. They are not merely lucky in their success, for they succeed out of competence. Yet they are not inflexible. Stable competences can be exercised in a range of environments. Moreover, the competence itself can change, though normally at a gradual pace. Aesthetic experts are nimble in their responses and can adapt to changing circumstances. This too a theory of aesthetic value should explain.

The network theory aims to explain all six observations (Lopes 2018b: chs 5–7). Here is the official statement:

an aesthetic value, V, is reason-giving = the fact that x is V lends weight to the proposition that it would be an aesthetic achievement for some A to φ in C, where x is an item in an aesthetic practice, K, and A's competence to φ is aligned upon an aesthetic value profile that is constitutive of K.

The theory is an answer to the normative question, what makes it the case that an item's having aesthetic value gives anyone reason to do anything? An answer to this question completes the schema:

an aesthetic value, V, is reason-giving = the fact that x is V lends weight to the proposition that ....

Aesthetic hedonism recommends filling in the dots by appeal to the fact that anyone always has reason to maximize pleasure. The network theory reduces aesthetic normativity to the normativity of achievement.

To achieve is to act successfully and as a result of competence. Achievement understood as performance that succeeds out of competence is a broader phenomenon than achievement where the exercise of the competence is difficult (Bradford 2015). Studying Kiswahili or scaling the Grand Wall of the Stawamus Chief are achievements because they are difficult. Success out of competence in the face of difficulty is good, but so is mere success out of competence. In this broader sense of achievement, anyone who acts at all thereby has reason to achieve. If the fact that a dash of coconut vinegar is an easy way to make a *caldinho* sing, then a cook has reason to use their skill to make it sing. In reducing aesthetic normativity to the normativity of achievement, the network theory reduces aesthetic normativity to plain vanilla practical normativity: whenever you act, you have reason to act as someone acts who acts well.

The achievement clause of the reduction does not by itself explain the six facts listed above; the rest of the theory is also needed. If reasons to act are thereby reasons to achieve, then it is a small step to the claim that they are also reasons to acquire competence, and reasons to acquire competence are very often reasons to specialize. Imagine a society that

48 AESTHETIC INJUSTICE

hits on the idea of dance. At first they simply perform dances, but as the dance culture begins to thrive, they also choreograph dances, compose danceable music, craft suitable masks and costumes, construct performances spaces, exchange critical commentary, and document dances for posterity. Perhaps everyone is a generalist who can and does perform all these acts. Nonetheless, as long as each has reason to achieve, each has reason to develop some of their competences at the expense of other competences, so long as they can expect their neighbours to fill in the gaps. Those who are adept at criticism have reason to leave choreography and performance to others, for example. As long as enough act on the reasons they have, labour divides, raising levels of achievement.

For the division of labour to work, all must be on the same page aesthetically. A dancer who has attuned their skill to the fluid and airy aesthetics of ballet is unlikely to perform in a way that boosts the achievement of a choreographer who has honed competence in the syncopated aesthetics of hip hop, and neither can rely on a costume designer whose training suits the taut and shimmering aesthetics of Kathakaḷī. Ballet, hip hop, and Kathakaḷī are aesthetic cultures with different aesthetic value profiles.

An aesthetic value profile is a correlation that obtains between the aesthetic values of items in the culture and the properties that ground the aesthetic values (for details see Lopes 2018b: ch. 10). A dancer makes a movement. In the vocabulary of human kinetics, they lower their foot to the ground in a direction with force and velocity. Executed in ballet by Misty Copeland, the move is vivid, but the very same gesture is lifeless when performed by Kanak Rele. Each dancer realizes an aesthetic value by making a movement, but the very same movement, as characterized in the vocabulary of human kinetics, grounds different aesthetic values. Equally, in different traditions, different movements ground the same aesthetic value. Vivid in Kathakaḷī requires a gesture different from Copeland's. Ascending a level, the properties that ground a vivid dance move are different from the ones that ground a vivid proof, a vivid melody, or a vivid sunrise.

Accordingly, for the division of labour to work, all must be on the same page aesthetically, in the sense that they have enough competence in same aesthetic value profile. Each will have reason to expect the rest to perform in compliance with the aesthetic value profile. They belong to group with a social practice constituted both by the profile and by a norm to comply

THE AESTHETIC CAPACITIES   49

with the profile. All elements of the network theory are now in place. What makes an aesthetic value reason-giving is that its instantiation in the fact that x is V lends weight to the proposition that anyone belonging to a group with the relevant aesthetic practice would be more likely to achieve by acting in accordance with the practice's aesthetic value profile.

Now to the six facts to be explained. First, the network theory explains why aesthetic agents will be found in almost all demographic niches. Folk thrown together in the same valley or online community, frequenting the same spaces, or belonging to the same social classes have reason to rely on each other for aesthetic support and so will coalesce around shared aesthetic value profiles. Second, add up all these aesthetic localizations and the sum leaves no remainder. Where there are agents there is a practice, and where there is a practice there are agents. Aesthetic agents jointly cover the whole aesthetic universe. Third, aesthetic cultures branch into more specific cultures when chances of achievement are thereby boosted, so aesthetic agents will specialize by aesthetic culture. Fourth, specializing by activity is a product of the same mechanism. People boost achievement by specializing. Fifth, specialization by activity and culture interact: as dance divides into practices with different profiles, choreographers must specialize further, and choreographic specialization drives further branching of aesthetic cultures. Finally, mutual reliance requires sufficient norm compliance, and norm compliance requires having capacities that secure compliance time and again under a range of ecologically valid conditions.

In *Being for Beauty*, the main argument for the network theory is that it explains the six facts listed above (in addition, it makes sense of aesthetic disagreement, the metaphysics of aesthetic value, and some of the personal and collective importance of aesthetic culture). Here, the question is whether it is cosmopolitan-friendly. It must explain why:

(1) aesthetic activities sort into diverse cultures

by appealing to the fact that:

(2) agents often enough act on their normative aesthetic reasons.

The network theory does explain (1) by appeal to (2). Aesthetic cultures are regularities of aesthetic acts in groups, where those regularities are

50   AESTHETIC INJUSTICE

explained by social formative conditions that equip agents with aesthetic capacities that are aligned on aesthetic value profiles and that raise their chances of achievement. We are not aesthetic monads because we do not have strong enough reason to be. We can each achieve more by co-operating with some others than by going it alone. Likewise, an aesthetic monoculture is not in the cards because we do not have strong enough reason to converge on one. Achievement is boosted by specialization in a context of cooperation: those who fare poorly at calibrating their responses to those of true judges have strong reason to nestle into their own local aesthetic niches, where they are more likely to achieve. The network theory explains why ours will be a massively diverse aesthetic ecosystem. It explains (1) by appeal to (2).

Rootedness and Practice-Internal Reasons

One core element of the cosmopolitan theory is the claim that aesthetic injustice involves harms to people in their capacities as aesthetic agents. The network theory portrays those capacities in a way that is friendly to cosmopolitanism. In particular, it reconciles cultural diversity with normativity. Meanwhile, the second core element of the cosmopolitan theory is that harms to people in their capacities as aesthetic agents subvert interests in aesthetic cultures that are not our own. We also need to characterize these interests in a way that is friendly to cosmopolitanism. In particular, cosmopolitanism is markedly rooted: it sources interests in other cultures at least partly within our own cultures. One might object that the network theory cannot represent interests in other aesthetic cultures as rooted.

After all, aesthetic values and normative aesthetic reasons are practice-internal. The network theory takes each aesthetic culture to be a social practice in a group of people interacting with one another around a shared aesthetic value profile. A gesture that is vivid in ballet is not vivid in Kathakalī. Moreover, the vividness of a ballet gesture is very strong reason for Copeland to dance it and for her audience to appreciate it, but it is no reason at all for Rele to dance it and little reason for Kathakalī audiences to pay it much attention. The strength of aesthetic reasons is asymmetrical: practice-internal aesthetic reasons are keys to achievement only for insiders. The aesthetic cultures of groups to which you and I do not belong cannot matter to us, at least in as much as they do not support our achievements. Put another way, if they matter at all, it is not by appeal to local reasons. Yet cosmopolitans need interests in other aesthetic cultures to be rooted in interests in our own aesthetic cultures.

Is there more to the network theory than appears at first glance? Might practice-internal reasons ground interests in other cultures? Happily, there is more to say. The network theory implies that aesthetic value schemes are plural and hence that we are in a position to respect the values of cultures that are not our own.

Pluralism and Respect

Obviously, there are many different aesthetic cultures. Each has its own aesthetic value profile, and each provides normative reasons that are valid for insiders. That a move is vivid in ballet might be a reason for Copeland to execute it; that a different move is vivid in Kathakalī might be a reason for Rele to dance it. However, the pluralism of aesthetic cultures goes beyond valid difference. Aesthetic cultures are plural because they have aesthetic value profiles that are (1) different and (2) valid, but also (3) incommensurable, (4) compatible, and (5) to some degree mutually comprehensible.

Values in commensurable profiles can be rank ordered. For example, the values of different types of investment are commensurable, because there is a common measure of their value, namely return on risk. By contrast, athletic values are incommensurable across sports. Which is better, a Venus Williams serve or a Sidney Crosby wrist shot? There is no correct answer to this question; tennis and hockey values are incommensurable. Likewise, the elegance of a cake and the elegance of a guitar riff cannot be ranked. Neither is better than the other, nor are they equal in value. Aesthetic value profiles are incommensurable.

Values profiles are compatible just when truths about the values in one profile do not speak against truths about values in another profile. The honour code of the medieval samurai is incompatible with the ideal of non-violence: the content of one is logically inconsistent with the content of the other. By contrast, tennis and hockey values are compatible

52 AESTHETIC INJUSTICE

because it is true both that the Williams serve is excellent and so is the Crosby wrist shot. In practice, limited resources might compel you to choose which values to bring about. More tennis lessons or more time on the rink? Incompatibility is not competition for resources, though. Just as tennis and hockey values are compatible, a cake's elegance is compatible with a guitar riff's being elegant. With enough resources, we could have both. Aesthetic value profiles are compatible.

Two value profiles are mutually comprehensible to the degree that competence in evaluating with respect to one profile is no barrier to competent evaluation with respect to the other. Some think that ethical values embedded in distant ways of life can be pretty incomprehensible to us. Perhaps the *bushidō* was so embedded in a lost way of life that we cannot genuinely appreciate how ritual suicide could be a way to restore honour (*chanbara* depict fantasies of samurai life). By contrast, a hockey fan who can see the value of wrist shots might also be able to see some of the quality of tennis serves. When it comes to comprehensibility, aesthetic evaluation is more like tennis and hockey than *bushidō* and *satyagraha*. To Rele, Bharatanatyam is more comprehensible than Noh, and Noh is more comprehensible than ballet. Degree of comprehensibility comes down to degree of overlap between aesthetic profiles.

In sum, aesthetic cultures are plural because they have aesthetic value profiles that are (1) different, (2) valid, (3) incommensurable, (4) compatible, and (5) mutually comprehensible to some degree. This pluralism of aesthetic cultures makes it possible for us to take several perspectives on aesthetic values.

Joseph Raz distinguishes engaging value from respecting it (2004: 160–164; see also Matthes 2015, Zuckert 2019: 151). To engage value is to act in response to the facts in which values figure. Copeland engages aesthetic value by dancing, and her audience engages it by appreciating. You might engage it by downloading Untitled Sans. In explaining what it is for aesthetic values to figure in normative reasons, the network theory treats aesthetic values as to be engaged. The networked agents whose interactions ground aesthetic value profiles are engaging value.

Respecting value does not entail engaging it. To respect the vividness of the gesture or the modest integrity of the typeface, one must take an attitude to each that is consistent with its value. However, respecting a value requires more than taking on board that it is a value. Respecting a value entails understanding it as a value. Since the modest integrity of Untitled Sans is a reason to engage someone in some specific way, someone who respects the value must have an inkling, however imprecise, of how its having the value is a reason to engage it in that specific way. Copeland respects Kathakalī values only if she sees how they engage Rele much as she is engaged by ballet values.

Aesthetic culture pluralism explains why respect is an alternative to engagement. Copeland can respect Kathakalī values because the Kathakalī aesthetic profile is different enough from ballet's that engagement is not on the cards, because Kathakalī values are nevertheless reason-giving for its practitioners, because there is no incompatibility between the values of ballet and Kathakalī, and because there is enough overlap between the aesthetic values profiles of ballet and Kathakalī that she can see how some Kathakalī values are reasons to act in specific ways. Nothing obstructs her respecting the values.

Raz's account of respect has an important repercussion. Copeland's respect for the values of Kathakalī is a function of her engagement with ballet. For one thing, her comprehension of Kathakalī depends upon the overlap between its aesthetic value profile and ballet's. More importantly, respecting Kathakalī values means seeing how they are reasons to engage Rele much as she is engaged by ballet values. For this reason, engagement in some home practice is a condition on respect for aesthetic values in any aesthetic culture that is not one's own.

Respect is an attitude that is rooted in the values of a culture that is one's own but that is taken in the values of others' cultures that are not one's own.

Engagement and rooted respect are not the only perspectives on aesthetic value. Comprehension is a matter of degree, because it is a function of profile overlap, and overlaps are contingent, often gifts of history and geography. The aesthetic value profile of Thai cuisine overlaps considerably with Vietnamese and Malay food, less with Chinese and South Asian food, and more with Mexican than with Newfoundland cooking. For any engaged aesthetic agent, there are likely to be some faraway aesthetic practices whose values do not position her for rooted respect. Aficionados of some dance traditions are likely to be flummoxed by Kathakalī, or ballet, seeing nothing but a lot of stomping, or fluttering, about the stage.

54 AESTHETIC INJUSTICE

For the flummoxed, rooted respect is not an option, but there is an option to take a third perspective. Call it "routed respect." Someone who is at home in some aesthetic culture and who has rooted respect for the values of some nearby aesthetic cultures can know that rooted respect for the values of a faraway culture is possible. In particular, they can know that there is a route through a sequence of aesthetic cultures with overlapping profiles that leads them to rooted respect and even engagement with the faraway aesthetic culture. The route might not be practical to follow, but its existence is sufficient for taking an attitude shaped by knowledge that there are values there worth somebody's engaging.

Cosmopolitan Interests Beyond Migration

Anyone who is engaged in aesthetic culture has first-hand experience of respect, for anyone now engaged in an aesthetic culture was once positioned only to respect its values, and it was respect that led to engagement. When respect leads to engagement, we have migration. Nonetheless, the capacity needed for us to act upon our cosmopolitan interests is not the capacity to migrate. It is not a capacity for respect as a promise of engagement. All we need in order to act upon our cosmopolitan interests is a capacity for respect, independent of engagement.

Migration through aesthetic cultures is a fact of aesthetic life. Growing up is a succession of initiations as a newly engaged member of aesthetic cultural groups. In societies where there is copious contact between people from different walks of life, opportunities abound for migration into their aesthetic cultures.

How is migration possible? How does respect lead to engagement? Manuel is a weaver, but he does not weave kente, though he has a respect for kente values that is rooted in his own weaving culture. He sees how the values figure in reasons for members of the kente cultural group to act as they do. However, a reason to engage is an aesthetic reason, and an aesthetic reason is an aesthetic value fact, a fact of the form $\ulcorner x$ is $V \urcorner$. For example, that this piece of cloth is dignified is a reason to weave it as a commencement stole. The trouble is that the fact about the cloth that is a reason for a kente weaver to weave it is not a reason for Manuel to follow suit. It is not a reason for him to follow suit because he is not likely to achieve by weaving kente. He is likely to achieve within his own culture.

This suggests how to answer the question how migration is possible—how respect sometimes leads to engagement. Manuel has reason to get into kente if he would achieve aesthetically, given his existing competences, were he to acquire a competence in kente. The overlap between his existing competences and the aesthetic profile of kente gives him "derived" aesthetic reason to learn kente (Lopes 2018b: 205–207). That is:

a fact about K is derived aesthetic reason for A to acquire competence in K = the fact lends weight to the proposition that A would achieve were A to acquire aesthetic competence in K.

The reason for Manuel to get into kente is not the aesthetic reason that this piece of cloth is dignified. Rather, his reason to get into kente is a fact about kente and his existing competences. The fact is that he would be able to achieve were he to get into kente and begin to engage aesthetic reasons for which he now only has rooted respect.

To act on our cosmopolitan interests in other cultures, we do not need reasons to migrate. Migration is often just fine, but sometimes it is better not to join others' cultures, even when one has derived aesthetic reason to do just that. Cosmopolitan interests are sometimes best accommodated by policies of non-engagement. They do not entail interests in engagement; they require nothing more than capacities for rooted or routed respect. These capacities are rooted in local engagement, but they need not be capacities to engage in others' cultures.

In sum, aesthetically unjust social arrangements are those that harm people in their capacities for acting on aesthetic evaluations in accordance with the aesthetic profiles of their own cultures. Harming people in this way subverts interests that call upon capacities for rooted or routed respect.

Does cosmopolitanism entail the network theory? It does not. Perhaps other theories can deliver similar results. If so, the network theory is a model of what to look for in those theories. On the network theory, we niche into aesthetic cultures because we act on our local, social aesthetic reasons. Having settled into our niches, and sometimes migrated to new ones, we acquire capacities for rooted and routed respect. As a result, the diversity of aesthetic cultures is normatively grounded.

4

The Cosmopolitan Interests

Building on the network theory, Chapter 3 portrayed capacities of aesthetic agents that can be harmed in large-scale social arrangements. Yet not all harms are injustices. According to the cosmopolitan theory, an aesthetic injustice occurs only when harms to people in their capacities as aesthetic agents subvert cosmopolitan interests. More can now be said about those interests. Whatever they are, we act on them through capacities for rooted and routed respect. And whatever they are, they must be justice-relevant. This chapter considers the circumstances in which threats to pluralism and respect are matters of injustice.

Circumstances of Justice

In addressing arrangements of social life at any scale, from the local community or association to global institutions, cultural cosmopolitism is only in a broad sense political. If the state is a special case, one among many social arrangements that can be more or less just, then what state-focused theories of justice leave out can provide clues to justice-relevant cosmopolitan interests.

The aim is not to downplay the importance of justice as a feature of the state. John Rawls (1971, 1993) foregrounds justice as a feature of the legal and constitutional provisions that manage a society's basic structure. The basic structure is a single system comprising key fields of social interaction—governance, economics, and the family—through which individuals seek to obtain the benefits of cooperation. Importantly, the subject of justice is the basic structure taken as a whole. Rawls sets aside justice within components of the basic structure taken individually, and he sets aside justice in fields of social interaction outside the basic structure. Granted, we need a theory of just legal and constitutional provisions

---

Aesthetic Injustice. Dominic McIver Lopes, Oxford University Press. © Dominic McIver Lopes 2024.
DOI: 10.1093/oso/9780198930983.003.0004

to manage the basic structure taken as a whole, but such a theory is incomplete. The circumstances of justice include local fields of social interaction, taken on their own, aesthetic cultures included.

Rawls's focus on justice in the state echoes a deep concern of political philosophy. Bringing out the concern can help us to think about justice more locally.

A just state is needed in circumstances of justice that meet two conditions (plus some further conditions that they entrain). One is that it be both possible and necessary for individuals to obtain the benefits of cooperative social interaction. Satisfying this condition does not yet suffice for circumstances of justice, though. Cooperation can occur in anarchic societies. The just state is needed only when some cooperative endeavours come into irreconcilable conflict. Since conflict undermines necessary cooperation, the state is needed either to impose uniformity or to negotiate and implement a consensus on how to manage the conflict and secure the benefits of cooperation.

With this in mind, we might ask whether circumstances of justice obtain in local fields of social interaction, taken on their own. Those fields do serve interests we have in getting the benefits of cooperation. That satisfies the first condition on the circumstances of justice. However, one might wonder whether the second condition, the requirement of conflict, is also necessary for circumstances of justice in local fields of social interaction, taken on their own. Put another way, is there no need for justice where there is no conflict?

From Contact to Conflict

Cosmopolitanism is one among several intellectual traditions that respond to a recognition that people come into contact with others who differ from them in ways that are significant or that pose a challenge. Contact is not yet conflict, however. States have to deal with conflict under four conditions.

First, there must be contact between groups with different cultures. Contact requires more than one party's awareness of the existence of the other and their differences. In contact, activity (or perhaps the known practical possibility of activity) by at least one party makes a difference to

58 AESTHETIC INJUSTICE

activity by the other party. What we intuitively consider to be an intervention is sufficient but not necessary for contact. Contact also occurs when one party's carrying on as they always did, without giving a thought to the other party, nevertheless affects what the other party does.

Second, without downplaying contact across state lines, it is contact within state territory that preoccupies political philosophy. External contact has rarely posed challenges without internal echoes. The European wars of religion, fought between states, were echoed by considerable internal friction, as English catholics and French protestants well knew. One effect of colonialism was to internalize, on a massive scale, contacts that had been external, impacting colonizers and colonized alike (Nandy 1988). Waldron lists the routes to the multicultural state, which range from confederation and territorial exchanges to migration and natural processes of internal differentiation to conquest, enslavement, and transportation (2003: 27–28). Yet the violent end of the spectrum should not be exaggerated. Human beings are violent, but also migratory, curious about others, willing to marry exogenously, ready to share what they know and what they can do, eager to engage in trade. As Waldron observes, it was part of the ideology of the nation-state, notably in the nineteenth century, that "distinct cultures would inhabit distinct territories apart from each other," so that all contact with difference could be managed on a state to state basis (2003: 30; see also Glover 1997). Needless to say, that is rare.

Third, cultures do not inhabit territories; people do. People occupying a territory have a single culture only on the organic conception of culture discussed in Chapter 2. On this conception, a group's having a culture is its having a complex property made up of its having a bundled epistemic, religious, athletic, linguistic, legal, economic ... and aesthetic culture. In as much as each element of the culture makes an essential contribution to the whole, the culture is the group's "comprehensive way of life." Unless they occur between groups with organic cultures, differences in culture will cut across groups. For example, the fact that any two people share a non-organic culture (e.g. street tango) will not predict their having another culture (e.g. bobsledding or speaking Kiswahili). Hence, what the state has to deal with are groups with different organic cultures all sharing the same territory (see also Benhabib 2002: 1–4).

THE COSMOPOLITAN INTERESTS   59

Summing up the first three conditions, states have to deal with conflict only when there is internal contact between groups with organic cultures. Cultural groups like these are seen as coexisting within a state and its territory, in an inward projection of circumstances of contact across state lines.

For a nice example of this thinking, take Kymlicka's (1995) recommendations on the rights of minority groups. Some minority groups are national minorities. For Kymlicka, a nation is a group that occupies a territory and has a societal culture—it uses a set of educational, communication, and trade institutions that enable it to maintain itself (see Chapter 2). In as much as a group has a societal culture, it is an organic culture. In as much as societal cultures enjoy and require comprehensive institutional backing, it is hard to move between them. Thus a national societal culture is an organic culture that can constitute a national identity, and national minorities maintain their societal cultures alongside other national groups in multinational states. A multinational state is not the same as a polyethnic state, which houses ethnic cultures that do not command the territorial and institutional assets needed to maintain societal cultures. Kymlicka argues that states should ensure that national minorities be equipped (with rights) in aid of their cultures' survival but that non-national minorities should receive support towards cultural integration (1995: ch. 2). Now consider: why just two options? The assumption is that what is at stake is the survival of organic culture, so integration is the only option for minorities who cannot command the institutional resources to maintain organic cultures. Cultural integration just is the dissolution of the organic whole, some of its elements being rendered out entirely, others remaining as vestiges.

A fourth condition is needed to characterize circumstances where it would seem that the state must deal with conflicting cultures. The cultures in question must be organic cultures of groups making contact within the state, but these three conditions do not suffice for conflict. Roughly put, the fourth condition is that the cultures' values speak against each other.

Sometimes groups compete for resources to realize values, each according to its own value scheme. The values each group wishes to realize are different, yet the groups must draw upon the same store of resources, which are not adequate to realize all the values. In our world, competition is routine. The Great Trail Association pitches for funds to complete

60 AESTHETIC INJUSTICE

their bike and hiking trail linking the Pacific, Arctic, and Atlantic coasts. Meanwhile, the Rick Hansen Foundation pitches for funds to complete their project of refitting playgrounds to make them universally accessible. The community chest can sponsor only one project. Competition conflicts need not turn on monetary resources. Resources include whatever is needed to realize value: space, air time, education and research, technology, public attention and endorsement, or simply a spot on the agenda.

Sometimes there are many values worth realizing, but it is impossible to realize them all, even with unlimited resources. Chapter 3 defined two value schemes as incompatible just when truths about the values in one scheme speak against truths about the values in the other scheme. Quakers cannot train in the *bushidō* without betraying their pacifist principles. Maple Leafs fans cannot remain true while cheering for the Penguins (unless the Penguins are playing the Red Wings). These can be called "incompatibility conflicts."

Incompatibility conflicts can turn on values that are mutually incomprehensible, in the sense defined in Chapter 3. Onora O'Neill highlights cases where we confront "a plurality of 'subjective conceptions of the good,' between which we cannot hope to arbitrate rationally" (2012: 16). Then "appeals to the actual norms of a society or tradition, or to the actual sensibilities, attachments or commitments of individuals will seem at worst incomprehensible to those who do not grasp those norms and commitments and at best merely conditionally reasoned to those who grasp but do not share them" (2012: 51). No doubt gaps in comprehension can occur, but incompatibility does not entail them. Not all incompatibility conflicts fit O'Neill's description.

Unlike competition, which makes life demanding, incompatibility conflicts need not be demanding. So long as those with different value schemes isolate themselves into separate spheres, where they are not in contact with each other, they will not be pulled into competition as they strive to realize their values. That said, when there is internal contact and groups have to divide scarce resources, incompatibility conflicts tend to generate or to coincide with competition for resources. Then, in a process of transference, incompatibility conflicts can come to feel demanding. Indeed, they can be felt as tragic for those who do not win the resources they need to realize the good as they see it. Matters are made worse when they cannot comprehend the values that get realized instead.

Once paired with an incompatibility conflict, competition can become intractable. After all, one way to resolve a competition is for the competing parties to converge on the same values. What prevents that is likely to be a deep, unshakeable incompatibility conflict. Moreover, the failure to secure resources to realize one's own values will seem like a tragic failure to secure resources to realize any values at all. When conflicts are demanding in this way, because competition pairs with and is exacerbated by incompatible values, the stable options are to turn to the state either to homogenize or to manage the contacts.

Appiah warns against the "common picture" that all conflicts trace to incompatible values: "we've been encouraged, not least by well-meaning intellectuals, to exaggerate their significance by an order of magnitude" (2007: xxvi). Perhaps he is right. All the same, incompatibility conflicts between organic cultures in internal contact do loom large in thinking about state-focused justice.

Justice for Cultural Conflict

Take the debate that culminated in the 1980s and 1990s between communitarians and those they took to be their liberal opponents. The "took to be" acknowledges that the debate's persistence was fuelled by overly strong positions, which eventually softened into a moderate consensus around liberal culturalism. Chapter 8 will revisit the consensus in more detail and suggest how to build upon it. For now, the debate nicely illustrates how thinking about state-focused justice centres on incompatibility conflicts between organic cultures within the state.

Communitarians offer a constellation of rationales for giving cultural interests considerable weight in the constitution of the state. Whether the rationales are, in the final analysis, inconsistent with liberalism depends on liberalism's core commitments. At any rate, begin with the rationales.

Alasdair MacIntyre voices one line of thought in *After Virtue* (1981). All genuine evaluative or normative reasoning is grounded in social practices and is articulated using schemes of thick concepts—such as concepts of honour, attentiveness, curiosity, or subtlety—that can only be

62 AESTHETIC INJUSTICE

grasped within the social practices that ground them. As O'Neill puts it, the reasoning is available only to "those who have internalized a given way of thought or life and its norms or traditions, its sensibilities, attachments or commitments" (2012: 53). Any attempt to forge a scheme of evaluative or normative reasoning that is thin enough to cross the borders between social practices is inadequate to its task: it cannot equip people to reason well and hence to flourish. If it catches on, it is liable to damage more adequate, local schemes. This is the format rationale.

A second rationale concerns the importance of having options. Having options might well be a final good, but the claim here is that since people are aware that they have lives to live and that they must make a go of living them well, they need to be able first to envisage and then act to realize their best lives. To do that, they need meaningful options. Yet, as Kymlicka writes, "it is only through access to societal culture that people have access to a range of meaningful options" (1995: 83). Why? Recalling the format rationale, perhaps meaningful options are those expressed in a vocabulary that an agent understands and that renders them imaginable (Dworkin 1985, Margalit and Raz 1990, Kymlicka 1995: 80–84). Perhaps, alternatively, meaningful options are those with a normative appeal available only to cultural insiders. This is the options rationale.

A third rationale, concerning recognition, features in the writings of Charles Taylor (esp. 1991 and 1994). A problem with the format and options rationales is that they imply only that people have an interest in having some culture, not that they have an interest in having the very culture that is their own (Margalit and Habertal 1994). On those rationales, a direct solution to any culture-based value conflict is for the parties to converge on the same culture. The recognition rationale does not yield this result, because it traces our interests in culture back to a more basic interest in authenticity. For Taylor, authenticity is the distinctively modern form in which people secure their dignity: their dignity consists in their being who they are (see also Dworkin 2013: 203–209). Being oneself is not, however, an entirely individual endeavour. People are social creatures, and who they are is partly a function of how they are seen by others. Moreover, there is no dignity in being seen by others merely as a member of some group. Recognition is more demanding than that: it requires that others see us as members of groups that are understood to have values and reasons to which their members rightly respond. Taylor argues that recognition, in this sense, "is not just a courtesy we owe people. It is a vital human need" (1994: 26).

Some communitarians oppose what they call a "classical liberal" picture of agency and human thriving. Classical liberals place fundamental importance on agents being able to realize the good as they conceive it, as individuals, hence as independent of tradition (Mill 1859, Waldron 1995: 753, Bourcier 2020). On this picture, agents can step back from their cultural background and, from that neutral viewpoint, select schemes of value by which to live. Taylor objects that "to bracket out history, nature, society, and the demands of solidarity, everything but what I find in myself, would be to eliminate all candidates for what matters" (1991: 45). Arguably most trenchant is Michael Sandel's (1998) analysis of the theory of agency upon which Rawls (1971) constructs his theory of justice.

Liberals need not (and most do not) accept the targeted theories of agency. Liberal culturalists take on board the communitarian critique of classical liberalism; they concur that the exercise of agency necessarily draws upon cultural resources (e.g. Mason 1993, Margalit and Halbertal 1994, Raz 1994, Taylor 1994, Galston 1995, Kymlicka 1995, Tully 1995, Waldron 1995, Kymlicka 2001b, Appiah 2005, Chambers 2008, Patten 2014). They also accept the observations about format, contexts for having options, and the importance of recognition. Thus Rawls takes it for granted that the crucibles of full agency are organic cultures, which generate comprehensive conceptions of the good. For the most part, liberals insist only that the state must treat conflicting organic cultures neutrally, ensuring especially that none is able to leverage state power and direct it against its competitors (cf. Chambers 2008).

This is not the place to adjudicate the dispute between communitarians and liberals. Rather, the task is to bring out how all acquiesce in the view that state-focused justice must deal with organic cultures locked in incompatibility conflicts internal to the state. Organic cultures so differ that it is impossible to extract from all of them any interests that can ground a shared vision of how to engineer their common social space. Any candidate for a shared vision endorsed by some will be rejected by others, and any candidate that can be endorsed by all will be too thin to provide robust reasons to act. For communitarians, it follows that there can be no shared vision of how to engineer a common social space. The

64   AESTHETIC INJUSTICE

only source of values and reasons is local culture. For liberals, it follows that a shared vision of how to engineer a common social space cannot have its source in local, culture-bound value schemes; it must abstract from their specificities (O'Neill 2012: 53–54).

The dialectic boasts a rich history. Thomas Hobbes saw the state as needed to manage "discord and strife" that inevitably grows out of the fact that people "mete Good and Evill by diverse measures" (1983 [1651]: 3.31). By the late eighteenth century, it had been settled that personal value schemes arise within and find their home in cultural groupings (the classic history is Berlin 1997 [1958]). Even John Stuart Mill, advocating "experiments in living," took them to be group, not solo, endeavours (1859: ch. 3).

Rawls's *Political Liberalism* could not be clearer. The "serious problem" for political philosophy is how there can be a just society of free and equal citizens profoundly divided by incompatible comprehensive conceptions of the good (1993: xviii). His paradigm is religion, which "introduces into people's conceptions of their good a transcendent element not admitting of compromise .... Political liberalism starts by taking to heart the absolute depth of that irreconcilable latent conflict" (1993: xxvi). (As an aside, not all religions function as Rawls assumes.) At any rate, a comprehensive conception of the good can only come from an organic culture; the key circumstance of state-focused justice is the fact of incompatibility conflict between organic cultures internal to the state.

Manufactured Conflict

Not all cultures are in internal contact, not all are organic, and not all have incompatible values schemes. Therefore, state-focused justice, which deals with incompatibility conflict between organic cultures internal to the state, provides a foil for thinking about justice in circumstances where there is contact, not necessarily internal to the state, between non-organic cultures with compatible value schemes.

If religious culture is Rawls's paradigm of the serious problem to which state-focused justice is the solution, then Alexander Nehamas provides a counterpoint to Rawls. Aesthetic cultures are, he writes, "less like Christian churches and more like the pagan cultures of Ancient Greece,

THE COSMOPOLITAN INTERESTS   65

which recognized their common concern with the divine despite the different forms in which they worshipped it, and acknowledged even foreign practices they had no desire to follow" (2007: 81–82).

Notice how the three communitarian rationales lose their grip once thinking turns away from organic cultures. Organic cultures might articulate webs of thick concepts that knit together ways of life and constitute the identities for which agents demand recognition. While some aesthetic cultures are parts of organic cultures, aesthetic culture certainly does not supply a thickly comprehensive vision of how to live, and it is not often a point on which recognition is a "vital human need."

Acknowledging this, state-focused justice defaults to privatizing aesthetic cultures, leaving their management to commerce and civil society. Only for special reasons is there a role for the state to play (see Chapter 8). Therefore, what considerations factor into what we should do when designing (privatized) social arrangements that manage contact between aesthetic cultures?

According to the network theory, aesthetic engagement channels into many cultures. Those aesthetic cultures are plural: their aesthetic value profiles are different but valid, incommensurable, compatible, and to some degree mutually comprehensible. Since aesthetic cultures are plural, we engage the aesthetic values of cultures to which we belong, and we can take attitudes of rooted or routed respect towards the aesthetic values of cultures to which we do not belong. So concluded Chapter 3.

Here is a further hypothesis. Since they are plural and welcome respect, aesthetic cultures are not natural sites of incompatibility conflict. They are naturally conflict-free zones. Of course, aesthetic cultures in contact with one another can and do compete for resources, but their competitions are not made intractable by an incompatibility conflict. One might say that incompatibility conflict is a degenerate condition for contact between aesthetic cultures.

The degenerate condition can be a symptom of weaponized aesthetics. Pecola's predicament requires that the beauty of white bodies be incompatible with any notion of black beauty. Nat's predicament stems from the aesthetic potential of tactile images being so unthinkable that nobody bids for the resources that would have made him an artist. Yahgulanaas suggests a predicament where too much admiration blocks the need to leave people in peace.

66 AESTHETIC INJUSTICE

If the hypothesis is correct that aesthetic culture is naturally a conflict-free zone, then a case can be made that weaponized aesthetics is unjust in two ways. It deploys aesthetic culture as an instrument of social injustice. At the same time, it subverts interests in aesthetic cultures being conflict-free zones. In particular, it subverts those interests by harming people in their capacities as aesthetic agents. In other words, among the circumstances of justice are those where the way to avoid having to manage conflict is to secure conflict-free cultural zones—to guard against manufactured conflict.

Value Diversity

According to the cosmopolitan theory:

> a relatively large-scale social arrangement is aesthetically unjust when and only when, and because, the arrangement is part of an aesthetic culture that harms people with a different aesthetic culture in their capacities as aesthetic agents and thereby subverts justice-relevant interests in the value diversity and social autonomy of aesthetic cultures.

The challenge has been to specify the two cosmopolitan interests as justice-relevant. The previous chapter sought their reflections in portraits of capacities for aesthetic activity, and this chapter has sought them in the circumstances of justice for non-conflicting cultures. The interests are ones we might have because aesthetic cultures are plural, affording rooted or routed respect, so that conflict is a degenerate condition for them. Here is the first cosmopolitan interest.

When it comes to plural fields of value, we have an interest in there being diverse cultures of value. That is, the interest is in there being diverse value cultures in fields where values sort into schemes that are different, valid, incommensurable, compatible, and to some degree mutually comprehensible. Since the field of aesthetic cultures is plural, we have an interest in there being aesthetic cultures with distinct aesthetic profiles. Call this the "diversity claim." The claim can be restated as a claim about value. All else being equal, it is good that there be diverse value cultures, for plural fields of value. Hence, all else being equal, it is good that there be diverse aesthetic value cultures.

Is it good, all else being equal, that there are diverse aesthetic goods? One option is to count realizations of aesthetic goodness: it is better that there be n + 1 rather than n graceful turns of phrase or n + 1 rather than n edgy typefaces. Arguably, however, it is not always good to realize more goods (Parfit 1984). An alternative is to count ways of being good: it is better that there be n +1 rather than n ways of being graceful or edgy, even if nothing realizes them. However, the network theory and its cousins (e.g. Walton 1970) imply that all determinates of aesthetic goodness exist, because all aesthetic profiles exist. All aesthetic profiles exist because they are abstracta (see Chapter 3, Lopes 2018b: ch. 10). Consequently, any interest in there being diverse determinates of aesthetic goodness is satisfied trivially.

The diversity claim is not that it is good that there be diverse aesthetic goods; the claim is that it is good that there be diverse aesthetic value cultures, hence diverse social arrangements where people realize aesthetic goods. From this it does not follow that it is always good to realize more aesthetic goods. Neither is the claim the trivial one that it is good for there to be diverse aesthetic profiles for cultures to coordinate upon. The diversity claim is that it is, all else equal, good that there be diverse aesthetic cultures, each being a pattern of behaviour in a social group whose members actually coordinate on an aesthetic profile.

Compare: there is no point in claiming that it would be good to have diverse languages, conceived abstractly as lexicons and grammars. An infinite number of those already exist. When it comes to language, one might suggest instead that it is good, all else being equal, that people know and use diverse languages (e.g. Nowak 2019, Nowak 2020).

Perhaps, as is often said, we should celebrate our differences. If we should, the reason is not simply that we are different. Difference is not by itself a source of value, for everything differs from everything else. Only some differences matter. The interest in the diversity of aesthetic value cultures is not an interest in the value of difference; it is an interest in having different values, in the sense of having cultures in which different values can be realized, in plural fields of value.

Is the diversity claim true? Do we have an interest in there being diverse aesthetic value cultures? The cosmopolitan theory asserts that we

68 AESTHETIC INJUSTICE

do indeed have this interest, and the main argument for the theory is that it explains scenarios where aesthetic injustice stems from and compounds weaponized aesthetics. By hypothesis, weaponized aesthetics functions partly by degrading the value diversity of aesthetic cultures, and degrading the value diversity of aesthetic cultures amplifies the harms wrought by weaponized aesthetics. The case for the hypothesis is made in Part II.

Since this is the argument for the diversity claim, no commitment is made to another argument for the claim. Moreover, an objection to the claim turns out to miss the mark.

The objection targets what Kymlicka calls a "quasi-aesthetic" argument (1995: 121–123). On this argument, we have reason to make social arrangements for cultural diversity because it contributes to quality of life by creating a more interesting world that enriches our experiences (Falk 1988). As Alan Patten puts it:

> Since people benefit in various ways from the flourishing of cultures they are not members of, they could conceivably have complaints based on justice when somebody else's culture enters into decline. In general, justice has to do with the distribution of benefits and burdens, and we benefit, all else being equal, from living in a richer and more diverse world. (2014: 149)

Kymlicka accepts the premise but doubts that it justifies social arrangements where group-differentiated rights favour minority cultural groups. The "quasi-aesthetic" benefits rarely outweigh the burdens on members of the majority. Moreover, the argument can be extended to argue that members of minorities have obligations to preserve their cultures for the common good, when insisting on their complying with such obligations would be illiberal.

Granting Kymlicka's concerns, they do not impeach the diversity claim. In the first place, pairing the diversity claim with the network theory of aesthetic value, an item's having aesthetic value does not amount merely to its enriching our experiences. More importantly, an interest in the diversity of aesthetic cultures does not entail the kind of group-differentiated rights or obligations that worry Kymlicka. Other kinds of policies can secure an interest in the value diversity of aesthetic cultures, as we shall see. The diversity claim's failure to do what philosophers have sometimes asked of it shows only that they have asked too much.

An argument for the diversity claim, following in the footsteps of Mill (1859), appeals to the instrumental benefits of having diverse value cultures (Page 2007, Gaus 2016, Muldoon 2016). In brief, we cannot know how to arrange our lives without trying out, hence making room for, many perspectives on what is good and on what realizes what is good; therefore, a diversity of cultures is an effective means to living well. For this reason, as Ryan Muldoon writes, "diversity is ... something that we should celebrate and encourage" (2016: 15). Richard Wollheim (1985) applies the argument specifically to the diversity of aesthetic cultures, which he takes to be an effective means to discover unexpected sources of pleasure.

Maybe this argument is sound, both in general and as applied to aesthetic culture. The art historian Thomas Crow hints at it when he describes avant-garde art as the research and development arm of aesthetic culture (1996: 35). Even so, one might accept the cosmopolitan theory of aesthetic injustice and still reject the instrumentalist argument. The cosmopolitan theory is consistent with cultural diversity being a final good, in plural fields of value.

Social Autonomy

Complementing and counterbalancing the interest in the value diversity of aesthetic cultures is a second cosmopolitan interest, an interest in their social autonomy. For plural fields of value, we have an interest in the social autonomy of cultures. Since aesthetic culture is plural, we have an interest in the social autonomy of aesthetic cultures. Like the value diversity claim, the social autonomy claim can be restated in terms of value: for plural fields of value, it is good, all else being equal, that cultures have social autonomy. Hence, all else being equal, it is good that aesthetic cultures have social autonomy.

What is a culture's social autonomy? Autonomy is standardly attributed to persons. Catriona Mackenzie provides a helpful three-part taxonomy (2014: 16–18). The core of autonomy is self-governance, which consists in a personal capacity to act on the basis of motives that are in

70 AESTHETIC INJUSTICE

an important sense one's own. Self-determination is a further capacity, a capacity to make and implement decisions about what to value and what kind of person to be. Self-authorization is a personal capacity to regard oneself as having normative authority with respect to self-governance and self-determination.

Each of these is a capacity of persons, even if nobody is likely to thrive except in a favourable social setting. Social obstacles to self-determination and self-authorization pose an especially obstinate challenge. For instance, adaptive preferences are widespread: people often act on the basis of motives that they endorse, although their endorsement is not self-determined. Liberals typically champion a conception of just social arrangements as ones that are favourable to personal self-determination and self-authorization, as well as self-governance (e.g. Raz 1986, Sunstein 1994, Chambers 2008, Mackenzie 2014).

Personal autonomy requires favourable social conditions, but social autonomy is not personal autonomy in favourable social conditions. Granted, aesthetic life invites the exercise of personal autonomy (Walden 2023). I decide to flavour this *caldinho* with lime juice, I have made it my mission to be someone who cooks Goan food, and I lay claim to my authority in these two matters of self-governance and self-determination. Nonetheless, the cosmopolitan theory appeals to a feature of cultures that is not reducible to the personal autonomy their members.

Might social autonomy be personal autonomy elevated to the group level? Some groups have capacities to make collective decisions about how to act in accordance with group values, to make and implement decisions about what to value and what kind of group to be, and to arrogate to themselves authority over group self-governance and group self-determination. Perhaps an example would be a university's strategic planning process? Be that as it may, few aesthetic cultural groups have the needed facilities for collective decision-making. Ballet and the typography scene are not group agents; they can neither deliberate nor act collectively. The proposal that they be more like universities, endowed with capacities for collective thought and action, has not a lot of prima facie appeal.

Suppose that we have certain interests because aesthetic cultures, being plural, are at home to rooted and routed respect, such that their coming into conflict is a degenerate condition. Starting on the aesthetic side of things, anyone who is engaged in some home aesthetic culture is

THE COSMOPOLITAN INTERESTS   71

equipped to respect the values of some neighbouring aesthetic cultures. They can see, to some degree, how those engaged in the neighbouring cultures act on genuine aesthetic reasons. (That is rooted respect.) Being so equipped, they are additionally equipped to see how it is practically possible for them to come to see how those engaged in faraway aesthetic cultures also act on genuine aesthetic reasons. (That is routed respect.) Switching to the justice side of things, anyone who is engaged in some home aesthetic culture is in principle equipped to regard the field of aesthetic cultures as degenerating into conflict through the erosion of respect. Obstacles to respect for the values of another culture will tend to make competition intractable. Competing parties will not have the option to converge on the same values, and a failure to secure resources to realize one's own values will seem like a tragic failure to secure resources to realize any values at all. The stable options are to turn to the state either to homogenize or to manage the contacts.

In short, members of any aesthetic culture have an interest in its being the case that, for any other aesthetic culture, aesthetic reasons for its members to act will continue to have normative weight. They will continue to be reasons for them to engage.

Many (but not all) aesthetic cultures are dynamic; their aesthetic profiles change over time. The claim is not that we have an interest in their never changing. We need a more flexible account of what it is for aesthetic reasons to continue to have normative weight in an aesthetic culture.

Members of an aesthetic culture determine its aesthetic profile by engaging value, but discourse plays a role too. Consider aesthetic disagreement, as in this exchange about a curry:

DOMINIC: Way too spicy!
AARON: Not at all.

Assume that the dish tastes the same to both and that they both like it just as much, or as little, so that the point of the exchange is not for the speakers to share information about themselves (Egan 2010). What, then, is its point? Suppose they go on:

D: It's so hot it obliterates the key ingredients of a *vindalho*.
A: I'm making a Yorkshire curry house vindaloo.

72 AESTHETIC INJUSTICE

The point of the exchange is to determine the social context (Sundell 2011, Sundell 2017, Lopes 2018b: ch. 9). That is, it determines what the aesthetic profile is in the context of the conversation. Is it the aesthetic profile of Goan cuisine or its northern English offshoot? This example of intercultural negotiation on aesthetic profiles has an intracultural counterpart. Disagreements between members of a culture can reorient thinking about the aesthetic profile so as to modify engagement, thereby putting pressure on the profile to change.

As a feature of aesthetic cultures, social autonomy does not consist in capacities for collectively acting on collective motives, collectively choosing the good, and collectively assuming authority in these matters. Rather, a culture has social autonomy just when and to the extent that its constitutive conception of the good—its aesthetic profile—is a product of group members' acts of engagement. An interest in its social autonomy is an interest in its being, in this way, true to itself.

Is the social autonomy claim true? Do we have an interest in the social autonomy of value cultures, for plural fields of value? The cosmopolitan theory answers that we do. The main argument is that the theory makes sense of scenarios where aesthetic injustice stems from and compounds weaponized aesthetics. By hypothesis, one of the effects of weaponized aesthetics is that people participate in aesthetic practices where their own engagement is not what determines the aesthetic profile—or at least not often enough. What determines the aesthetic profile is (too often) forces from which they are alienated. This hypothesis had better do some heavy lifting in Part II.

Interactions

According to the cosmopolitan theory, we have interests in the value diversity and social autonomy of aesthetic cultures. How might the interests interact?

Pursuing one interest can promote the other. The social autonomy of aesthetic cultures tends to diversify them, because a group whose members' engagement determines the aesthetic profile is likely to steer a course of its own. Likewise, value diversity paves paths to social autonomy: the more aesthetic cultures there are, the higher the chance that people will make their way to cultures where their engagement actually

THE COSMOPOLITAN INTERESTS 73

does determine their culture's aesthetic profile. As long as they get in where they fit in, they can make a difference.

At the same time, the two interests counterbalance each other. On the one hand, fanatical or over-zealous pursuits of the interest in value diversity are held in check by deference to the power of members to determine the aesthetic profile of their culture through their own acts of engagement. On the other hand, the interest in social autonomy can be checked by an interest in value diversity. It matters that members' engagement determines the aesthetic profile in part because the culture has its own character, its own scheme of values. There is something members' engagement can be true to.

Neither interest is more basic than the other. Appiah champions the lexical priority of personal autonomy over any interest in diversity. "There is," as he remarks, "no place for the enforcement of diversity by trapping people within a kind of difference that they long to escape" (2007: 105). Indeed, he adds, homogeneity is a worry only when it is a result of "a previous crime against autonomy" (2005: 153). Granting Appiah is right about this, it would be a mistake to apply the point about personal autonomy to social autonomy. Suppose that, having secured the personal autonomy of aesthetic agents, we thereby secure the social autonomy of their aesthetic cultures. Also suppose that those socially autonomous cultures began to converge on homogeneity. Surely we would continue to have an interest in the value diversity of aesthetic cultures. The interest need not imply trapping people in difference that they long to escape. Policies that implement the interest need not be illiberal (Chapter 8).

A cosmopolitan approach to aesthetic injustice need not appeal only to interests in the diversity and autonomy of aesthetic culture. Those interests are prominent, however, and we will need to appeal to both in mounting the argument, in Part II, that aesthetic injustice stems from and compounds weaponized aesthetics.

Rooted Capacities

Aesthetic injustices are harms to aesthetic capacities that subvert interests in the value diversity and social autonomy of aesthetic value cultures. Chapter 3 located the capacities in a theory of aesthetic value.

74 AESTHETIC INJUSTICE

That procedure was not mandatory. An alternative is simply to cite aesthetic capacities in a list of those that should carry weight in designing just social arrangements. One of Martha Nussbaum's central capabilities is "being able to use imagination and thought in connection with experiencing and producing works and events of one's own choice ... literary, musical, and so forth" (2003: 41). Nobody can complain that the inclusion is erroneous: the goods of aesthetic life belong on any list of goods whose pursuit is central to human well-being. However, Nussbaum does not attempt to reason from an account of the capability to its belonging on her list. There might be value in a richer picture of aesthetic capability that brings out why it merits its place in a list like Nussbaum's.

In view of their pluralism, aesthetic cultures give their members reasons to respect, and these capacities for rooted or routed respect are key to serving cosmopolitan interests. Recall that rooted respect is not merely an awareness that others have their own values; it is an awareness of how those values are reasons for others to engage in specific ways. Copeland respects Kathakalī values by seeing how a movement's being shimmering would be a reason for Rele to execute it, even though it is no reason for her to do the same. Respect is rooted when and because it implicates engagement in this way. (Routed respect requires an additional ability to think counterfactually about rooted respect.) At any rate, capacities for rooted and routed respect include all the capacities that are core capacities for engagement, with the addition of the capacity for comprehension—for evaluating in an overlapping profile.

Engagement's core is the capacity to make accurate evaluations in alignment with the aesthetic profile of a culture (Lopes 2018b). Practical capacities are also crucial because members of the culture determine the aesthetic profile only by acting, with effect, on their evaluations in culture-specific ways—by making, appreciating, or performing some other aesthetic act-type. Engaging in a social practice also exploits the skills needed to learn, to communicate, and to coordinate with others.

What is not required is what Raz, in passing, calls "enlightenment" (2004: 3). Enlightenment is an explicit understanding of the pluralism of aesthetic cultures and their affording rooted and routed respect. The cosmopolitan theory does not go so far as to claim that, in order to act on interests in the value diversity and social autonomy of aesthetic cultures, ordinary aesthetic agents must apply a concept of plural value schemes as different but valid, incommensurable, compatible, and to some degree mutually comprehensible. Nor need they apply concepts of rooted or routed respect. Concepts such as these—and the understandings in which they figure—are achieved only on a theoretical plane, by those who can step back from the thick of aesthetic engagement and take the kind of bird's eye perspective on the whole field of aesthetic cultures that was offered in Chapter 3. This special achievement is not an option in every cultural setting. We live our aesthetic lives in practice and not in principle.

Since they do not require enlightenment, our cosmopolitan interests are served by capacities that we have just because we inhabit local aesthetic cultures. We need not step outside the confines of our local cultures in order to have interests in things going well in our contacts with other aesthetic cultures. Just as testimony is a mechanism by means of which your evidence can become my evidence, cosmopolitan interests are a mechanism by means of which values in your aesthetic culture can give adherents of my aesthetic culture reasons to act. In this way, cosmopolitan interests are rooted: that values in your culture are reasons for adherents of my culture to act is partly a function of facts about my culture.

Policy Considerations

Where there are unjust social arrangements, there must be considerations to take into account in crafting policy. The circumstances of justice shape the kinds of considerations that should inform policy. Incompatibility conflicts between organic cultures in internal contact might favour the design of states whose legal and constitutional arrangements can manage the conflicts. Since the cosmopolitan theory does not take justice to be a state monopoly, it is natural to ask what entities should be equipped with what policy tools in order to counteract aesthetic injustice. However, we cannot directly deduce from the cosmopolitan theory either a list of policies or a list of the non-state entities that should implement them.

As we saw in Chapter 2, aesthetic engagement permeates just about every sphere of human activity. In addition to the arts, aesthetic cultures are found in commerce, agriculture, domestic life, entertainment, the sciences, and the applied sciences. The entities whose policies can produce

76 AESTHETIC INJUSTICE

or remedy aesthetic injustice come in all shapes and sizes. Arts institutions stand out: galleries, auction houses, labels and producers, publishers, performing arts companies, arts journalists, patrons and granting bodies, the schools for the arts, and manufacturers of arts materials, from pencils to pianos. Add in their counterparts outside the arts. There is the design world, of course: fashion, domestic design, cuisine, and the like. Educational institutions, social clubs, neighbourhood associations, developers, many manufacturers and retailers, farmers, and academic disciplines are sites of aesthetic culture, too.

Few, if any, policies promoting aesthetic justice are likely to be effective in the hands of all of these entities. Just consider, very briefly, the three scenarios of cultural appropriation, bodily beauty ideals, and unjust access to aesthetic infrastructures that were presented in Chapter 1 and that are going to resume centre stage in a page or two. One tool that can be brought to bear on cultural appropriation is intellectual property law, an instrument of the state, but that tool is not well suited to address Yahgulanaas's concern about the medusa syndrome. He is not at all concerned about a breach of intellectual property. The most effective tools to remedy gendered and racialized bodily beauty norms are those in the hands of image-makers: the movie business, fashion, advertising, and social media platforms. Reversing the distributive injustice brought out by the case of Nat might require allocations of public funds, but the most direct impact will come from energy put into curriculum reform and messaging the public. Obviously, then, no one policy tool is suitable for every entity that is in a position to address some scenario of aesthetic injustice. Modesty is in order about the prospects of extracting one size fits all—or even one size fits most—policies from the interests in the value diversity and social autonomy of aesthetic cultures.

Might one at least hope to land on general policies to be adopted by states in support of aesthetic justice? Many state policies set environmental conditions that can favour or disfavour aesthetic injustice: protections for freedom of association and expression, legal provisions recognizing intellectual property rights, and general commitments to fair allocations of public funds, just for starters. However, the precise content of these policies rarely takes aesthetic culture into account. As implemented, they might fail to curb aesthetic injustice. Examples pepper Part II.

The work of Brian Soucek (2017 and 2019) gives further reason to be wary of directly deriving state policies from the cosmopolitan theory. An overemphasis on constitutional provisions that limit state action obscures the myriad laws and regulations that cannot help but impact aesthetic culture, often in unforeseen ways. Examples include import tariffs, tax laws, land use ordinances, one percent and beautification bylaws, and regulations for historic preservation. Safety standards for food, playgrounds, and vehicles also belong on Soucek's list (Herrington and Nicholls 2007). A dramatic example is how high taxes on U.S. cabarets drove the shift from the big band to the bebop eras. The "tax efficiency" of the small ensemble drove big bands off the stage.

A theory of aesthetic injustice should provide considerations to take into account in crafting policies. The interests in the value diversity and social autonomy of aesthetic cultures had better fit the bill. However, the policies to which it points us must be sensitive to the settings where they are applied and the characteristics of the group that is to apply them.

This concludes Part I. Aesthetic cultures are patterns of behaviour explained by shared formative conditions. Being plural, they afford rooted and routed respect; they are not, by nature, sites of incompatibility conflict. This chapter added that interests in the value diversity and social autonomy of aesthetic cultures require capacities for respect, and they are justice-relevant because interests of justice include any interests in ensuring that naturally non-conflicting cultures do not degenerate into manufactured conflict. If there is any aesthetic injustice, then we can understand it as a large-scale social arrangement that undermines interests in the value diversity or social autonomy of aesthetic cultures by harming people in their capacities as aesthetic agents. Part II argues that the cosmopolitan theory earns its keep because there is some aesthetic injustice, so described.

PART II

5

Aesthetic Appropriation

The main argument for the cosmopolitan theory is that our understanding of weaponized aesthetics is incomplete until we see how it spawns and is compounded by aesthetic injustice. Weaponized aesthetics comes in many guises, and the following chapters discuss some, beginning with weaponized appropriation of aesthetic culture. The place to start is with existing scholarship (e.g. Nicholas and Wylie 2012, Matthes 2016, Ypi 2017, Liao 2018, Matthes 2019, Nguyen and Strohl 2019, Rings 2019, Lenard and Balint 2020, Mejía Chavez and Bacharach 2021, Pearson 2021, Tuvel 2021, Young 2021). This scholarship is not wrong, but it is incomplete in as much as it overlooks aesthetic injustice. A full understanding of weaponized aesthetics must heed Yahgulanaas's concerns about the reception of Reid's *Spirit of Haida Gwaii*. In the Medusa syndrome, people are harmed in their capacities as aesthetic agents in ways that subvert an interest in the social autonomy of aesthetic cultures.

From Contact to Weaponized Aesthetic Appropriation

The appropriation of aesthetic culture—call it "aesthetic appropriation"—is a special case of cultural appropriation. To see how badly the broader phenomenon of cultural appropriation can go wrong, it helps to situate it against a background of cultural contact that is often harmless or mutually beneficial. Characterizing aesthetic appropriation as neither good nor bad per se makes vivid how much is lost by its being weaponized.

People with different cultures come into contact with one another. Chapter 4 defined contact as more than people with different cultures catching sight of one another. Contact occurs just when activity (or the

Aesthetic Injustice. Dominic McIver Lopes, Oxford University Press. © Dominic McIver Lopes 2024.
DOI: 10.1093/oso/9780198930983.003.0005

82 AESTHETIC INJUSTICE

known practical possibility of activity) by at least one party makes a difference to activity by the other party. So understood, contact is routine among human beings, because we are on the whole curious, migratory, on the lookout for new information, new technologies, and new experiences.

Such traits as these do not turn every contact into conquest or colonialism. In his history of some major seventeenth-century contacts, Timothy Brook underlines how contacts at that time featured:

> selective adjustment, made through a process of mutual influence. Rather than complete transformation or deadly conflict, there was negotiation and borrowing; rather than triumph and loss, give and take; rather than the transformation of cultures, their interaction .... The age of discovery was largely over, the age of imperialism was yet to come. The seventeenth century was the age of improvisation. (2008: 21)

The takeaway is not that we must admire, or excuse, the people of that century; it is that contact runs from mutually enriching exchanges to vicious colonialism.

For excellent reasons, the vicious end of the spectrum tops the agenda. Yet, even as we regret the worst of the past and strive for reparation and reconciliation, those writers have a point who seek to remind us how much advantage there can be for all parties to contact, when conditions are right. Cultures mix. What we call "China" was Chinese porcelain decorated to suit the taste of the Persian market, where gold plate was prohibited. British curry houses serve vindaloo, a dish derived from Goan *vindalho*, whose Portuguese name reflects some of its distinguishing flavours. Jazz without the saxophone, a fixture of the nineteenth-century orchestra, is hard to imagine. Today, *kyogen* troops fruitfully collaborate with *commedia dell'arte* companies, Aboriginal artists in Australia use acrylics to make dot paintings, and stoles made of *kente* have been incorporated into the academic and clerical regalia of black people in the United States. A touchstone for many commentators is a passage from Salman Rushdie's *Imaginary Homelands* in praise of "hybridity, impurity, intermingling, the transformation that comes of new and unexpected combinations of human beings, cultures, ideas, politics, movies, songs." Rushdie adds that "*mélange*, hotchpotch, a bit of this and a bit of that is *how newness enters the world*" (1991: 394). (Caveat: newness is not invariably a good thing, and we must not scorn the impulse to prevent oldness from leaving the world.)

Put broadly, aesthetic appropriation is a form of contact, a practice of using the resources of an aesthetic culture in the expressive practices of those who are not its members—call them "outsiders"—in a way that makes a difference to insiders. Notice that the focus is on practices, not specific acts.

What are the resources of an aesthetic culture? This is hardly the time to be stingy. They include material or symbolic artifacts; practices of using motifs, themes, subject matters, vocabularies, genres, or styles; methods of performance and display; conventions or norms; or techniques for manipulating other resources. They also include aesthetic profiles. On the network theory, its profile is essential to the coordinated activity that constitutes an aesthetic culture.

Uses of resources such as these in the expressive practices of outsiders run the gamut from taking to a new location, displaying, and modifying to reproducing or representing in various media for any of a number of purposes.

Ivan Gaskell helpfully labels some significant points along a spectrum of uses (2018: 161). In what he calls "assumption," outsiders use bits of another culture while valuing them in what they take to be the very same way as insiders value them. The values are assumed to be shared. In "translation," outsiders adopt elements of culture, in the belief that their doing so will be to their benefit, knowing full well that the benefits are not those that insiders expect to accrue. In "supersession," outsiders treat elements of another culture either oblivious to or aiming to expunge the value it holds for insiders. If Brook is right about the seventeenth century, assumption and translation are not always covers for supersession.

So conceived, aesthetic appropriation is normatively neutral, neither good nor bad per se (see also Rogers 2006, Young 2008: 3–5, Matthes 2016, Nguyen and Strohl 2019, Pearson 2021, Tuvel 2021). The alternative is to define it as necessarily bad, wrong, or unjust (e.g. Heyd 2007, Nicholas and Wylie 2012, Lenard and Balint 2020). As Erich Matthes points out, the alternatives are terminological and heuristic, not metaphysical (2016: 347–348). Going neutral, the task will be to mark out the practices of aesthetic appropriation that are bad, wrong, or unjust. Going

84 AESTHETIC INJUSTICE

loaded, we start out by pinning the label, "aesthetic appropriation," only on those cases of a broader phenomenon that are bad, wrong, or unjust.

Technically, we should be able to say what needs saying whether we go neutral or loaded, but normative loading tends to muddy a useful truth. As we have seen, when conditions are right, contact is perfectly fine, a powerful engine of cultural change. Therefore, one question will be, how can this good thing sour? Another will be, what can we do to keep it healthy? Both questions are worth asking, and their answers are important, but normative loading tends to distract us from them.

On a broad and normatively neutral theory that reduces appropriation to use:

> aesthetic appropriation is any practice of using the resources of an aesthetic culture in the expressive practices of outsiders in a way that makes a difference to insiders.

This theory of aesthetic appropriation can be woven into the theory of weaponized aesthetics stated in Chapter 1. The result is a theory of weaponized aesthetic appropriation. That is:

> a relatively large-scale social arrangement weaponizes aesthetic appropriation when and only when, and because, it includes expressive practices of using the resources of another aesthetic culture, and these practices stem from and compound social injustice by licensing or normalizing the acts and interlocked harms that constitute social injustice.

In short, aesthetic appropriation is weaponized just when it impacts insiders by exposing them to social injustice. The next four sections draw from existing scholarship to present four takes on weaponized aesthetic appropriation.

Dispossession

For better or worse, the law regulates cultural appropriation within a property framework (Merryman 1986, Harding 1999). Examples include the United States's Native American Graves Protection and Repatriation Act of 1990 and, at the international level, the Hague Convention of 1954, the UNESCO Convention of 1970, and the Bellagio Declaration of 1993. Across the decades, the trend has been to extend what counts as property and who owns it. Thus the Hague Convention protects the "tangible" property of nation-states in times of war, and the Bellagio Declaration also covers the "intangible" cultural property of Indigenous peoples. Presumably, the expressive practices of outsiders using the resources of an aesthetic culture can stem from and compound social injustice by violating property rules. Letting "theft" refer to any practice of use that violates property rules, we can ask when a practice of use of the resources of an aesthetic culture counts as theft.

Things can be property, but property is not a set of things. Property is a type of social institution whose tokens are systems of rules that empower some to exclude others from the use of resources. Resources can be material, such as land and manufactured goods, or intangible, as in the case of intellectual property. Private property rules give individuals limited power to exclude others from some uses of a resource. Collective property rules give groups limited power to exclude people from some uses of a resource. Common property rules give anyone use of a resource, limited by the condition that their use not deprive others of the same use. Different property systems have different rules allocating resources into the three categories. Other features of property can also vary from one system to the next—for example, many rules for transfer and alienability are possible. However, these are special exclusions derivative upon the prior existence of property. Rules for exclusion from use are fundamental to the institution of property.

The function and hence the justification of a property system, with its own constitutive rules, is to serve some interests of parties to the system. The interests can be economic—interests in incentivizing productive labour, for example. However, there is no reason to restrict the interests served by property systems to economic ones, and economic interests are not always paramount (see Waldron 2020 for examples).

James O. Young proposes what he calls the "cultural significance principle" (2008: 91; see also Thompson 2003: 252, Young 2012). According to this principle, the fact that the resource of an aesthetic culture has value for the members of a cultural group lends weight to an exclusion

86   AESTHETIC INJUSTICE

of outsider use. Notice that any kind of value will do—not just economic value.

At the same time, Young adds three further principles (2008: 98–101). The principles are that it lends weight to an entity's owning a cultural resource that the entity is best able to preserve the resource, to make it accessible to all those for whom it has value, or to supply it with an interpretive context. Young reasons that when these three kinds of considerations outweigh the value of a cultural resource to insiders, then they should not have the power to exclude its use by outsiders—it should not be their property.

This reasoning fails to accommodate the realities of weaponized aesthetic appropriation. Right off the bat, note that the three further principles (concerning preservation, access, and interpretive context) are supposed to apply only to cultural resources and not to other kinds of resources. The asymmetry is surprising—imagine applying the further principles to car ownership! Worse, the asymmetry is especially concerning when a group is unable to preserve, share, or provide appropriate context for a cultural resource precisely because it has suffered social injustice and, indeed, a flagrant disregard for the cultural significance principle in the first place.

Kicked off the land, depopulated, their political and legal structures disrupted or dismantled, many Indigenous peoples endure unconscionable levels of abuse and violence, and they suffer disproportionately bad health, education, and economic outcomes. All this severely strains their capacity to preserve their cultural resources, to provide access, when access is warranted, and to maintain the integrity of cultural items. Records exist of Indigenous elders—for example, Billy Assu, a Ligwilda'xw Kwakwaka'wakw chief—whose obligation to preserve cultural resources compelled them, as a last resort, to turn their treasures over to outsiders, in the hope that they might some day return to the community (Coleman, Coombe, and MacArailt 2009: 186–189). Only this history tips the balance of interests away from ones that favour vesting insiders with ownership of cultural resources. At the same time, in a cruel irony, cultural resources have more value for groups who, having faced repeated assaults on their existence, are left with little else. As Roslyn Langford put it in "Our Heritage—Your Playground," "if we Aborigines cannot control our own heritage, what the hell can we control?" (1983: 4).

The preservation, access, and interpretive context principles compound social injustice; they become the very means by which aesthetic appropriation is weaponized. Their asymmetrical application to cultural resources and not other kinds of resources reads like an ad hoc apology for weaponized aesthetic appropriation by outsider institutions. Once weaponized, aesthetic appropriation radically changes the calculation of the interests captured in Young's four principles. Only the cultural interest principle survives this critique.

We can now see how weaponized aesthetic appropriation both stems from and compounds social injustice by means of theft. Theft disregards the exclusions of outsider use that secure the cultural values in which insiders have an interest. Sometimes the disregard is a symptom of social injustice. At the same time, the loss of the goods in which insiders have an interest can weaken insiders to the point that their interests in those goods seem to lose purchase. That more deeply compounds the injustice.

The proposal so far is that a practice of outsider use of the resources of an aesthetic culture can stem from and compound social injustice because it violates property rules. However, the proposal cannot stand on its own. Grant that some weaponized aesthetic appropriation violates property rules in a way that stems from and compounds social injustice. Having granted that, one might wonder why the property rules were justified in the first place. As we saw, the function and hence the justification of a property system is to serve some interests of parties to the system. The cultural significance principle, with its appeal to the value of a resource for a cultural group, echoes the same thought. So, the question is, what values or interests are to be secured by excluding outsider uses of the resources of aesthetic cultures? In particular, what values do the resources of an aesthetic culture have for insiders, such that securing the values warrants excluding outsiders from using the resources?

Taking the question seriously also takes seriously that not all aesthetic appropriation is weaponized. Tommie Shelby itemizes some benefits of aesthetic appropriation for insiders and outsiders alike: it can broaden the audience, stimulating cultural production, and it can be "a form of homage, a way of acknowledging the value of the culture and paying tribute to its founders … done with integrity and respect" (2005: 194). Exclusions of use might not be in order if they thwart insider interests in getting respect and widening audiences.

88 AESTHETIC INJUSTICE

The next three sections examine some values whose vulnerability to aesthetic appropriation can stem from and compound social injustice. None are economic, except indirectly. For the record: economic considerations do matter. We should avoid the error of further disadvantaging people by depicting them as not having an interest in full participation in economic life. At the same time, economic interests are not our only interests; some others are profoundly important.

Misgivings about property-oriented approaches to aesthetic appropriation deserve to be taken seriously (e.g. Coombe 1993, Brown 1998, Harding 1999, Coleman 2005: ch. 4, Mezey 2007; cf. Thompson 2003, Thompson 2004, Thompson 2012). Those who share the misgivings might take solace in the fact that property-oriented approaches do ultimately kick the can down the road. If a cultural property system is meant to protect what is of value to members of a group by excluding others from its use, then we must ultimately come to terms with the value itself.

Misrepresentation

Weaponized aesthetics often involves misrepresentation. As we saw in Chapter 1, the expressive practices that figure in weaponized aesthetics often deploy stereotypes or controlling images, and these are typically (though not always) inaccurate representations (Kim-Prieto et al. 2010). They predictably stem from social injustice because subordinated groups are ill equipped to combat unfavourable representations or to replace them with favourable ones (Young 2008: 107). They predictably compound social injustice because they license or normalize the acts and interlocked harms that are constitutive of social injustice. Tragically, members of subordinated groups are more likely to come to see themselves and their cultures as others see them, hence to acquiesce in their status. This section considers a special case of misrepresentation in weaponized aesthetics, namely misrepresentation in weaponized aesthetic appropriation.

Weaponized aesthetic appropriation involves expressive practices, on the part of outsiders, of using the resources of an aesthetic culture, where the practices stem from and compound social injustice by licensing or normalizing the acts and interlocked harms that constitute social injustice. Among these expressive practices are ones that misrepresent a subordinated group's aesthetic culture or its resources. Here are some examples, some informal and some formal, some obvious, some more subtle (see also Mezey 2007, Brown 2009, Shim 2021).

Starting with an obvious example, minstrel shows misrepresent the music of black people in the United States, depicting it as expressing happy acquiescence to their mistreatment (Jones 2014). Turning to less obvious cases, much appropriation of aesthetic culture is done through sampling or its low-tech antecedents (Coleman, Coombe, and MacArailt 2009). Sometimes, the intention is to pay tribute to the source culture, but extracting a bit of a larger whole runs the risk or caricaturing it. As the ethnomusicologist Steven Feld writes, we too often get "a single, untexted vocalization or falsetto yodel, often hunting cries rather than songs or musical pieces. This is the sonic cartoon of the diminutive person, the simple, intuitively vocal and essentially non-linguistic child" (1996: 27). Complex improvisational and compositional forms are reduced to whoops. In cases like this, obvious or not, insiders struggle to counteract caricatures that subvert their power to represent themselves accurately to others.

The same dynamic is present in more formal institutions. Schools, sports teams, and consumer brands notoriously propagate caricatures of black and Indigenous people, elements of which appropriate aesthetic culture, from Aunt Jemima's head scarf to First Nations regalia.

Again, it is important to look beyond the notorious cases to more subtle, perhaps more insidious, phenomena. By the early twentieth century, the Euro art world had begun to reorient its relationship with aesthetic cultures that had previously been seen as ethnographic curiosities (Eaton and Gaskell 2009). Although one might suppose that the art world's embrace of what it had excluded should have been a welcome development, it tended to revolve around a false choice between making exotic and assimilating, both being modes of misrepresentation.

William Rubin's Primitivism exhibition, mounted at the Museum of Modern Art in 1984, illustrates the assimilationist manoeuvre, which is to establish the credentials of "primitive" art by arguing for its deep affinity to modernist visual art. By placing a Nukuoro carving alongside a casting by Brancusi, MoMA invited its audience to apply their modernist

90 AESTHETIC INJUSTICE

expectations to something unfamiliar. The move builds audience, which is good, but at the expense of misrepresenting the carving, whose aesthetic and artistic value has, in fact, nothing to do with modernism (Karp 1991).

Collectors' insistence on a form of authenticity illustrates the manoeuvre of representing aesthetic cultures as exotic to Euro culture. Larry Shiner argues that collectors have operated with a conception of "primitive" or "traditional" art as made in small-scale societies in a traditional style to serve a traditional social function (1994: 226; see also Clifford 1988, Dutton 1993, Thompson 2004: 551–554, Coleman 2018). Anything is discounted that has not been danced or that has been made for a Euro audience. Indeed, while a Euro influence is intolerable, an influence in the other direction, on Euro culture, is fine. The direction of appropriation must be one-way, for the whole point of the conception is for what is collected to be purely non-Euro. This nostalgia for pre-contact culture, which has to mean pre-Euro-contact, disregards the reality of contact for almost all cultures and treats source cultures as either extinct or as persisting only in impure, hence degraded, derivatives of the past.

The irony of the art world's reorientation of its relationship with "primitive" aesthetic cultures is that it acknowledges them at the expense of misrepresenting them, because it acknowledges them not for what they are but through an exotic lens. In the notorious cases of lampooned regalia, misrepresentation via aesthetic appropriation obviously stems from and contributes to social injustice. Can the same be said of the practices of museums and collectors? The question is empirical, but it beggars belief that the answer is neither "yes" nor "yes, often enough to be a concern."

Rosemary Coombe observes that a central theme in complaints about cultural appropriation comes from "the experience of everywhere being seen, but never being heard, of constantly being represented, but never listened to, being treated like an historical artifact rather than a human being to be engaged in dialogue" (1993: 279–280; see also Todd 1990: 24). The bind is that to be heard at all, you must speak from the past, but your words will count only if spoken in the language of today. Perhaps this is good reason to exclude outsiders from uses of resources that tend to misrepresent.

Disrespect

Google searches for "cultural appropriation" reveal considerable personal anxiety about giving offence. People fret about (being called out for) offending members of groups by appropriating resources from their aesthetic cultures. Young argues that aesthetic appropriation can be wrong when it triggers profound offence (2008: ch. 5). However, if being offended is a reactive response, it might be worthwhile to consider the condition to which it is a response, and profound offence is merited principally in response to disrespect. Some practices of aesthetic appropriation stem from and compound social injustice because they imply disrespect (see also Keene 2014, Tuvel 2021).

On Joel Feinberg's (1985) classic account, offence is a state of mind that one dislikes being in. Profound offence is also state of mind that one dislikes being in, but it stands apart from garden variety offence in four ways. It is extremely unpleasant and therefore strongly motivating. Mere knowledge of something offensive is enough to bring it on. Someone is profoundly offended not merely in their sensibilities but more deeply, in who they are, in their sense of self. Yet profound offence is impersonal because it is a feeling in protection of an impersonal value.

Granting that profound offence exists, some cases of aesthetic appropriation surely occasion it. Take the custom of dudes wearing Sioux trailer war bonnets to music festivals. Just knowing that this happens can be sickening to a person because it affronts a commitment that goes to the heart of who they are. They are not the kind of person who can countenance a practice of random youth wearing Sioux honours and regalia to music festivals, on top of a history of ill treatment of Indigenous people.

That said, the proposal that aesthetic appropriation can be weaponized by triggering profound offence puts the focus on the attitudes of insiders from whom some culture is appropriated. What about the outsiders who do the appropriating? Surely the penchant for wearing Sioux trailer war bonnets at music festivals merits profound offence precisely because it is disrespectful.

Two considerations favour replacing appeals to profound offence with appeals to disrespect. In the first place, disrespect merits profound offence, but a response that a person is merited in having need not be a response that they actually have. Great achievement merits a feeling of

92 AESTHETIC INJUSTICE

pride, but we sometimes fail to muster the pride we merit. The point is crucial in circumstances of social injustice. Social injustice very often persists because it inhibits those on the downside from having the responses that they are merited in having. Profound offence is a reactive attitude, hence a demand for respect for the value that is at stake, and a demand for respect requires some degree of power. In the worst circumstances, a history of disrespect for a group's values is coupled with severe material and political depravations that together cause group members to internalize the outsider's attitude, so that they cannot to take offence in what is disrespectful. The injustice is amplified, not diminished, by the absence of feelings of profound offence.

In the second place, profound offence is by definition a state of mind, whereas profound disrespect might be a feature of an activity or a practice, as well as a mindset. Some of those wearing Sioux trailer war bonnets at music festivals probably intend no disrespect. The point is not to exonerate their behaviour. On the contrary, the point equips us to appreciate some powerful instances of weaponized aesthetic appropriation. For example, critiques of aesthetic appropriation as commodification are best understood using the concept of disrespect (e.g. Todd 1990: 30, Rogers 2006: 488–489). Industrial manufacturing processes output goods that are fungible with respect to their use value. Therefore, to drive sales, marketers create an appearance that their product is different, and then sell the appearance of difference. When Victoria's Secret marketed lingerie incorporating vaguely Native American motifs using models wearing Dakota Sioux trailer war bonnets, the company reduced the value of the regalia to bare difference for the sake of marketing, disrespecting its significance in Dakota Sioux aesthetic culture. The critique holds even if Victoria's Secret intended no disrespect.

Aesthetic appropriation manifests "profound disrespect" just when outsiders use the resources of an aesthetic culture in a way that is cavalier about the value or meaning of the resources to insiders. A use of the resources of an aesthetic culture is cavalier if predicated on the proposition that insiders' interests are not owed serious consideration, just because they are interests of those people. That is an extreme case, involving malicious intent, but malicious intent is not necessary for profound disrespect. Lingerie manufacturers and dudes at music festivals are cavalier because, entirely out of negligence, they give no weight to the value, to insiders, of the resources they appropriate. Needless to say, circumstances of social injustice licence and normalize the negligence.

When weaponized by profound disrespect, aesthetic appropriation is a failure to make relatively large-scale social arrangements that give due weight to the values of the resources of aesthetic cultures as they are seen by insiders. Failures such as these are not accidental: they are far more likely to occur in contexts of social injustice, where those on the downside have less voice and less economic and political heft. They stem from social injustice. They can also compound it. Frantz Fanon, writing "On National Culture" (1963), documents how central profound disrespect for aesthetic culture is to the enterprise of colonialism and how essential it is to the post-colonial struggle to regain self-respect.

Assimilation

Aesthetic culture can ground and promote a sense of belonging to a community, linking the community's members to their ancestors and heirs, equipping them "to achieve confidence in themselves and, thus, to imagine their future" (Moustakas 1989: 1195; see also Thompson 2004, Jeffers 2015). Without their aesthetic culture, the community might face dissolution. Thus practices of aesthetic appropriation are weaponized when they undercut community cohesion, raising the chances that the community will suffer further disadvantages. The threat of assimilation can be felt very keenly in circumstances of social injustice. With the land taken, with political and family structures disrupted, the aesthetic culture that remains might be the sole remaining ground upon which a community can stake a claim to self-determination (Coombe 1993: 283–285).

An insight at the heart of Elizabeth Coleman's work on cultural appropriation is vividly portrayed in the testimony before an Australian court of John Bulun Bulun, a Ganalbingu artist. He explained that copying his paintings:

> interferes with the relationship between people, their creator ancestors and the land given to the people by their creator ancestors. It interferes with our custom and ritual, and threatens our rights as traditional Aboriginal owners of the land and impedes in carrying out the

94 AESTHETIC INJUSTICE

obligations that go with this relationship. (John Bulun Bulun & Anor v R & T Textiles Pty Ltd 1998 FCA 1082, quoted at Coleman 2005: 47)

Coleman argues that paintings like Bulun Bulun's serve a social function essential to Ganalbingu social life and that appropriation impairs the function. As a result, the paintings should be protected against appropriation. To flesh out the reasoning, Coleman provides a theory of the function and makes a case for how appropriation impairs it.

Most communities cohere through shared institutions where individuals are empowered to act, and are responsible for acting, on behalf of the group (Bicchieri 2006, Epstein 2015, Guala 2016). These individuals have "functional roles, obligations, and rights, determined by institutions" (Coleman 2005: 113). The institution must include practices for placing individuals in social roles, for marking them as occupying the roles, and for marking the acts they perform within the institution. A commander in the Royal Canadian Navy holds a commissioning document issued by the crown, and she wears insignia that indicate her rank. The commission gives her powers and obligations that she would not otherwise have, and the insignia identify her as so empowered and obligated. Moreover, insignia can do double duty, signalling that someone occupies a role but also making it the case that they occupy the role.

Insignia can take many different forms. Coleman proposes that, in some societies, elements of aesthetic culture function as insignia marking social roles (2005: 54–60, 111). She also proposes that, in some societies, insignia function as legal instruments that constitute the social roles, "demonstrating and enacting ... the transfer and possession of those rights which define the central bonds of the society" (Coleman, Coombe, and MacArailt 2009: 186). This is precisely how Bulun Bulun describes his paintings. He does not claim copyright or ownership of a trademark, like a corporate logo; he claims that his paintings are instruments that signify and constitute Ganalbingu social life. What some societies do via written orders, others do via paintings or songs. Chief Assu entrusted his songs to outsiders because they were instruments that signified and constituted his social role, which gave him an obligation to preserve them as a guardian and protector of Kwakwaka'wakw social life (Coleman, Coombe, and MacArailt 2009).

Appropriating insignia in Coleman's sense is not like infringing copyright or trademarks; it is more like impersonating a public official. That is, practices of appropriating insignia erode the capacity of members of a group to have and to fulfill their social functions, thereby eroding the group's capacity to act collectively (Coleman 2005: 117–118).

Insignia are more vulnerable to harm in contexts of social injustice. A practice of civilians wearing the rank insignia of a commander in the Royal Canadian Navy is unlikely to erode naval organization: false insignia are apt to be detected—and punished (Young 2008: 123). Conditions of social injustice can change the equation, because they characteristically include patterns of thought and behaviour that inhibit recognition of the legal cultures of communities whose aesthetic cultures are appropriated (Coleman 2004). The patterns of thought and behaviour breed practices of assimilative aesthetic appropriation, and they are entrenched by them in turn. In so far as Ganalbingu social institutions have already been weakened by the failure to see them for what they are, undermining what is left of them can be devastating. Indeed, what is undermined can include instruments of territorial recognition and even the capacity for individuals to perform the obligations that give their lives meaning (Coleman, Coombe, and MacArailt 2009: 193–195).

Thi Nguyen and Matt Strohl (2019) argue that cultural appropriation can also breach group intimacy. Group intimacy is not the same as intimacy in personal relationships, but they are analogous. Thi and his spouse have a funny dance that they do when one of them is sad. Whether or not others are allowed to witness or use the dance is entirely up to the two of them: they decide where the boundary should be, and their setting it generates normative constraints upon others. If they do not want to let anyone else in, then we should oblige them. Analogously, intimate groups are ones that are bound together by practices that function to embody or promote a sense of common identity and group connection. Their having this function means that it is up to the group to decide whether or not to let others in, and if they decide not to, then others should oblige them. As Nguyen and Strohl acknowledge, contexts of injustice heighten the normative claims: "if a group is socially and politically marginalized, it becomes especially important to defer to the group in matters relating to its practices and institutions, to afford the group as much self-determination as possible" (2019: 990). Practices of failing to recognize the intimacy

96 AESTHETIC INJUSTICE

function of a group's "funny dance," which results in the dance's being appropriated, stems from and compounds social injustice.

One might think that assimilation comes not from outsiders appropriating a group's culture but rather from the group's importing too much from outside. The thought is tenable only when groups interact equitably. In conditions of social injustice, outsiders are especially apt to overlook the importance of aesthetic practices to a community's cohesion and identity, hence to engage in assimilative appropriation. When this happens, a case can be made for excluding outsiders from use of the community's aesthetic culture.

The Medusa Syndrome as Aesthetic Injustice

Although it depicts central elements of Haida life and thought, Reid's *Spirit of Haida Gwaii* has also become an icon of Canada's aspiration to foster cross-cultural recognition and respect. Yet it is precisely the adoption of *Black Canoe* as a national symbol, up to and including its circulation on the twenty dollar bill, that Yahgulanaas sees as a potential problem. Following a quick review of social autonomy, this section argues for three claims. First, the Medusa syndrome, as triggered by the national use of *Black Canoe*, might harm members of the Haida aesthetic cultural group in some of their capacities as aesthetic agents, subverting an interest in the culture's social autonomy. Second, this is not identical to weaponized aesthetic appropriation. Nonetheless, third, it typically stems from and compounds weaponized aesthetic appropriation. From all this we can infer the existence of a case of aesthetic injustice: it exists because we must appeal to it to form a complete picture of weaponized aesthetic appropriation.

Any culture enjoys social autonomy to the extent that it is, as it were, true to itself—that is, to the extent that its constitutive conception of the good is a product of its members' acting on their culture-given reasons. According to the network theory, the conception of the good that constitutes an aesthetic culture is its aesthetic profile, a correlation that obtains between the aesthetic values of items in the culture and the properties that ground the aesthetic values (see Chapter 3). The profile enables the coordinated acts of engagement of members of the group that has the culture. For example, a Haida carver's success inter-depends with success on the part of critics, members of the intended audience, tool makers, foresters, and many others. All raise their chances of performing well by converging on an aesthetic profile. In the usual course of events, the aesthetic profile is also a product (as well as an enabler) of group members' acting on their aesthetic reasons. Their so acting might change the aesthetic profile of the culture, or it might keep it from changing.

Another element of the network theory will be useful. Aesthetic experts are members of a group with an aesthetic culture who reliably succeed in their acts of engagement as a result of their competence. Competence for aesthetic expertise centrally includes competence in the aesthetic profile. An important principle follows:

> the aesthetic profile of an aesthetic culture is determined by the acts (hence the knowledge) of experts in the culture.

As they achieve in new ways and bring others along with their innovations, they change the profile. Others are brought along to the extent that their personal prospects for achievement hinge on their performing in line with experts within their community. So, an aesthetic culture enjoys social autonomy to the extent that expert knowledge and action determine the aesthetic profile.

Non-experts have little impact on the aesthetic profile. One kind of non-expert is the insider whose lack of competence in the aesthetic profile curtails their chances of reliable success. Another kind of non-expert is the outsider. If they act on aesthetic reasons, then their reasons are not, except by accident, the ones upon which experts would act. An aesthetic culture in a group none of whose members are experts—none of who reliably get success out of competence—enjoys no social autonomy. It is pushed about by whatever happens to motivate its members, which are not accurate representations of their aesthetic reasons.

Haida aesthetic cultures are social practices where individuals perform many different types of aesthetic acts, achieving success because they coordinate with one another. To coordinate, they comply with norms. Central among these is the norm to act in accordance with the aesthetic profile that is constitutive of the aesthetic culture. Reid is one among many experts who helped revive coordination around an aesthetic profile

98   AESTHETIC INJUSTICE

where facts about certain graphic and sculptural forms—the formline vocabulary of ovoids, S-forms, and U-forms—ground aesthetic value facts. What can be said, aesthetically, is a function of the vocabulary in which it is said.

Yahgulanaas's concern is that the national veneration of *Black Canoe* sets an expectation that the aesthetic profile, as it stands now, will continue to supply the aesthetic vocabulary for Haida form-making. In the Medusa syndrome, one is frozen, unable to act, by an awareness of another's regard. Elevated to a cultural level, patterns of engagement among insiders are held fixed, no longer free to change, as a result outsiders' intense attention. The proposal is that, in the Medusa syndrome, what is frozen is the aesthetic profile.

Stasis is not a problem per se; rather, the concern is about its causes. Outsider expectations subvert the normal process whereby the aesthetic profile is determined by the acts and hence the competence of experts. The expectations subvert experts acting in ways that impact the profile to enable them to achieve in their own terms. In effect, to externalize the expectations that set the aesthetic profile is to externalize expertise.

Chapter 4 emphasized the role of discourse in how experts determine the profile. The function of the exchange between Aaron and Dominic about curry is to determine what the context is. Is the context Goan cooking or Yorkshire curry houses? They negotiate the context. When expertise is externalized, expert insiders are no longer in a position to negotiate the context. Outsiders determine what the context is.

The result is a hit to the culture's social autonomy, as measured by the degree to which the aesthetic profile is a product of experts' acts. The Medusa syndrome is a harm to members of the Haida carving culture in some of the very capacities that are needed to secure the culture's social autonomy. Since the syndrome is an impact on insiders resulting from a national use of *Black Canoe*, we can conclude that Yahgulanaas's concern is about aesthetically unjust aesthetic appropriation. That was the first claim.

Before proceeding to the second claim, it is important to note that some Indigenous writers already articulate something akin to the first claim, though they use the metaphor of voice. For example, Loretta Todd, the Métis–Cree filmmaker, explains that appropriation is a problem "when someone else becomes the expert on your experience and is deemed more knowledgeable about who you are than yourself" (1990: 24–26).

The second claim was that the account of the Medusa syndrome as aesthetically unjust appropriation does not reduce it to weaponized aesthetic appropriation. Weaponized aesthetic appropriation stems from and compounds social injustice by means of theft, misrepresentation, disrespect, or assimilation. The reception of the *Spirit of Haida Gwaii* does not involve any of these. It accurately and respectfully represents a thriving and distinct Haida culture, from which it takes nothing away.

Aesthetic injustice and weaponized aesthetics are distinct, but they are not disjoint. The third claim is that aesthetically unjust appropriation sometimes, and perhaps often, stems from and compounds weaponized aesthetics.

When appropriation is aesthetically unjust, it harms insiders in the capacities that undergird their culture's social autonomy. This is more likely to occur when the exclusionary rules that make up a group's property system are violated. After all, those rules are designed to secure their interests, and practices that weaken a group in its aesthetic interests are likely to expose it to higher rates of aesthetically unjust appropriation. Aesthetically unjust appropriation is also more likely when practices routinely misrepresent a group's aesthetic culture, treat its values in a cavalier manner, or undercut its role in building community.

Running in the opposite direction, a hit to an aesthetic culture's social autonomy exposes it to weaponized aesthetics. A loss of aesthetic voice is a loss of a crucial tool in responding to aesthetic misrepresentation, disrespect for aesthetic value, assimilation, and hence disregard for property. For example, one of the first steps in setting up a colonial system is refusing to see Indigenous people as possessing the least understanding of themselves and their world. The abrogation of voice includes aesthetic voice.

The Medusa syndrome can be an aesthetic injustice that is distinct from but can also stem from and compound weaponized aesthetic appropriation. Sometimes, to fully understand weaponized aesthetic appropriation, we must see how it implicates an aesthetic injustice grounded in an interest in social autonomy. It follows that we have the interest that the cosmopolitan theory ascribes to us.

Policy Considerations

Cosmopolitan interests are not grounded in transcultural principles; they are interests that anyone has just in so far as they engage in some local aesthetic cultures. From within the perspective of their own cultures, anyone has an interest in the social autonomy of other aesthetic cultures. Having an interest is one thing, and recognizing it is another. Moreover, recognizing it is not yet adopting policies, within one's own aesthetic cultures, to secure it in other aesthetic cultures. Chapter 4 conceded that the most the cosmopolitan theory supplies is considerations to shape policy-making. Those policies must be sensitive to the settings where they are applied and the characteristics of the group that is to apply them. Here a few remarks to get the ball rolling.

The argument that the Medusa syndrome subverts an interest social autonomy brings out how much space has to be bridged from having an interest to recognizing it. For one thing, the interest has to be seen as an interest in justice, not personal ethics. In addition, the interest has to be seen as weighty. Often it is not weighty, though it is likely to be more weighty when its subversion is entangled with weaponized aesthetics. Weaponized aesthetics amplifies its seriousness, giving us much stronger reasons to seek remedies. Finally, since the phenomenon of aesthetic injustice is unfamiliar, policies are needed to place it on the agenda for deciding more direct policies.

What might more direct policies look like? The policies need not limit contact. Stephen Davies (2017) documents some of the policies implemented in Bali in order to secure the social autonomy of its aesthetic cultures in face of strong pressures from mass tourism. Tourist revenues have been used to subsidize expensive gongs. Arts schools were created to preserve knowledge of classic forms. When it was seen that the schools undercut local control and the diversity that comes with it, a national arts festival was put on, exploiting regional rivalries to foster stylistic variety. New techniques, materials, and ideas from the expatriate community helped to reinvigorate the culture and to balance pride in tradition with a love of innovation. Notice the mix of state-funded formal institutions, such as schools and festivals, with informal human resources, such as expatriate experiences.

Only having examined cultural interests are we in a position to decide when property rights—and which property rights—safeguard against aesthetically unjust appropriation. The question is whether some cases of aesthetically unjust appropriation warrant some exclusions of use. Is it ever the case that the norm for outsiders should be to leave insiders to get on with things on their own, without making any use of their aesthetic culture? An answer in the affirmative is what makes their aesthetic culture their property.

Some trace competing claims in public disputes over cultural appropriation to differences in value (e.g. Nicholas and Wylie 2012: 199). Others remind us that we all share aesthetic interests, so that cultural appropriation goes sour when appropriators forget or ignore the significance of their own culture when dealing with others' cultures (Harding 1999: 312–315). The cosmopolitan theory of aesthetic injustice concludes that both have it right.

Appendix: Aesthetic Versus Epistemic Injustice

The idea that externalizing expertise subverts an interest in the social autonomy of aesthetic cultures was unpacked above by quoting Todd's remark that "when someone else becomes the expert on your experience and is deemed more knowledgeable about who you are than yourself." Readers who are familiar with the recent literature on epistemic injustice and who noticed Todd's epistemic vocabulary might wonder whether aesthetic injustice is an epistemic injustice. It is not.

An important species of epistemic injustice is testimonial injustice. Taking testimony from a speaker implicates a judgement as to their credibility. Miranda Fricker (2007) argues that epistemic injustice occurs when a speaker suffers a credibility deficit because of an identity prejudice. Hearers underestimate the credibility of the speaker because they accept false stereotypes about members of the speaker's identity group. Kristie Dotson (2011) adds that testimonial injustice is even more acute in cases of silencing and smothering. Silencing occurs when hearers fail to recognize the speaker as a knower—they do not even get as far as making a credibility judgement about the speaker. In smothering, a speaker truncates their own testimony to meet the audience's low expectations.

Externalizing expertise no doubt goes hand in hand with testimonial injustice: they are likely to co-occur and to reinforce one another in conditions of weaponized aesthetics (remember that injustices cling together like burrs). Early anthropologists who wrote about Haida form-making sometimes discounted the credibility of insider experts or failed even to recognize them as experts in the first place. As a result, insiders were sometimes pushed to smothering. However, by the time he was commissioned

102 AESTHETIC INJUSTICE

to create the *Spirit of Haida Gwaii*, Reid's expertise and credibility were not in question, and his successes had done a great deal to restore his peers' voices. Granting that externalizing expertise often accompanies epistemic injustice, one can occur without the other, and they are distinct phenomena.

As characterized by the cosmopolitan theory, aesthetic injustice is not an epistemic phenomenon, for the theory does not represent aesthetic experts merely as sources of knowledge. The claim is rather that what experts know—their competence for reliable achievement—is in large part what determines what the practice is. It makes the practice one with that very aesthetic profile.

Consequently, the aesthetic injustice of externalizing expertise does not lie in its excluding insiders from what Fricker calls the "credibility economy." It rather consists in an abrogation of constitutional authority, as it were—the power to determine what the context is, hence what the aesthetic profile is, hence what the culture is. The injustice is metaphysical rather than epistemic (Lopes 2024b).

6

Beauty Ideals and Ideologies

Widdows opens a recent paper on bodily beauty by announcing that her task is to explore its "neglected harms" (2017: 1). Just a few decades ago, talk of the harms of beauty would have sounded as paradoxical as "the harms of virtue" or the "harms of intelligence." Nowadays, in the wake of trenchant critiques by feminists, from Simone de Beauvoir (1953 [1949]) to Naomi Wolf (1990), expectations about bodily beauty evoke suspicion (see Martin-Seaver 2023 for an overview). Obviously, bodily beauty ideals vary by gender; the new claims are that the ideals are key factors in gender formation and gender-based injustice. Analogues of both claims apply to race thinking, too (Appiah 1994, Mills 1997, Taylor 1999, Taylor 2016). The second iteration of the main argument for the cosmopolitan theory is that our understanding of weaponized ideals of bodily beauty is incomplete until we see how they spawn and are compounded by aesthetic injustice—by harms to people that subvert an interest in aesthetic value diversity, in particular. A full understanding of weaponized aesthetics will tell the whole story of Pecola in *The Bluest Eye*.

Ideology

Human beings share with other primates an acute sensitivity to perceived unfairness (Brosnan and de Waal 2014). We do not tolerate injustice without coercion or ideology. Predictably, ideology plays a lead role when aesthetics is weaponized, but it does not follow that the ideology is itself aesthetic. To see this, take a closer look at ideology and then at aesthetic ideals.

Following Shelby, let an ideology be any pattern of thought in a group that stems from an unjust social arrangement and constitutively functions to perpetuate it (2003: 183–186). This is a normatively charged

Aesthetic Injustice. Dominic McIver Lopes, Oxford University Press. © Dominic McIver Lopes 2024.
DOI: 10.1093/oso/9780198930983.003.0006

104   AESTHETIC INJUSTICE

theory of ideology, since it rules out good ideologies. A neutral characterization is possible, and it might be useful in some contexts, but this chapter relies only on bad ideology.

Notice that the proposed theory does not circumscribe how ideologies can perform their constitutive function: a group's pattern of thought can function in any of a number of ways to perpetuate an unjust social arrangement. Nonetheless, as broad as it is, the theory determines some important properties of ideologies having to do with their scope, vehicles and formats, sources, proximal impacts, and cognitive defects.

The scope of an ideology is not individual: it is a pattern of thought across members of a group. Moreover, ideologies need not be—and they are typically not—avowed in any explicit way by members of the group. Typically, they are disavowed. In Shelby's parlance, they belong to "social consciousness;" they are "implicit in the behavioral dispositions, utterances, conduct, and practices of social actors" (2003: 161). Even those subordinated by an unjust social arrangement tend to implicitly accept and support its ideology.

The vehicles of ideologies are not limited to beliefs, desires, or other propositional attitudes. In Haslanger's metaphor, an ideology is a "palette of psychological content," which includes concepts, scripts, and heuristics alongside beliefs and principles (2017: 155–156). We should add metaphors and stereotypes to the list (Camp 2017). Noël Carroll (1990) and Anne Eaton (2016) emphasize how dispositions to affective response—to respond with emotion, feeling, pleasure, or pain—can perform what amounts to an ideological function. The same goes for dispositions to make perceptual discriminations and classifications, and to engage in mental imagery (Clavel-Vazquez 2023). In as much as cognitive materials such as these operate relatively automatically and resist rational persuasion, they serve ideological functions exceptionally well. Indeed, differences in vehicles explain why ideological content can be norm discordant (Young 1990: ch. 5). As Eaton puts it, "one can have both the justified belief that fat hatred governs social relations and the conviction that this is morally wrong yet nevertheless find oneself disgusted by fat bodies" (2016: 48). The recalcitrance of disgust to rational oversight abets norm discordance.

Turning to sources, ideological patterns of thought also resist rational persuasion because they are not typically products of inference.

Metaphors, stereotypes, heuristics, scripts, and perceptual, imagistic, affective, and conceptual dispositions are acquired through habituation, or repeated exposure with rewarded performance. For example, perceptual learning results from exposure to sampled classes of stimuli (Ransom 2020a, Ransom 2020b). Ronnie de Sousa proposes that emotional learning occurs as responses come to be keyed to paradigm scenarios. Paradigm scenarios have two components: "first, a situation type providing the characteristic objects of the specific emotion type, and second, a set of characteristic or 'normal' responses to the situation, where normality is first a biological matter and then very quickly becomes a cultural one" (de Sousa 1987: 182). The cultural aspect includes artistic and aesthetic culture, since paradigm scenarios "are drawn first from our daily life as small children and later reinforced by the stories, art and culture to which we are exposed" (de Sousa 1987: 182). Work in feminist aesthetics emphasizes the sources of gender ideology in works of art, but it has to be said that art hardly dominates the ideological economy, whose principal products are non-art stories and images.

Given its scope, vehicles, and sources, it will come as no surprise that an ideology's proximal impact, through which it ultimately achieves its constitutive function, will be pragmatic. That is, ideological patterns of thought chiefly motivate acts, especially everyday, prosaic, person-to-person interactions. Iris Marion Young offers two examples:

> A Black man walks into a large room at a business convention and finds that the noise level reduces, not to a hush, but definitely reduces. A woman at a real estate office with her husband finds the dealer persistently failing to address her or to look at her, even when she speaks to him directly. (1990: 133)

At the same time, ideologies profoundly impact our self-conceptions. Haslanger writes that "living together requires social fluency, skills for interpretation, interaction and coordination that we exercise 'unthinkingly.' In a social world structured by practices, performing what the practices require of us is just what we do, it becomes who we are" (2017: 158; see also Shelby 2003: 158). To the extent that who we are is, under the right conditions, just what we do or are prepared to do, and to the extent that it is difficult to change who we are, ideologies become deeply entrenched.

106 AESTHETIC INJUSTICE

Ideologies are defective because unjust—they are defects of the social fabric. They are also cognitive defects, though not necessarily because they yield false or unwarranted beliefs. Ideologies can so structure social arrangements that they turn out to be true (Haslanger 2017; cf. Sunstein 1994: 2416–2417, Shelby 2003: 158, Manne 2018: 79). A widespread belief that, for instance, people with a certain kind of body are incompetent performers in some domain is self-fulfilling when it ensures their exclusion from learning and participating in the domain (see Chapter 7).

Two cognitive defects of ideologies stand out: they project illusions and they mask important regions of reality. Cognition is defective when it delivers false beliefs but also when it fails to deliver those true beliefs that are crucial for understanding the social world. Ideological patterns of thought typically function to perpetuate injustice by masking facts about what matters, what is good, or what reasons we have to act, by masking or distracting us from suffering, and by masking a complete accounting of the available alternatives. The more effectively an ideology masks, the stronger the illusion among people, including those on the downside of social injustice, that there is no injustice (Shelby 2003: 177). Notice how much stronger the illusion will be when an ideology outputs true beliefs that are conspicuously useful in navigating social life (e.g. that people with that body perform incompetently in a domain). Also notice a bone chilling consequence: the cognitive resources available in the kinds of unjust social arrangements that are buoyed by ideologies are rarely going to be up to the task of detecting the injustice (Haslanger 2017: 160).

To summarize, the scope, vehicles, sources, proximal impacts, and cognitive defects of an ideology are tailored to contribute to its performing its constitutive function.

Beauty Ideals

Some aesthetic ideologies leverage aesthetic ideals. An aesthetic ideal is a kind of aesthetic evaluation. Evaluations are states of mind—beliefs, perceptions, affects—that represent values (see Chapter 3). One might see how Kramer's logo for the CBC and Radio Canada is economical with meaning, or one might judge that Milton Keynes does not invite textured exploration. An aesthetic evaluation becomes an aesthetic ideal when it applies to all items of a kind and has a normative content, a content expressed using a "should," "ought," or "must." A pug must be cute. Corporate logos should be economical in conveying meaning. Cities ought to invite textured navigational choices.

Human bodies can be beautiful in many ways. We have radiant faces, generous smiles, elegant curls, cute derrières, chiselled abs, and rugged jaws. The list illustrates that beauty is not homogenous when it comes to human bodies. Matching the positives—being chic, handsome, or sexy—are negatives too—being dumpy or dowdy. The list also illustrates that bodily beauty extends to how we move and use our bodies, care for and groom them, or dress and adorn them. Bodily beauties are not always off the rack; some are fruits of craft and labour. Rugged jaws are usually a gift of nature; elegant curls are usually the hairdresser's handiwork. In between are cute derrières and chiselled abs, which might come naturally or from engineering in the gym. Generous smiles, radiant faces, and confident strides are typically byproducts of personality, perhaps cultivated, perhaps inborn. Grooming and dress usually involve careful choice and self-expression. That bodily beauty runs a gamut from mutable to immutable characteristics will be important in what follows.

In *Adornment*, Davies spotlights some acts of bodily adornment (2020: chs. 2–3). To adorn a body is, for Davies, (1) to intend to endow it with aesthetic merits, (2) to intend to win audience recognition of the attempt and of the success, and (3) to succeed to some degree with respect to (1) and (2)—or to follow a social practice that originated in successful cases meeting conditions (1) to (3). As he observes, though, "we do many things to alter our bodies and our appearance with aesthetic enhancement in mind. And we desire that the improvements are noticed. But we do not necessarily want the effort at improvement to be noticed" (2020: 39). In the cases of full-blown adornment that Davies spotlights, we intend our efforts to be seen as deliberate. However, the wider domain of bodily beauty includes what comes naturally, as well as modifications made without an intention that anyone notices the effort, maybe in the hope that nobody does.

Although human bodies can be beautiful in many ways, ideals of bodily beauty are doubly narrow. They are meant to apply to all humans or all humans of a kind—all children, for example, or all women. In addition,

108 AESTHETIC INJUSTICE

they single out which aesthetic merits all of them should or must possess and which aesthetic demerits none may possess.

Given these theories of ideology and ideals of bodily beauty, we are now equipped to ask how bodily beauty ideals function ideologically, weaponizing aesthetics. Adapting the theory of weaponized aesthetics given in Chapter 1 to beauty ideals, the claim is that:

> a relatively large-scale social arrangement weaponizes bodily beauty when and because it includes ideological beauty ideals that stem from and compound social injustice by licensing or normalizing the acts and interlocked harms that constitute social injustice.

In particular, beauty ideals are key elements of some social positions—expectations and norms governing how members of a group should behave. The expectations and norms stem from and compound social injustice. Scholarship on weaponized aesthetics brings out how the narrowness of some ideals of bodily beauty stems from and contributes to social injustice.

Beauty × Gender: Sexual Objectification

What Paul Taylor calls the "beauty–gender nexus" comprises large scale social arrangements that promulgate ideals of bodily beauty that in turn encode the social meaning of gender (2016: 21). The task is to understand how bodily beauty ideals are gender-linked, how they function ideologically, and then how they burden genders asymmetrically. To this end, some feminists defend a pair of claims, about gender and sexual objectification, on one hand, and about sexual objectification and bodily beauty ideals, on the other.

The classic treatment of sexual objectification in gender-formation is what Kathleen Stock dubs the "MacKinnon–Haslanger account" (MacKinnon 1987, Haslanger 2012: 57–63, Stock 2015). Haslanger (2000) argues that genders are hierarchical social positions whose occupants are marked, in a context, for social positioning by perceived or imagined bodily traits thought to have to do with reproduction. Thus, to be a woman, in some context, is to be marked for social positioning by certain perceived or imagined bodily traits, where the social positioning subordinates women to men along some dimensions (legal, economic, educational, athletic, artistic, etc.). (On social positions, see Chapter 1.)

An account of genders as hierarchical social positions, achieved by some means or other, along some dimension or other, is schematic. Its abstraction is a merit, because it allows the details to vary from one social context to the next. Put another way, the account invites an investigation, for any given social context, of how women are subordinated to men along dimensions that are salient in that context. Haslanger accepts the standard account on which social positions include social norms, some of which set the standard of goodness for occupants of the positions. The broadest constitutive norm governing women is, "be subordinate," which makes a good woman a subordinate one. Since norms are typically sanctioned, women who violate the constitutive norm of their social position are typically subject to sanctions (Manne 2018). Yet, a norm as generic as this cannot structure social relationships in a meaningful way. Be subordinate how? With respect to what dimensions? We need an investigation, for any given social context, of ancillary norms, each setting a standard of goodness, each typically backed up by a suite of sanctions.

It would be astonishing (albeit logically possible) to find that the bodily traits perceived or imagined to be those of male and female humans figure in none of the norms positioning gender. Catharine MacKinnon argues that a norm of sexual objectification is focal, explaining the other norms and social structures that position women. A person objectifies another just when, first, the objectifier perceives, treats, and evaluates the objectified as a means to satisfy their desires, and, second, the objectifier has the power to make it the case that the objectified has the properties needed to satisfy the objectifier's desires. So understood, objectification is a subordinating exercise of power. Moving from the personal level to the social level, objectifying social arrangements are ones where a group is subordinated because its members are typically perceived, treated, and evaluated as means to satisfy others' desires and where the social arrangements ensure that the subordinated group's members will have the properties needed to satisfy others' desires. For MacKinnon, the focal norm positioning gender is sexual. Haslanger puts the norm succinctly: "she is for the satisfaction of his desire" (2012: 60). Supporting this norm are a slew of more specific norms compliance with which makes it the case

110   AESTHETIC INJUSTICE

that women come to have the properties needed to service men's sexual desires—and also that men have the desires. In sum, hierarchical gender positioning occurs at least in part through compliance by men and women with norms that sexually objectify women.

Neither MacKinnon nor Haslanger links bodily beauty ideals to sexual objectification, but a link is plausible (e.g. Bartky 1990, Jeffreys 2005). Compliance by men and women with norms that sexually objectify women is not entirely a result of coercion. Maybe it rarely is. Ideology is in play when bodily beauty ideals are patterns of thought that motivate women to make their bodies such as to satisfy men's desires, when they motivate men to have those desires, and when the ideals stem from and reinforce the gender hierarchy. Bodily beauty ideals are the ideological machinery at work in positioning gender by sexual objectification.

Being ideological, they are implemented in perception and affect, which insulates them against rational critique. After all, we learn to see people as women and men (and girls and boys), and there is more to seeing gender than seeing the bodily traits associated with reproduction that target people for social positioning. These traits are not always easy to see, yet infants begin to see gender at four months (e.g. Walker-Andrews et al. 1991). Presumably, the signal for the presence of the targeting traits is boosted by association with other, more visible traits. Each gender acquires a characteristic and legible look (Weiser and Weiser 2016: 215–217). Added to that, people whose looks approach the average for their gender are perceived with pleasure and are judged more beautiful (Langlois and Roggman 1990). Hence, the processes by means of which we learn to see people in gender categories are also ones that generate hedonic responses. Hedonic responses are strong pragmatic motivators—that is why we have them—and hedonically charged perceptual responses are not readily amenable to rational critique. We should predict that we learn them from artifactual images, such as advertisements and movies (e.g. Mulvey 1989, Carroll 1990).

If bodily beauty ideals mediate sexual objectification, then they burden women and men asymmetrically. Burdens can distribute asymmetrically in one or both of two ways. The content of the ideals can differ: ideals of masculine beauty do not make men objects of female desire. Alternatively, even when the contents of the ideals are the same, they can be differentially enforced: men and not women can get away with flouting them.

Either way, bodily beauty ideals are ideological materiel in weaponized aesthetics.

Beauty × Gender: Premium and Penalty

Ideological ideals of bodily beauty might stem from and contribute to gender-based injustice without mediating sexual objectification. Some critiques of bodily beauty ideals emphasize how they entrain asymmetrical beauty premiums and penalties that sustain unjust discrimination. As Sherri Irvin puts it, "women are disproportionately subject to narrowly defined standards of beauty ... and compliance with these standards is unfairly used as a criterion for the allocation of a wide variety of social and economic goods" (2016: 1).

Among the best studied are effects on employment and income (mostly in the United States), which are summarized by the economist Daniel Hamermesh in *Beauty Pays* (2011, esp. chs 3–4). The direct effect of compliance with bodily beauty ideals on the labour markets is equivalent to a year of additional education. On top of this, women endure an additional penalty for weight, and men enjoy an additional premium for being tall. Moreover, the effects are evident across a wide range of occupations, where they impact hiring decisions and also performance evaluation. For example, evaluations of beauty skew voting during elections and students' assessments of teaching in higher education. Aggravating the direct effects, bodily beauty ideals alter preferences. For instance, fewer women who fall short of the ideals seek employment.

The ideals also impact the distribution of other resources (Rhode 2016: 83–86, Irvin 2017: 3–6). Weight is a factor in educational outcomes, criminal sentencing, and damages awarded in civil suits. Being beautiful raises the chances of securing a loan ... and then defaulting on it (Hamermesh 2011: 145). Evaluations of beauty have significant effects on social esteem and power. They correlate with marriage rates, happiness, and self-esteem, and they correlate inversely with anxiety and depression. The health risks that come with dieting, surgery, and the use of body-shaping drugs regularly make the headlines. Quoting Susan Sontag's observation that "our manner of appearing is our manner of

112 AESTHETIC INJUSTICE

being," Deborah Rhode argues that bodily beauty ideals harmfully limit self-expression (2010: 99–100).

Expenditures of time and money for adornment are sizeable (Widdows 2018: 148–149). The global market for grooming products alone exceeds two hundred billion US dollars annually, and women spend twenty to thirty minutes a day on self-adornment, which totals a year in the average lifetime. To make matters worse, return on investment is poor. Dieting is known to be ineffective, and studies indicate that efforts at adornment make only a small difference to beauty ratings and to employment outcomes—four cents on the dollar (Hamermesh 2011: 36). The opportunity costs are presumably considerable. Widdows (2017) also urges attention to the costs borne by third parties, especially workers in the beauty services sector, who are underpaid and must often handle toxic materials.

Yet there are positives, beyond the premiums mentioned above. Self-care and pampering are sources of pleasure, self-esteem, and pride (Rhode 2010: 86–89). Some philosophers argue that the pursuit of bodily beauty affords opportunities for the exercise of autonomy or for achievement in realizing value (Heyes 2007, Parsons 2016, Protasi 2017, Ravasio 2023). Communal beauty practices—such as sharing clothes, paying compliments, and group exercise—strengthen intimate social bonds, especially among women (Cahill 2003, Widdows 2018: 153–155). Widdows must be right to observe that human beings need to touch and be touched, but some—think of the elderly, for example—are deprived of this good, and beauty practices provide one of the few settings where non-sexual touch is acceptable (2018: 152–153). Like most complex social phenomena, bodily beauty ideals yield a mixture of benefits and harms.

Three claims are needed: bodily beauty ideals asymmetrically burden women, the asymmetry is unjust, and the ideals stem from and contribute to the persistence of the injustice. Two interpretations of these claims articulate two indictments of bodily beauty ideals.

In 1961, H. L. A. Hart remarked that:

> in contrast with morals, the rules of deportment, manners, dress, and some, though not all, rules of law, occupy a relatively low place in the scale of serious importance. They may be tiresome to follow, but they

do not demand great sacrifice: no great pressure is exerted to obtain conformity and no great alterations in other areas of social life would follow if they were not observed or changed. (1994 [1961]: 173–174)

The passage betrays a double standard and double bind in the application of bodily beauty ideals. Only for men might the ideals be merely tiresome to follow, demand no great sacrifice, and affect little else. That is the double standard. The double bind is that women fail when they are not beautiful, yet being beautiful "lacks serious importance." As Rhode writes, "even as the culture expects women to conform, it mocks the narcissism in their efforts" (2010: 44). Indeed, the gendering of beauty as superficial was one cause of its banishment from serious art in the early twentieth century (Danto 2003, Nehamas 2007). The asymmetry claim is true. So is the injustice claim: combined with the double standard, the double bind is subordinating (Widdows 2018: 233). After all, women are sanctioned if they fail to meet the ideal, but their meeting it counts as nothing significant, and men are not in the same predicament. In short, bodily beauty ideals both reflect and reinforce gender hierarchy: they function ideologically.

In *The Beauty Bias*, Rhode reproduces a *New Yorker* cartoon that depicts a young executive reassuring his boss: "Not to worry—I'm going to put our best-looking people on the job" (2010: 91). The cartoon encapsulates the standard social science interpretation of the three claims (e.g. Rhode 2010, Hamermesh 2011). Studies of some social settings indicate that the harms that result from attempting to conform with bodily beauty ideals fall disproportionately on the shoulders of women. Among these are effects on employment and health, for example. Yet people should not be treated on the basis of irrelevant physical characteristics, and social arrangements are unjust when they provide for this kind of discrimination (Mason 2021). Therefore, the demand that women be beautiful, in the way the ideal prescribes, is unjust because it is discriminatory. Finally, the discrimination reinforces gender-based disadvantage, which reduces opportunities for women to develop their full potential, which generates stereotypes that either seem to confirm or else make it hard to overturn the ideal (Rhode 2010: 93–96; see also Sunstein 1994: 2416–2418). Bodily beauty ideals function ideologically.

114 AESTHETIC INJUSTICE

That bodily beauty ideals function ideologically explains what we see about their scope, sources, vehicles, proximal impacts, and cognitive defects. They are spread non-propositionally through images and hedonically charged perceptions of our own and others' bodies—eating disorders increased dramatically in Fiji in the 1990s within three years of the introduction of television (Rhode 2010: 60). They are sanctioned mainly by pleasures and emotional responses coupled to perceptual responses (we need to expand on Manne 2018: 68). As a result, they are especially effective in determining immediate behaviour while obscuring the presence of injustice.

Beauty × Race

Pecola is caught at the intersection of ideological bodily beauty ideals that are inflected by race as well as gender. Ideologies are patterns of thought, and racially inflected bodily beauty ideals are to be found in what Taylor calls "race thinking" (2016: 9). Race thinking might be thinking about nothing, if there are no races, or it might be thinking about races, which might be biological or social entities (e.g. Glasgow et al. 2019). What matters for present purposes is that race thinking includes ideals of bodily beauty that encode the social meaning of race so as to perpetuate race-based social injustice.

Central to race thinking is a set of dispositions to perceive people as grouped according to certain anatomical features—skin, eye, and hair colour, hair texture, lip, nose, and eyelid shape, and physique. Since these features are thought to indicate shared ancestry in distinctive geographical regions, what is perceived is geographically marked bodies (Hardimon 2003). As Taylor puts it, "often enough, we just see race, the way we just see home runs and rude gestures" (2016: 22).

Dispositions to see geographically marked bodies do not yet encode the social meaning of race in circumstances of social injustice. Taylor adds that "differential modes of treatment that mark the boundaries between racial populations can be reliably underwritten by aesthetic perceptions—by the affectively and symbolically loaded workings of immediate experience" (2016: 22). This needs unpacking.

BEAUTY IDEALS AND IDEOLOGIES   115

Classical racism in the United States represents black people as morally and intellectual inferior—as unreliable, dependent, dangerous, undisciplined, unintelligent, and inarticulate. That is not all: black bodies are also thought to be ugly. Recall how Franklin opposed slavery on the ground that transporting black people to the new world would mar its beauty (Mills 1997: 62). Thomas Jefferson, conceding that what he took to be the moral and intellectual inferiority of black people might be due to their living conditions, found in aesthetics an unshakeable bedrock for racism:

> The first difference which strikes us is that of colour.... And is this difference of no importance? Is it not the foundation of a greater or less share of beauty in the two races? Are not the fine mixtures of red and white, the expressions of every passion by greater or less suffusions of colour in the one, preferable to that eternal monotony, which reigns in the countenances, that immoveable veil of black which covers all the emotions of the other race? Add to these, flowing hair, a more elegant symmetry of form, their own judgment in favour of the whites, declared by their preference for them, as uniformly as is the preference of the Oranootan for the black woman over those of his own species. The circumstance of superior beauty, is thought worthy attention in the propagation of our horses, dogs, and other domestic animals; why not in that of man? (quoted in Appiah 1994: 68)

In an aesthetic counterpart of the Cartesian cogito, the unshakeable ugliness of black people turns out to vindicate beliefs about their intellectual and moral traits. In the stories we tell and depict, villains are ugly, and heroes, handsome. A tendency for running beauty together with goodness, intelligence, and civilization primes us to apprehend geographically marked bodies as signs of socially important intellectual and moral features (Mills 1997: 61, Taylor 1999: 16). So, the sight of a black body is "affectively loaded" because it is an experience of ugliness, hence viscerally aversive; it is "symbolically loaded" because the aversive response motivates acts that trade on an association of ugliness with moral and intellectual traits.

Among the vestiges of classical racism are racially inflected ideals of bodily beauty, whose scope, sources, vehicles, impacts, and cognitive defects equip them to function ideologically. Visual images flooding the

116 AESTHETIC INJUSTICE

representational environment equate beauty with fairness. Once internalized as perceptual and affective dispositions, they are hard to dislodge and indeed to discern. They persist even as individuals explicitly disavow them. Safe from rational critique, they have outsized practical impacts. In so far as the impacts disadvantage black people, the injustice tends to be masked, for its origins in affectively loaded perception are at odds with people's explicit avowals. In sum, aesthetic responses occur at the intersection of race-detecting perception and race-directed affect; they are learned through narratives, metaphors, perspectives, and images that encode the ideal; and they mask discriminatory treatment even on the part of those who oppose it intellectually.

Ideals of bodily beauty can weaponize aesthetics in two ways, in circumstances of racial injustice. Once imprinted on perceptual and affective tendencies, the ideals might shape how those on the downside are treated. They might facilitate unfair practices around employment, housing, education, and health care, while masking the unfairness. In addition, the ideals might damage the self-image of those on the downside, leaving them unable to cope with and combat unfair treatment.

Taylor writes that Morrison's portrait of Pecola "poignantly delineates the links between race-related unease with one's own body image and broader forms of self-hatred" (2010: 11). If she is fictional, she might nevertheless illustrate a truth. The same truth is expressed in what is perhaps the most widely quoted passage in Fanon's *Black Skin, White Masks*:

> My body was given back to me sprawled out, distorted, recolored, clad in mourning in that white winter day. The Negro is an animal, the Negro is bad, the Negro is mean, the Negro is ugly…
>
> …
>
> I sit down at the fire and I become aware of my uniform. I had not seen it. It is indeed ugly. I stop there, for who can tell me what beauty is? (2008 [1952]: 86)

Pecola's Predicament as Aesthetic Injustice

Existing scholarship on weaponized ideals of bodily beauty leaves out how they spawn and are compounded by aesthetic injustice. It overlooks, in particular, how they harm people in their capacities as aesthetic agents and thereby subvert an interest in the value diversity of cultures of bodily beauty. To see this, contrast two interpretations of Morrison's story.

Pecola has seen distaste "lurking in the eyes of all white people" (Morrison 1970: 49). However, she does not wish to have blue eyes just so that she can be beautiful. Taylor interprets her as struggling against losing sight of herself (2016: 40–42, 46–47; see also Mills 1997: 62). In as much as evaluations of bodily beauty encode visceral, reason-resistant judgements about deeper traits of character, they play a key role in how we imagine our prospects and mold our own personalities. In coming to see herself through the eyes of white people, Pecola becomes unrecognizable to herself. She can no longer see herself as a creature whose embodiment fits and is welcome in the world. Her once beloved dandelions stand for a wider world that does not see her for who she is.

That is not the whole story, though. With their gaze averted, Pecola also loses sight of the dandelions' beauty. They are now ugly.

Why? What could Morrison mean by this?

Perhaps Morrison means nothing more than to project onto the flowers Pecola's shame and anger, but here is a bold interpretation. Suppose that deep insults to aesthetic self-regard can impair aesthetic capacity across the board. Then the bold interpretation is that an anti-black beauty ideal has harmed Pecola in her general capacity as an aesthetic agent (John 2012). She loses the capacity to apprehend beauty.

The bold interpretation has its attractions. It predicts that, when beauty ideals are weaponized, targeted groups must struggle to regain an aesthetic voice. Two threads are woven into Taylor's *Black Is Beautiful*. One exposes the workings of anti-black ideals of bodily beauty; the other articulates how any achievement of black aesthetic culture must confront the anti-black ideals. If Pecola's misperception of the dandelions as ugly results from the ideals' injuring her general ability to apprehend beauty, then she can engage beauty only by defying the ideals. The same link between bodily beauty ideals and the power of aesthetic agency is in the background of early feminist art, where it is a given that restoring women's aesthetic agency means standing up to gender-oppressive bodily beauty ideals. If Morrison and the pioneers of feminist art have it right, then bodily beauty ideals contribute to gender-based and race-based

118   AESTHETIC INJUSTICE

injustice partly by harming people in their global capacities as human agents.

Still, the bold interpretation is too bold. No doubt, bodily beauty ideals sometimes cause global injuries to aesthetic agency, but most targets of weaponized aesthetics nonetheless enjoy rich aesthetic lives. Aesthetic agents find resources in the harshest conditions, even war and famine; we must not underestimate their resilience. The bold interpretation takes the metaphor of the ugly dandelions too literally.

Here is a more modest interpretation. Pecola's dandelions personify her. If they are her, then her seeing them as ugly is her seeing her own body as ugly. More accurately, her seeing them as ugly, when they are not, is her seeing her own body as ugly, when it is not. Her eyes are now blue, for she mistakenly sees herself with the same distaste as "lurk[s] in the eyes of all white people."

So interpreted, Morrison tells a tale of aesthetic injustice. To begin with, bodily beauty ideals harm Pecola in her capacities for evaluating bodily beauty—black bodily beauty in particular. After all, she has internalized a gendered and racialized ideal of bodily beauty that rules out the possibility of beautiful black bodies. Now Pecola represents us all, no matter what the colour of our skins, in as much as we have all internalized the same ideal of bodily beauty. We see bodily beauty too narrowly, and that is a harm to our capacities as aesthetic agents.

The next question is whether the harm amounts to an aesthetic injustice. It does amount to an aesthetic injustice if the hypothesis that the harm subverts an interest in the value diversity of aesthetic cultures is needed to fully understand weaponized aesthetics. We ask: does an aesthetic injustice stem from and compound the weaponized aesthetics?

The aesthetic injustice does compound weaponized aesthetics. The harm to our capacities to perceive the beauty of black and brown bodies is precisely what licences and normalizes the harms of social injustice. To make matters much worse, internalizing bodily beauty ideals causes people like to Pecola to struggle against losing sight of themselves, and their struggles take a psychological toll (see also Fanon 2008 [1952]). Their sight in the eyes of others further curtails their opportunities, and that is weaponized aesthetics.

By the same token, the aesthetic injustice stems from weaponized aesthetics. The harm to our capacities as aesthetic agents is not the result of merely flooding the informational environment with certain kinds of representations. Weaponized ideals of bodily beauty work ideologically, masking the true diversity of bodily beauties. The ideology that secures social injustice is what deprives us of an opportunity to multiply cultures of bodily beauty that can shelter and invite rooted or routed respect for multiple valid, incommensurable, logically compatible, and sometimes mutually incomprehensible ideals of bodily beauty.

To sum up, we fail to fully appreciate how Pecola is put down by the blue-eyed beauty ideal as long as we overlook the aesthetic injustice. We fail to appreciate weaponized aesthetics until we acknowledge that it subverts an interest of ours—an interest in the value diversity of cultures of bodily beauty. That is an argument in favour of the cosmopolitan theory of aesthetic injustice.

New Beauty Ideals

In *Perfect Me*, Widdows argues that new ideals of bodily beauty are emerging but that what is troublesome about them is not explained by accounts of their role in social injustice. They are troublesome because they are narrow in content and wide in scope, hence too demandingly ethicized. Widdows's diagnosis of the new ideals also suggests that they are aesthetically unjust.

Starting with content, the new ideal prescribes that beautiful bodies be young, thin, and firm and smooth (Widdows 2018: 21–26). Youth might be the controlling value, if it is what being thin, firm, and smooth emulates. Since the features go together in this way, the ideal is narrow, even as it admits a range of ways to be thin, firm, and smooth. Thin can come with curves, or not, and big but fat-free can count. Firm can be slim and buff or built. Smooth skin is hairless, wrinkle-free, and glowing but need not be white—the global trend is to "golden." All the same, thin, firm, and smooth are criterial.

A narrow ideal that applies to few is not automatically demanding, but the new bodily beauty ideal applies to increasingly more types of people. Thus it applies to more and more women: girls and elders, as well as young adults, and the poor or working class, as well as socialites, celebrities, professionals, and the middle class (Widdows 2018: 54–68). Men

120   AESTHETIC INJUSTICE

and boys are now under its sway too (Widdows 2018: 236–240). Finally, it covers more races and ethnicities, allowing for local differences in how it is interpreted, negotiated, and justified (Widdows 2018: 71).

Given the ideal's wide scope and narrow content, very few are able to comply with it except with great effort. In that sense, it is demanding. However, an ideal with wide scope and narrow content might generate only weak reasons—ones that are easily outweighed by other considerations. As we know, bodily beauty ideals greedily intrude on the daily regimen, call for continual self-monitoring and self-discipline, and soak up resources. The beauty ideal is only as greedy as it is because it is an ethical ideal.

The claim is descriptive: it says that the ideal is treated as ethical, not that it is correctly so treated. For better or worse, it provides an evaluative framework that is valid in all contexts, that sets a standard for success, that apportions praise and blame, and that engenders shame and disgust, where engagement is virtuous and failure is vicious, where it is desired as both a final and an instrumental good, and where it promises to deliver the goods of the good life, including personal and collective meaning (2018: ch. 1). The list bespeaks the "two faces" of the bodily beauty ideal: it is at once demanding, even punishing, but also a source of considerable rewards (Widdows 2018: 38). As we have seen, engaging it can pay off materially, it can bring pleasure, self-esteem, and health, and it can enrich our relationships with others, but its deep appeal does not lie in its promising these goods.

By engaging the new bodily beauty ideal, we endeavour to locate our selves in our bodies, fashioning ourselves by fashioning our bodies (Widdows 2018: chs 7–8; see also Heyes 2007). Identifying the self with the body is not objectification; it is, as Widdows writes, a "reconstruction of subjectivity located in, and symbolized by, the body" (2018: 187). The reconstruction is a project of self-transformation where we see the flawed bodies we actually have as potentially beautiful, where perfect beauty is a notional or nominal endpoint, and where the process of transformation is empowering and expressive. For Widdows, we judge ourselves and others not as inert objects but as "becoming, promising, and potential objects" (2018: 185–186). As a result, the stakes are high. Failure to engage the beauty ideal is not merely a failure to comply with a prudential, aesthetic, or social norm; it is "a failure of the self" (Widdows 2018: 32).

A demandingly ethicized bodily beauty ideal is well suited to function ideologically in gender-based or race-based injustice, but it need not weaponize aesthetics. Granted, the new ideal continues to mark gender and racial difference. For example, hairlessness signifies girlishness for women but masculinity for men (Widdows 2018: 245). Nevertheless, marking difference is not sufficient for injustice. Widdows contends that the new bodily beauty ideal does not figure in sexual objectification because sexual desire is more diverse than the narrow beauty ideal permits (2018: 174). She also contends that the double bind unravels if beauty is anything but trivial (2018: 235). Moreover, gendered burdens are evening out: "that men increasingly have to engage in body work and that appearance is important to male identity is a significant change, and one that upsets the traditional critique" (Widdows 2018: 248).

This conclusion is hardly cause for celebration. Widdows laments that "a world in which both men and women were equally subject to ever more punishing demands of beauty is not a desirable end point" (2018: 250). One might wonder whether the new ideal continues to produce aesthetic injustice. Here is reason to think that it does.

Widdows argues that the only alternative to the new beauty ideal with its narrow content and wide scope is to regard to beauty practices as blown about by the whims of taste and fashion. Whimsical taste and fashion cannot deliver opportunities for striving, self-control, self-esteem, and pleasure; they are not sources of personal and collective meaning. To get these benefits, we need ethicized beauty ideals, with wide scope and narrow content, that can generate weighty reasons.

A third option is implied by the network theory. Each aesthetic culture is an arrangement of social life that sources local aesthetic reasons. Those reasons can be very weighty for insiders to engage, even if they carry little weight for outsiders to engage. In other words, evaluations of bodily beauty have narrow scope. What about content? From within the perspective of any one aesthetic culture, their content is narrow. A Tlingit woman might have reason to pierce her lip for an abalone labret, but not to wear a miniskirt. At the same time, stepping back from any given aesthetic culture, evaluations of bodily beauty have an enormously wide range. In many cultures of bodily beauty, an abalone labret is not beauty-making; in many, the new ideal is alien. In other words, evaluations of bodily beauty have wide content. Evaluations with narrow scope and

122 AESTHETIC INJUSTICE

wide content are not fit to be ethicized. Nonetheless, they source practice-internal reasons that are weighty enough to yield the benefits that accrue from participation in any normatively structured endeavour.

If this is correct, then the new beauty ideal harms people in their capacities to make evaluations within local cultures of bodily beauty. The hypothesis is that, in doing so, it subverts an interest in the value diversity of aesthetic cultures. If the hypothesis explains what is troublesome about the new ideal, then the ideal is aesthetically unjust. The cosmopolitan critique of the new beauty ideal is a critique of its being ethicized.

Beauty Policy

The cosmopolitan theory of aesthetic injustice should generate considerations that can shape policy. Perhaps the most important point on this score is that we should not rely too much on policies to be enacted either by the legal system or by individuals.

Rhode's detailed survey of legal instruments deployed in various jurisdictions to target appearance-based discrimination concludes rather pessimistically (2010: 120–125). In the United States, a handful of city and state ordinances directly proscribe appearance-based discrimination, but they are rarely enforced. The same goes for truth in marketing laws, which have not proven useful as a remedy for discrimination based on bodily beauty ideals (Rhode 2010: 141–142). Meanwhile, the courts are unwilling to remedy discrimination based on bodily beauty ideals by invoking general protections against discrimination on the basis of gender, race, or disability. Interestingly, the exception is discrimination against physically disabled and extremely obese people. At any rate, statutory approaches are indirect. They leave bias in place and promise at most to dampen its impact.

Rhode also warns that we must not "ask too much of individuals and too little of society" (2016: 90). Widdows (2022) adds that placing the burden for change on individuals is not likely to succeed. She argues that individual efforts to combat sexism and racism have succeeded only because they have involved consciousness-raising—that is, revealing the fact of the injustice. Consciousness-raising with respect to bodily beauty ideals has not worked, despite decades of trying, for two reasons. Bodily beauty ideals have benefits, and that is reason to stick with them. In addition, they are a powerful source of adaptive preferences, which are rational in the short run, even if not in the long run (Chambers 2008). As a further reason for skepticism, consciousness-raising loses its urgency as bodily beauty ideals apply yet more widely and thereby dissociate from sexism and racism.

If Rhode and Widdows are right, then the focus should be on policies to be adopted by entities below the state and above the individual. How can schools, athletic institutions, social clubs, and the worlds of entertainment, advertising, and the arts be effective agents of change?

Alfred Archer and Lauren Ware (2018) advocate lightening the normative load of bodily beauty ideals. In fact, they argue, compliance with the ideals is aesthetically supererogatory; it is not obligatory from an aesthetic perspective, though it is aesthetically better than the obligatory minimum. We go wrong in treating what is supererogatory as obligatory. More fundamentally, we go wrong in failing to see the distinction between the supererogatory and the obligatory. Marking the distinction "has a crucial role to play in persuading people of their freedom not to feel obligated to meet the standards of aesthetic perfection" (Archer and Ware 2018: 125). That seems right, but what policies are liable to improve normative reasoning? Obviously, lectures on normative theory are not the right approach. What we need is to portray bodies as sites of aesthetic engagement that is either compatible with or entails a vision of bodily ideals as normatively weighty yet highly variable.

Bodily beauty ideals are transmitted principally through images, and many writers advocate propagating more diverse images of bodily beauty (Widdows 2018: 259–260). Eaton (2016) observes that exposure to images can change our emotional responses. After all, emotional responses are keyed to situation types learned in part by exposure to images. Bence Nanay adds that we can harness the mere exposure effect, where the more frequently we are exposed to an image without recognizing it, the more we like it (Lopes, Nanay, and Riggle 2022: 100–101). Surely schools, athletic institutions, social clubs, and the worlds of entertainment, advertising, and the arts all have roles to play in a project of enriching the diet of images of bodily beauty. Indeed, some have recently been on the case.

Diversifying the informational environment is a way to implement either of two strategies whose goal is to portray bodily ideals as normatively weighty yet highly optional.

124   AESTHETIC INJUSTICE

One might be called the "Benetton strategy," after the retailer whose marketing campaigns accommodate many skin tones into one clothing style. On this strategy, everyone has a place within one, overarching and welcoming aesthetic culture. The cosmopolitan theory suggests a different strategy, namely, to propagate images of bodies from diverse cultures of bodily beauty. Instead of finding everyone a place in an overarching aesthetic culture, the strategy is to promote and portray many cultures, such that everyone can find one in which to thrive. Images that convey the variety of bodily beauty cultures can train us to see bodies as complying with local ideals that might carry great weight for insiders but that are obviously not obligatory for everyone. In short, more abalone labrets, please.

A similar strategy animates black and second-wave feminist art. Shelby writes that, "Black people have a long and remarkable history of using various cultural practices, not only to express themselves aesthetically and spiritually, but to resist and subvert the forms of racial domination that oppress them" (2005: 181). Among the forms of domination to be subverted by expressions of black culture were bodily beauty ideals and what the ideals made of black bodies. Black artists undercut the ideals by representing black bodies as part of black aesthetic culture. The strategy can be exported beyond art and also beyond race and gender (e.g. Eaton 2016, Frazier 2023).

The main argument for the cosmopolitan theory of aesthetic injustice is cumulative. This chapter and the chapter on appropriation make the case that we do indeed have cosmopolitan interests in the value diversity and social autonomy of aesthetic cultures. The next two chapters appeal to both interests together.

7

Outlier Aesthetics

Being blind, Nat was told that he could not draw and should not try, yet one of his pictures made the cover of the *New Scientist*. His triumph is a (modest) step toward a world that contains less aesthetics weaponized against disabled people. At the same time, it also hints at a decrease in aesthetic injustice—that is, in relatively large-scale social arrangements that subvert interests in the value diversity and social autonomy of aesthetic cultures. The main argument for the cosmopolitan theory of aesthetic injustice is elastic and cumulative. Aesthetic injustice, as characterized by the cosmopolitan theory, is real because it stems from and compounds aesthetics weaponized through appropriation and ideological ideals of bodily beauty. This chapter adds that it stems from and compounds aesthetics weaponized in aid of disability-centred injustice too.

Justice for Minority Bodies

What justice demands for disabled people depends on what it is to be disabled. Anita Silvers makes the connection lucid. Since disabled people differ from others (and each other), the question is "how to distinguish the kinds of differences that should matter for justice, and how to delineate the difference(s) for justice these should make" (Silvers 2009: 166–167). Indeed, theories of disability seek to unify the phenomenon in a way that is both informative and also fit for confronting injustice (Barnes 2016: 10–12 and 39–43, Francis and Silvers 2016).

Theories of disability are too numerous to sum up here, but we can make do by contrasting evaluative with neutral theories. On evaluative theories, disabilities are intrinsically bad. Neutral theories deny that disabilities are intrinsically bad. They are "mere differences," in Elizabeth Barnes's phrase (2016). As a result, whereas evaluative theories see

Aesthetic Injustice. Dominic McIver Lopes, Oxford University Press. © Dominic McIver Lopes 2024.
DOI: 10.1093/oso/9780198930983.003.0007

126 AESTHETIC INJUSTICE

disabilities as differences for just social arrangements to mitigate, neutral theories are poised to represent disabilities as differences for just social arrangements to "embrace" (Silvers 2009).

Until recently, the debate about the nature of disability has centred on two families of evaluative theories. Both articulate, albeit in very different ways, the commonly held position that to be disabled is a misfortune, something that makes one's life worse, so that we have weighty reason to avoid or mitigate it (Kahane and Savulescu 2009: 17).

One family of evaluative theories identifies disabilities with certain physiological or psychological traits. Obviously, the traits are massively heterogenous at a superficial level. Some philosophers seek to unify them as traits that deviate from normal function for the species; others unify them as functional deficits that substantially impact daily life (e.g. Daniels 1985, Bickenback 1993; see Silvers 1998: 59–74 for an overview and Kahane and Sevulescu 2009 for an alternative). The trouble is that many physiological or psychological traits meet these conditions and are not disabilities. Michael Phelps's enormous feet and arm span deviate from normal species functioning, but he quite rightly did not swim in the Paralympics (Barnes 2016: 14–15). My anomalous chromatopsia, which means I see some blues as green, is no disability, although it messes with my attempts at clothes shopping. The fix is to add that a deviation or deficit is a disability only when it is not easily mitigated and it makes one worse off beyond a high threshold. Making this fix nicely serves the purpose of representing disability as calling for collective action. As Jerome Bickenbach puts it, "many impairments are painful or otherwise intrinsically bad, and access to impairment-related health care resources is an important human rights issue for people with disabilities, around the world. Assuming otherwise ... will hardly serve the human rights cause of people with disabilities" (quoted in Silvers 2003: 478).

Another family of evaluative theories represent facts about disability as social facts, rather than physiological or psychological facts. For example, a theory of disability might adapt Haslanger's theories of gender and race (see Siebers 2006, Silvers 2010, Barnes 2016: 28–33, and arguably Thomson 1997; for alternatives, see Howard and Aas 2018, Jenkins and Webster 2020). To be disabled is to be socially positioned as subordinate to others along some dimensions, having been marked for positioning by certain perceived or imagined physiological or psychological

OUTLIER AESTHETICS 127

traits. A principal mechanism of social injustice is stereotyping, and, when it comes to disability, we very often construct social worlds where stereotypes are made true. If sight is considered necessary to be able to draw, blind people are going to be deprived of basic drawing lessons, and will therefore end up without competence in drawing. Social injustice also results from norms having been built into the environment. Buildings that have been designed around defaults that assume and secure compliance with various mobility norms will harm, in morally significant ways, those for whom compliance is a challenge. Thus a wheelchair user is disadvantaged for social reasons when building codes omit to mandate spaces for wheelchairs. Notice that subordination, secured in this way, is at best distally but not proximally explained by stigmatizing attitudes. It can and does outlast them. In sum, disability is a state of a minority of people that disadvantages them in society only (or largely) because a state of society disadvantages a minority of people (Silvers 2002: 28).

Both families of theories construe disability as intrinsically bad, so that being disabled makes one worse off. Whether they are intrinsically bad physiological or psychological traits or whether they are subordinate social positions associated with the traits, disabilities are to be mitigated, ideally eliminated. Either the bad effects of the traits themselves are to be remedied or the social infrastructure should be redesigned so that it no longer disadvantages people with the traits. Indeed, those who identify disabilities with intrinsically bad physiological or psychological traits will acknowledge a history of neglecting or disregarding the interests of disabled people, and their remedies will encompass renovations of the social environment.

Turn now to value neutral theories of disability, as pioneered by Silvers (2003, 2009 and Francis and Silvers 2016) and Barnes. In Barnes's striking statement, being disabled is:

> A way of being a minority with respect to one's body, just as being gay is a way of being a minority with respect to sexuality. It is something that makes you different from the majority, but that difference isn't by itself a bad thing. To be disabled is to have a minority body. (2016: 6)

Needless to say, the statement is striking because it downright contradicts the widespread belief that being disabled is a misfortune that makes one

128   AESTHETIC INJUSTICE

worse off. To take it seriously, we must get a grip on what it is for a trait to be value neutral. For that, we need a pair of orthogonal distinctions.

First is a distinction between dimensional and all things considered values (Barnes 2016: ch. 3). Being F can be good or bad for an agent in the sense that it positively or negatively impacts some dimension of their well-being. Being paraplegic might be bad for someone because it causes them pain, negatively impacting them on a hedonic dimension. Yet the same condition might be good for them because it affords athletic achievement, positively impacting them on the achievement dimension of their well-being. When we add up how being F is good and bad for someone along all dimensions of well-being, the result indicates how good or bad it is for them to be F, all things considered.

Second is a distinction between intrinsic and non-intrinsic values. For being F to be intrinsically bad for anyone is for being F to have a negative impact on anyone's well-being, just in virtue of what it is to be F. Evaluative theories characterize disability as having a negative impact on anyone's well-being "by definition," as it were. Some values are instrumental, of course. Being paraplegic might be good for someone in so far as it compels them to learn the virtues of patience and persistence. Importantly, not all non-intrinsic values are instrumental. Some are constitutive. Being paraplegic can be good for an agent in as much as it is part of belonging to a community with which they positively identify. Being paraplegic can be instrumentally or constitutively bad for someone, too. Examples are hardly needed.

Value neutral theories deny that being disabled is intrinsically bad in the sense that anyone takes a hit to their well-being, all things considered, just by dint of being disabled. True, being disabled is sometimes, perhaps always, intrinsically bad along some dimensions. Nonetheless, the very same trait that is bad for an agent along some dimension of their well-being can be good for them along other dimensions (Barnes 2016: 79). Moreover, instrumental and constitutive credits and debits vary along various dimensions of well-being. Whether or not being disabled is good or bad for an agent all things considered depends on how it combines with other conditions of their life.

Our two orthogonal distinctions help to state value neutral theories, but they also guard against some errors that make evaluative theories seem obvious. For one thing, that a feature is bad along some dimension of one's well-being does not entail a net hit to well-being all things considered. Another error is more subtle: the absence of a dimensional good might not be at all bad, or it might be bad only marginally (Silvers 1998: 89–90, Barnes 2016: 94). Folk conceptions of being blind virtually equate it with the loss of intrinsic goods such as seeing the beauty of sunsets and paintings. For those who make such goods prominent in their lives, being blind seems tragic. However, many sighted people are not keen on sunsets or paintings. If they are missing anything, what they miss barely nudges the needle on their well-being all things considered. Silvers observes that "it is odd to deem [these goods'] absence disadvantageous to those who cannot enjoy them but indifferent to those who can but do not enjoy them" (1998: 90).

In company with evaluative theories, value neutral theories are geared to aid thinking about justice. In failing to represent the disadvantages associated with disability as contingent, and as interacting with other conditions of individual lives, "we contribute to the barrier that distances disabled people from realizing the promises that justice should hold for them" (Silvers 2016: 846). Barnes makes the same point from the perspective of a disabled person:

> the high achiever who doesn't see themselves as limited or lacking feels pressure to say that they don't think of themselves as disabled.... the better response in this case seems to be rejecting the characterization of disability as nothing more than loss or lack, rather than granting that such people are not in fact disabled simply because their positive self-conception doesn't match their negative conception of disability. (2016: 35)

An aim of value neutral theories is to bring into view how disabled people are poised to flourish, so as to attune our thinking about justice accordingly. Silvers writes that "justice for outliers to develop and express their talents is and should be as much a value as remedying their deficiencies" (2009: 184). Barnes expresses the point in the language of pride, noting that the disability rights movement has evolved from demanding equality to celebrating difference: it "includes not just protests and demands for legislation, but disability pride parades, disability-centric art and theater, and an emphasis on shared community" (2016: 42).

130 AESTHETIC INJUSTICE

For present purposes, we need not decide between evaluative and value neutral theories. Both seek to supply tools to think through justice for disabled people. Evaluative theories emphasize the need for policies that either mitigate the disadvantages that stem from having certain physiological or psychological traits or from inhabiting the social structures that disadvantage people with the traits. Neutral theories additionally emphasize the need for policies that give disabled people opportunities to fully flourish, by exercising talent. Perhaps evaluative theories can be rejigged to accommodate the importance of such positive policies as Barnes and Silvers emphasize. At any rate, let us benchmark justice for minority bodies as putting a stop to disadvantage and discrimination and also as fostering flourishing, where there is more to the latter than the former.

Beauty × Disability × Art

Having sketched the character of social injustice facing disabled people, and having benchmarked what justice requires, the next task is to look at how aesthetic culture has been weaponized in ways that stem from and compound social injustice. Unsurprisingly, scholarship focuses on beauty ideals. The claim is that:

> a relatively large-scale social arrangement weaponizes bodily beauty when and because it includes beauty ideals that stem from and compound social injustice by licensing or normalizing the acts and interlocked harms that constitute socially unjust treatment of disabled people.

The aim is not to critique existing work on weaponized aesthetics. That work tells a large part of the story, even if it leaves a gap. The next section will return to Nat, who occupies the gap.

An aesthetic ideal is an aesthetic evaluation that applies to all items of a kind and that has a normative content expressed using a "should," "ought," or "must." Bodily beauty ideals dictate, in particular, that all human bodies should conform to a particular aesthetic profile: all beautiful bodies will be beautiful because they have certain narrowly circumscribed non-aesthetic features. As we saw in the previous chapter, ideals of bodily beauty can function ideologically, where an ideology is a palette of thought that stems from and secures the persistence of an unjust social arrangement, partly by obscuring the fact that the arrangement is unjust. The palette has a scope, vehicles and formats, source, proximal impacts, and cognitive defects that all contribute to its masking function.

Many scholars maintain that aesthetic culture promotes an ideological ideal of bodily beauty that privileges the normal human body and that licences or normalizes unjust treatment of people whose disabled bodies are seen as deviating from the ideal (e.g. Mitchell and Snyder 1997, Thomson 1997). Unjust treatment might amount to a distribution of resources that fails to alleviate morally significant disadvantages that come with being disabled. Alternatively, the treatment might catalyze the social subordination that constitutes being disabled. Either way, practices of representing human bodies implicate ideals on which disabled bodies are ugly and, by association, pitiable, dependent, and unable to cope in a self-reliant manner. Seeing people as having traits such as these makes it seem natural to treat them as incompetent.

Ideological ideals of bodily beauty are typically propagated through vehicles whose formats obscure their cognitive defects and tend to shape everyday, personal interactions. Children learn how to perceive and affectively respond to minority bodies by referencing the adverse reactions of adults. Perceptual and affective dispositions immediately prime pragmatic interactions; moreover, they are sticky, since not directly susceptible to rational critique. Scholars in the humanities mostly focus on artistic sources of ideologies around disability. In her classic study, Rosemary Garland Thomson (1997) argues that stories, images, and performances representing disabled people are metonyms for all minority bodies. Seeing some people as disabled, because deviating from normal, is the key to seeing women and people of colour as deviating from normal. "The disabled figure" is, as Thomson puts it, the "paradigm of what culture calls deviant" (1997: 6).

However, some warn against a focus on art. Silvers worries that the critique presumes that "art must be oppressive when it references disability, for otherwise it could not be valued by a society that discriminates against disabled people" (2002: 236; see also Siebers 2006). She points out that writers, painters, and performers have, for more than a century, presented some disabled people as beautiful, thereby challenging

132   AESTHETIC INJUSTICE

conceptions of normalcy and celebrating anomaly. Some art brings alive how "the diversity occasioned by disability is meaningful in furthering enduring human purposes" (Silvers 2002: 242). Perhaps it is harder to see this when one assumes an evaluative theory of disability.

Setting aside worries about the frequency of positive portrayals of disabled people in art, the remedy to weaponized ideals of bodily beauty is to modify our representational practices so as to disarm the ideals. Recall that to function ideologically, the ideals must have narrow content and wide scope: the ideals hold, of everyone, that their bodies are beautiful only if they are the kinds of bodies that few people have.

With respect to scope, Widdows argues that the new, increasingly dominant bodily beauty ideals have a narrower scope than traditional ideals: they specifically exempt disabled people, because the ideological function of the traditional ideals is now too conspicuous (2018: 150). Still, the trouble with the scope exemption for disabled people is that it continues to countenance treating them as not equipped to aspire to the rewards of bodily beauty.

As to content, we have just seen that Silvers points to art works that broaden the content of our ideals of bodily beauty (2002; see also Siebers 2006). In some art, disabled bodies are shown as beautiful, in novel ways. Moreover, the effect of this kind of art is to draw attention to the narrowness of the content of bodily beauty ideals, exposing their ideological function. All the same, broadened conceptions of bodily beauty in art might not colour personal interactions on a daily basis. Positive portrayals of disabled people in art go back more than a century, but serious reforms to social policy around disability are recent.

Two modest conclusions are in order. Some (but not all) artistic representations of disabled bodies weaponize aesthetics by engaging ideological ideals of bodily beauty. A remedy (albeit an imperfect one) is to promote representations that narrow the scope and broaden the content of the ideals in ways that expose the ideals' ideological function.

An Aesthetic Capacity: Tactile Drawing

The mantra of this book is that weaponized aesthetics and aesthetic injustice are causally intertwined, but nevertheless distinct. Weaponized aesthetics involves any expressive practices that are drawn from aesthetic culture and that stem from and compound social injustice. By contrast, aesthetic injustice involves harms to people in their aesthetic capacities that subvert certain justice-relevant interests. To show that aesthetic injustice stems from and compounds aesthetics that has been weaponized to target disabled people, the first step is to identify the harms to their aesthetic capacities. The second step brings in the interests. Start with step one.

Nat's accomplishment in making the cover of the *New Scientist* signals a high point in a history of intellectual advances, which begin with an empirical discovery, lead to a conceptual revision, and suggest an aesthetic conjecture.

The empirical discovery is simply that blind people, by means of touch, can comprehend and create raised-line drawings, notably drawings using the full range of projective geometries that are found in drawings by sighted people (Kennedy 1993, Lopes 1997). Performance is not perfectly uniform across blind and sighted subjects. Blind people are not accustomed to using tactile drawings, they have little practice in making them, tactile acuity falls below visual acuity, and raised-line drawings are relatively low resolution. For these reasons, blind people are less accurate at recognizing depicted scenes, and their drawings are on average less precise and controlled. Nonetheless, at the level of psychological capacities, they have what it takes to interpret and make pictures.

Some conceptual revision is needed once we take on board that drawings are amodal, as are the psychological capacities that underlie interpreting and making them. Colour aside, drawings turn out to be spatial representations that engage generic spatial skills needed to navigate the environment (Lopes 1997). As a result, there is no essential tie between vision and depiction. Yet a great deal of thinking, both among the folk and among scholars, assumes such a tie. When the art historian and critic Leo Steinberg wonders what a picture is, he imagines a dialogue between a painter and a blind person. In part:

PAINTER: A picture, you see, is a piece of cotton duck nailed to a stretcher.
BLIND PERSON: Like this? (He holds it up with its face to the wall.)
P: A picture is what a painter puts whatever he has into.
B: You mean like a drawer?
P: Not quite; remember it's flat. (1972: 48)

134 AESTHETIC INJUSTICE

Vision, blindness, and depiction are so conceptually intertwined that blindness is seen as a pictorial incapacity by definition. This is a mistaken conception of blindness and of pictures.

Competence in making and interpreting pictures does not imply competence in exploiting the aesthetic possibilities of tactile images. One conjecture is that tactile pictures do indeed afford some aesthetic possibilities. That is unlikely to be news, as just about anything affords aesthetic possibilities (Chapter 3). A more interesting conjecture is that tactile pictures afford distinctive aesthetic possibilities. That is, their particular non-aesthetic features can ground aesthetic values in aesthetic profiles that are not suited to other kinds of pictures. Why? As noted above, tactile acuity is not as fine as visual acuity, and the resolution of tactile media is not as fine as that of visual media. That can make an aesthetic difference. Robert Hopkins (2000) further argues that the relation between the representation of outline shape in ecological and pictorial vision has aesthetic significance, but the same relation does not obtain between the representation of outline shape in ecological and pictorial touch. He concludes, pessimistically, that tactile pictures cannot afford the same aesthetic possibilities as do visual pictures. The conclusion can be turned on its head: one might conclude, optimistically, that tactile pictures could have something new to offer, aesthetically (Lopes 2002). For instance, it might make a positive aesthetic difference that tactile pictures are to be perceived through physical contact (Korsmeyer 2016).

Nat's triumph is more extraordinary that it should be. Too many blind people are worse off than they would be otherwise because they have been deprived of an opportunity to foster and exercise one of their aesthetic capacities as aesthetic agents, namely a capacity to make images.

Tactile Drawing and Aesthetic Injustice

Harm is not sufficient for injustice; the next step is to close the gap between harm and injustice by making the case that the harm subverts interests in the value diversity or social autonomy of aesthetic cultures. The hypothesis is that we have interests such as these. That hypothesis is true if it is needed to fully understand weaponized aesthetics. The question is whether aesthetic injustice stems from and compounds aesthetics weaponized against disabled people.

Aesthetic injustice compounds weaponized aesthetics. Weaponized aesthetics portrays disabled people as pitiable, dependent, and unable to cope in a self-reliant manner. Indeed, the blind person is a trope of visual art in the Euro tradition, which features images that are meant to pack an emotional punch because they depict people who cannot appreciate their own reflections on canvas. As a result, weaponized aesthetics inhibits thinking of disabled people as talented, and thereby equipped to flourish, in their own ways. Spotlighting how disabled people thrive will tend to undermine the social injustice. An especially powerful way to spotlight how disabled people thrive is to see them engaged in activities that we would not recognize as worthwhile until we see them as activities where they are apt to thrive. Wheelchair-based dance and tactile drawing share this in common with wheelchair fencing and sledge hockey: seeing them as worthy activities for human beings discredits the thought that worthy activities are just those best suited to majority bodies. When blind people are not given a chance to learn to interpret and make tactile images, they cannot engage in a practice through which they might realize their potential as aesthetic agents and also through which their flourishing can enjoy the limelight. So, aesthetic injustice compounds weaponized aesthetics: some harms to people in their aesthetic capacities compound weaponized aesthetics by subverting an interest in the value diversity of aesthetic cultures.

Reversing directions, aesthetic injustice stems from weaponized aesthetics. Nat's story—the story of tactile images—exposes mistakenly narrow conceptions of perception and depiction. A conception of blindness joins with a visually oriented conception of depiction to make it seem absurd that blind people could make and use images, but these conceptions of blindness, vision, and depiction are not mandatory. They are products of processes of inquiry, and those processes of inquiry saddled us with mistakenly narrow concepts because they excluded proper attention to and input from blind people—they involved hermeneutical marginalization (Fricker 2007: ch. 7). Plausibly, blind people were excluded from the process of developing the relevant concepts because they are stigmatized as pitiable, dependent, and unable to cope in a self-reliant manner. In the end, weaponized aesthetics obscures from view how a

136 AESTHETIC INJUSTICE

disability might provide an opportunity to participate in aesthetic life. It inhibits thinking of disabled people as talented, and thereby equipped to flourish as aesthetic agents in distinct aesthetic cultures.

Not until we appreciate how it spawns and is compounded by aesthetic injustice do we plumb the full depths of weaponized aesthetics. When it comes to disability, the point is profoundly important. Weaponized aesthetics leverages aesthetic injustice to deprive disabled people of opportunities to foster and exercise some their capacities, when the thought that they are not fully capable is exactly what is used against them. We have further reason to believe that we do indeed have an interest in the value diversity of aesthetic cultures, just as the cosmopolitan theory would predict.

Justice for Talent

Blind people have not (yet) developed aesthetic cultures around tactile pictures. So far, raised-line drawings have been used principally to give them access to the history of visual art (Axel and Levent 2002). Access to visual art history is wonderful, of course, and it is hardly surprising that a new resource would be used to surmount access barriers. That granted, access to visual art is not the same as having aesthetic cultures of tactile imaging. Silvers holds that justice for disabled people requires more than measures to counterbalance discrimination. In her resonant phrase, "talent should command justice" (2009: 197). What does this principle come to, in practice?

The question is sharpened when cast as asking what we are committed to by an interest in the value diversity of aesthetic cultures. The interest need not be an interest in having marginally more aesthetic cultures: it is arguably not the case that, for any n, we should have n + 1 aesthetic cultures (Chapter 4). By the same token, the interest is compatible with our having n−1 aesthetics cultures, for some n. Nothing in the main argument for the cosmopolitan theory suggests an absolute threshold for sufficient value diversity in aesthetic cultures. So, it is fair to wonder in what conditions we have a cosmopolitan interest in there being n + 1 aesthetic cultures—an interest that is weighty enough to give us reason to take steps to foster its emergence.

The two cosmopolitan interests generate considerations for groups and institutions to weigh (against various other considerations) in determining policies. In general, the interests carry some weight, but not a great deal of weight. They must compete with many other considerations. One clear exception is when aesthetic injustice stems from and compounds aesthetics weaponized in aid of an egregious social injustice. In that case, the connection with weaponized aesthetics amplifies the strength of reasons to remedy aesthetic injustice. Does this give us special reason to increase the value diversity of aesthetic cultures that have been suppressed by social injustice? That is, do we have reason to make it the case that we have n + 1 aesthetic cultures, for some instances of +1?

Above it was noted that seeing wheelchair-based dance and tactile drawing as worthy activities for human beings discredits the thought that worthy activities are just those best suited to majority bodies. That is a reason to promote those activities, but it is not a very strong reason. Its being sufficient reason to engage in those cultures would burden disabled people with the task of reversing a stigma that we all have a duty to reverse.

One might reason as follows. Blind people have been dealt some great intrinsic bads. Among the bads is this: it is bad for them that they do not make or enjoy images. Justice requires a remedy, namely to make sure that blind people can make and enjoy images.

The reasoning rests on the false premise that missing out on a dimensional good is dimensionally bad. Recall Silvers's observation about the oddity of thinking that missing out on drawing is a tragedy for blind people but not for sighted people who are simply indifferent to it. In the same vein, the cosmopolitan theory claims that, in situations of aesthetic injustice, people are harmed in their capacities as aesthetic agents. To be harmed is to be less well off than one would otherwise be, but the state in which one ends up, having been harmed, need not be a bad state. This is the point of calling for justice for talent. Justice for talent does not run out at mitigating badness.

An even worse piece of reasoning appeals to what Barnes calls the "X-Men view," on which disabled people enjoy special, enhanced abilities (2016: 96). Presumably, the view invites the thought that special enhanced abilities merit special consideration. Setting aside that

138   AESTHETIC INJUSTICE

questionable thought, it is simply not true that tactile imaging skills are unique to blind people.

The problem generalizes. Blind people have many talents, and there are countless capacities that they might acquire. Some are aesthetic—writing poetry or preparing chaat—others are not—writing code or resolving diplomatic disputes. Granting Silvers's principle that talent should command justice, why should any particular talent command justice? Why this one, rather than those? Why aesthetic cultures of tactile imaging, for example?

One option is to throw in the towel on Silvers's principle. Maybe it is too much to ask that talent command justice. Or maybe the principle is attractive enough to stand up for. If any field of human striving is at home to Silvers's principle, then it is the field of aesthetics. The final chapter takes up the gauntlet.

8
Identity Aesthetics

Writing on multicultural policy, Chike Jeffers observes that the indifference towards his culture of a French immigrant to New Zealand is far less worrying than the indifference of an Anishinaabe woman living in Winnipeg to Anishinaabeg culture (2015: 216; cf. Shelby 2005: ch. 5). Her indifference predictably reflects how the culture has been denigrated and weakened. Likewise, the indifference of some sighted people to drawing might be far less worrying than indifference on the part of blind people to drawing. Suppose that we take the heightened worries seriously; suppose that justice calls for measures tailored in aid of some aesthetic cultures— for example, the aesthetic cultures of tactile imaging and Anishinaabeg beadwork. Some political philosophy already countenances measures to support the cultures of minority identity groups, but we shall see that those measures are inadequate. They do not warrant support tailored in aid of cultures to which identity group members are indifferent: they leave Nat and the Anishinaabe Winnipegger to their own devices. The cosmopolitan theory fills the policy considerations gap.

Identity and Minority Identity

The first task is to adopt a working conception of minority identities. The cosmopolitan theory does not make constitutive appeal to identity—in this respect, it contrasts with Fricker's (2007) theory of epistemic injustice, on which epistemic injustices necessarily involve identity prejudice. True, aesthetic injustice is causally implicated in identity prejudice when it stems from and compounds weaponized aesthetics. Yet aesthetic injustice need not implicate identity prejudice, and so far the argument for the cosmopolitan theory has not required a theory of minority identities. Only now, as we weigh how a theory of aesthetic injustice can

Aesthetic Injustice. Dominic McIver Lopes, Oxford University Press. © Dominic McIver Lopes 2024.
DOI: 10.1093/oso/9780198930983.003.0008

140 AESTHETIC INJUSTICE

contribute to multicultural policy, do we need a working conception of minority identity. The working conception should articulate what minority identity has to do with culture, aesthetic culture in particular.

"Minority" is a bad noun and a good adjective. If a minority is a smallish subpopulation of individuals who share some feature in common, then there are myriad minorities in any sizable population, of which very few should figure in thinking about justice—people who have visited Niagara Falls and people who revile cilantro, for example. Tourists and people with mutations of the OR6A2 gene are not identity groups; what matters is minorities that are identity groups.

If, like any group, an identity group comprises individuals who share some feature in common, then the question is what sorts of features are constitutive of identity groups in particular. Not being averse to cilantro or living in Moose Jaw. We need a working conception of identity groups such that minority identity groups correctly figure in thinking about justice.

Let an identity group comprise individuals who either identify with their being F or are taken in the larger society to be F, where being F is an identity group marker—being black, being gay, being South Asian, or being disabled, for example. These markers are contingent and vary by social circumstances, of course, but every identity group must have some marker, some feature with which identity group members can identify. In a genuine identity group, some members of the group do in fact identify with their being F. Groups whose members are all conscripts—none of whom identify with their being F—are not genuine identity groups (and no doubt the same goes for groups where too few identify). Perhaps few identity groups are genuine to begin with, but most eventually become genuine (Appiah 2005: 65–68). A label applied by outsiders is adopted by those who come to see themselves as belonging to the group. Since genuine and non-genuine identity groups might require somewhat different treatment in an account of justice, henceforth restrict identity groups to genuine ones.

It kicks the can down the road to take an identity group, the Fs, to comprise people who identify with their being F. What, after all, is it for someone to identify with their being F? Akeel Bilgrami (2015) proposes that for A to identify with their being F is for A (1) to value their being F and (2) to endorse (1), where (3) the endorsement is relatively resistant to revision, involving a commitment to try to make sure that A will continue to meet (1) in the future. Condition (3) confers Quinean central status on valuing being F. When someone ceases to endorse their being F, "it is not clear whether it is a change in the ordinary sense where the overall identity remains constant, but a change in value takes place, or whether the overall identity itself is changed" (Bilgrami 2015: 522). The idea is that what one values can change without a change in the self, and so can the values that one endorses. One's identity is anchored in the attempt to bind future selves to valuing what one values and endorses valuing now.

Bilgrami's account raises a conundrum whose solution will bring in aesthetic culture. Members of an identity group value their being F, where being F is an identity group marker, such as being black, gay, South Asian, or disabled. But what is it for A to value their being F? Presumably, identity groups do not matter as long as their members routinely value what is not in fact good. For being disabled to matter as an identity, valuing being disabled must be valuing what deserves to be valued. The conundrum is that being F is arguably not intrinsically good. Silvers and Barnes argue that being disabled is neither good nor bad intrinsically (see Chapter 7), and the same arguably goes for being black, gay, or South Asian. It hardly helps that the alternatives, evaluative theories, construe disability as a bad condition.

The conundrum's solution lies in recognizing that identity groups stand in close relation to some cultural groups, including aesthetic ones. South Asians are into chaat, for example. Indeed, desi, or South Asians in diaspora, are even more likely to link the aesthetic culture of chaat with their identity. Similar observations can be made about the aesthetic tendencies of those who identify with being black, gay, or disabled. Perhaps, then, for A to value their being F is for them to value the goods of the cultures that stand in close relation to being F. One way for a desi to value their being desi is for them to value the goods of chaat.

"Stands in close relation to" is a fudge made in recognition of the fact that identity groups do not reduce to cultural groups. A culture, in the minimal sense articulated in Chapter 2, is a pattern of behaviour in a population that is explained by members of the population sharing formative social conditions. By extension, a cultural group is a group of people whose behaviours comply with the pattern constitutive of the culture because they have shared the relevant formative social conditions.

142 AESTHETIC INJUSTICE

Many cultural groups are not identity groups—board game players and coffee drinkers, for instance. Board game players often value being board game players and endorse their valuing the board game lifestyle, but they typically do not commit themselves in Bilgrami's sense. The same goes for many aesthetic cultures, such as coffee culture. This is a useful result: the importance of identity groups for thinking about justice might outstrip that of aesthetic culture, minimally conceived.

Equally, it would be a mistake to suppose that members of an identity group must all belong to the same cultural group or groups. People who identify with being black participate in different cultures. Granted, in as much as members of an identity group share formative social conditions, they will tend to share at least some cultures. Discrimination and disadvantage, let alone segregation, provide for a shared history and shared experiences that can foster cultural commonality (Alcoff 1995). All the same, it does not follow that identity groups are culturally homogenous. Their members very often have many, overlapping cultural affiliations (Waldron 2000, Shelby 2005: 206–209, Scheffler 2007: 105–106). Correlations between identity and culture are causal and contingent; their presence and significance is to be discovered, not presumed.

Identity groups do not reduce to cultural groups, yet some of the cultures that contingently and dynamically pair up with identity groups are special. For instance, a desi might value being desi by valuing chaat, but not by valuing bossa nova. Bossa nova simply lacks the right linkage to being desi. Call chaat a "cultural associate" of desi identity. Bossa nova is not, then, a cultural associate of being desi. The question is, what is it to be a cultural associate of an identity? How is valuing chaat neither constitutive of nor a merely accidental correlate of being desi? What is there in between these options?

Chapter 2 characterized cultural cosmopolitanism as markedly normative: it views cultures as sources of goods and reasons, while denying that what makes a bit of culture good, hence reason-giving, is just that the goods and reasons are those of my group. That said, denying that my identity grounds the values and reasons of chaat aesthetic culture is compatible with holding that identity adds further value to cultural goods. What is good independently of its being ours might be all the better when we make it ours: identification adds value to cultural goods. Valuing being F by valuing the goods of the cultural associates of being F augments those goods. Thus, provided that chaat aesthetic culture delivers various goods anyway, the goods accrue additional value precisely because people value them as a way of valuing being desi.

In sum, to identify with being desi, one must value being desi. One values being desi by valuing some of the goods that come through its cultural associates. Valuing those goods as a way to value being desi augments the goods. The same goes for endorsing one's valuing being desi and one's committing to continue to value being desi. These amount to endorsing one's valuing and committing to value the goods of the cultural associates of being desi, thereby augmenting the goods.

Stipulate that the cultural associates of being F are just the cultures whose goods are augmented when and because valuing them, endorsing valuing them, and committing to value them is a way to value being F.

How are the goods augmented? No single answer needs to cover all cases. When they are associates of identity, elements of culture can source personal meaning and provide resources for composing a life for oneself (e.g. Appiah 2005). Those resources are subject to the social reality of identities. As Appiah puts it, "we make our lives *as* men and *as* women, *as* gay and *as* straight people" (2005: xiv). Andrew Mason (2004) argues that a community is a group that shares a range of values and a way of life, where members of the group identify with the group and recognize one another as members of the group. Some communities provide for solidarity and mutual concern in conditions free of exploitation and injustice (Mason 2004: 27). They satisfy a need for belonging, enhance cooperation, and unify efforts to protect against external threats. These goods come with forming a community by identifying with being F, hence valuing the goods of its cultural associates.

A working conception of identity groups that articulates their importance also applies to minority identity groups. Minority identity groups are identity groups that comprise relatively small subpopulations within a larger society. So understood, it is easy to see why we should consider measures to support the cultures of minority identity groups. Majority identity groups are in a position to see to it that their interests are well served. Not so minority identity groups.

Adopting the working conception of minority identity suggests a more precise statement of the thesis of the chapter: the cosmopolitan theory of

144 AESTHETIC INJUSTICE

aesthetic injustice warrants measures tailored specifically in aid of aesthetic cultures that are associates of minority identities.

From Basic to Robust Liberalism

Some versions of liberalism already go some distance in the same direction, though the argument will be that they do not go far enough. Most far-reaching is Patten's robust liberalism, which permits or mandates customized forms of accommodation of identity-related components of conceptions of the good (2014: 160).

Incidentally, robust liberalism makes a good foil to the cosmopolitan theory in one respect. Patten's identity-related components of conceptions of the good can be understood as cultural associates of identities. In another respect, the pairing is less ideal, for robust liberalism concerns state policy in particular, whereas the cosmopolitan theory concerns social arrangements at all levels. This point of difference matters, but it does not undermine the argument. If the cosmopolitan theory wins out by going far enough in warranting state policies tailored in aid of aesthetic cultures that are associates of minority identities, then it goes far enough in warranting non-state policies too.

Patten first contrasts robust liberalism with basic liberal proceduralism, identifying a shortcoming in the latter. A robustly liberal policy of customized accommodation patches the flaw, and that is the argument in its favour.

According to basic liberal proceduralism, state treatment of a minority identity group is just if the group enjoys the "standard liberal package" (Patten 2014: 150). Included in the package are Rawls's basic liberties, freedom from discrimination in the economy and civil society, a minimum with respect to income and essential goods, and policies to secure equality of opportunity. Basic liberalism is proceduralist when justice is to be obtained through policies of equal treatment, rather than policies that seek equal outcomes (more on this below).

Basic liberal proceduralism is compatible with two policies for allocating resources to the cultural associates of identities (Patten 2014: 119–122). One is privatization, where the state lets markets allocate resources to cultures, and the standard liberal package ensures that the markets are fair. As is well known, though, privatization fails for public goods. The fall back is what Patten nicely calls "generic entanglement." The policy is to support general purpose capacities that underlie participation in a variety of cultures, where the standard liberal package ensures that all can take advantage of that general purpose support. Examples of policies of generic entanglement include the state's provision of public security and secondary school writing classes. Both policies permit the state to be neutral, not directly favouring any group of citizens.

Right off the bat, it has to be said that basic liberal proceduralism promises a great deal to minority identity groups—even if, as a matter of fact, the promise remains to be kept. Making good on the promise would represent an advance towards justice (Barry 2001, Patten 2014: 8–9).

Nonetheless, basic liberal proceduralism has nothing to offer to address the decline of the cultural associates of minority identities, except in so far as they issue from violations of the standard liberal package. Unfortunately, the standard liberal package does not protect the cultural associates of minority identities against decline. Even with the steadfast support of identity group members, their cultural associates rarely withstand the assimilatory pressures of isolation from one another, immigration to a new society, or globalization.

For this reason, Patten proposes another approach. Like basic liberal proceduralism, his approach is proceduralist. To see the significance of proceduralism, contrast it with a non-proceduralist alternative, the capabilities approach. Silver's critique of Nussbaum's application of the capabilities approach to disability brings out a key advantage of proceduralism.

According to Nussbaum, a social arrangement is unjust unless it secures those human capabilities—including a capability for aesthetic participation—that are central to living a dignified human life (Nussbaum 2006: ch. 3). The standard liberal package fails to secure the central capabilities for disabled people when they need more resources to attain the same degree of capability as others. Therefore, what must be added to the standard liberal package is policies of special consideration in the distribution of resources to erase capabilities deficits. Nussbaum recommends allocating resources to achieve an outcome, a level of capability for all.

146   AESTHETIC INJUSTICE

Silvers (2009) objects that the outcome to be guaranteed is a minimum threshold of capability for all, but bringing everyone to a minimum threshold falls well short of justice for talent. As she explains, "erasing the disadvantage of deficit is a principle that must acknowledge and defer to a ceiling above which justice no longer cares whether individuals rise, even if they have the potential to do so, because they no longer are perceived as being in deficit" (2009: 184). Making the concern concrete, she reviews some United States case law where the high court considered an action against a school that had refused to provide an intellectually gifted deaf child with ASL interpretation (2009: 180–181). Without ASL interpretation, the child's scholastic performance fell below what it would have been otherwise, but the court found that her instruction met the legal threshold, which requires a minimal level of competence as an outcome.

Unlike the capabilities approach, Patten's robust liberalism is procedural. In place of policies to obtain equal outcomes, its core policy of customized accommodation is designed for equal treatment. Customized accommodations consist in allocations of resources that are tailored to fit specific cultures (Patten 2014: 157–158). The policy has two features.

First, tailoring is achieved procedurally, by allocating resources pro rata, given the standard liberal package. In Patten's favourite example, a municipality whose inhabitants prefer playing baseball to cricket in a ratio of four to one should allocate resources for each in the same ratio. The resources include funds but also physical space, time on the competition schedule, prizes and accolades, and whatever else is needed to make each viable. In this way, accommodation is customized to preferences. Since preferences are notoriously adaptive to contexts of discrimination, the standard liberal package also has a role to play. So, resource allocations are to be customized to preferences, provided that the preferences are not distorted by discrimination or anything else that ought to be eliminated by the standard liberal package.

Since customized accommodation is procedural, it does not secure outcomes. For Patten, responsibility for outcomes is divided between the state and cultural or identity group members (2014: 139–140; see also Rawls 1993: 189). The state provides facilities for the growth of talent, but citizens must take advantage of them. Cricket might decline without injustice if cricketers simply cool to the game. By the same token, they have

IDENTITY AESTHETICS 147

an opportunity to develop their cricketing talent to the full. Robust liberalism implements justice for talent.

Second, as the sports example makes clear, the beneficiaries of customized accommodations are members of identity associated cultures, in the minimal sense. Patten's phrase, "an identity-related component of a conception of the good," might seem to suggest that he has organic cultures in mind (see Chapter 2). However, in defending the policy of customized accommodation, he is careful not to rely on liberal culturalist arguments, familiar from the 1990s, that construe minority identity groups as approaching organic national or societal cultures (Kymlicka 1995; see also Patten 2014: ch. 3). The sports example recurs throughout the book, and sports are obviously cultures in the minimal sense. For this reason, the policy of customized accommodation can be neatly applied to identity-related conceptions of the aesthetic good, or to aesthetic cultures associated with identity groups.

Customized Accommodations

A policy of customized accommodation is warranted when two conditions are met (Patten 2014: 165–171).

To begin with, the culture to be accommodated is an identity associate. This means that its decline is highly consequential for members of the relevant identity group. The decline of cricket deprives members of cricket culture of the goods of cricket, but it also deprives black West Indians living in Toronto with a vehicle for valuing being who they are, and that is a far more serious loss.

The second condition is that policies of privatization and generic entanglement fail. Patten argues that these policies will tend to fail when the culture to be accommodated is an associate of a minority identity group and is expressed in a distinctive format. As he explains, groups,

> function in some language or languages and not others. They recognize some days as holidays and weekly days of rest and not others. The present themselves to the world—with flags, uniforms, anthems, coats of arms, and so on—through certain symbols and not others.

148 AESTHETIC INJUSTICE

They apply to people defined in one way and not another. And so on.
(2014: 169–170)

The fact of format distinctiveness is a problem for both privatization and generic entanglement.

Here is the reasoning. The formats of cultures associated with majority identity groups will typically have no trouble carrying on from generation to generation. Markets will see to that. By contrast, format distinctiveness dampens demand for elements of minority culture, and minority identity groups often lack the purchasing power needed to ensure that markets transmit their culture. Meanwhile, the distinctive format of the cultures prevents generic entanglement from curing the market failure.

Sometimes, then, a policy of customized accommodation is warranted. In particular, it is warranted for cultures that have distinctive formats and are associated with minority identity groups in ways that are highly consequential for them. When it comes to these cultures, allocations should not always be left to the market or funnelled to inculcate generic competences. Resources should be allocated to the culture, pro rated to preference. Customized accommodations afford members of minority identity groups with opportunities to nurture their talents.

Customized Aesthetic Accommodation

So far no reference has been made to aesthetic culture in discussing robust liberalism. Yet any identity group is liable to have or acquire one or more aesthetic cultures. Aesthetic cultures associate with being black, gay, South Asian, and disabled. In some contexts, these are minority identity groups—black West Indians in England, desi inhabitants of Mississippi, or people with minority bodies or sexualities just about anywhere. A general problem for aesthetics concerns policies for the just allocation of resources to sustain aesthetic cultures. A special problem concerns policies for the just allocation of resources to aesthetic cultures associated with minority identity groups. This section sees how far we can get in addressing the special problem by adopting policies of customized accommodation. The next section goes further and proposes a policy of cosmopolitan accommodation.

IDENTITY AESTHETICS   149

Aesthetic cultures and the activities they house consume resources. Decorating our dwellings and adorning our bodies, downloading books and movies, travelling to new places—all this hits the pocketbook. Writing with a bit of style takes time and energy. We see to it that our children receive an education that opens them to a world of aesthetic opportunities, and our taxes afford others' children the same education. Fine arts subsidies are common, if controversial in some quarters. We routinely allocate resources to aesthetic cultures in accordance with a mixture of policies of privatization and generic entanglement.

Privatization often works well at supporting aesthetic cultures for those who wish to participate in them. Markets support hip hop, Bollywood movies, clothing and automobile design, and dog breeding.

When markets fail, policies of generic entanglement might kick in, and philosophers have invoked them, particularly to justify state subsidies of the fine arts (see Lopes 2018b: 218–221 for an overview). Three conditions must be met to warrant a policy of state support for the fine arts as a form of generic entanglement. First, capacities to participate in fine art cultures must carry over to other cultures: there must actually be generic entanglement. Second, carrying them over into other cultures must yield important benefits. Third, the benefits cannot be obtained through privatization—there must be a market failure.

Assuming that some fine arts markets do fail, we can focus on the benefits of entanglement, and the benefits need not be aesthetic. Ronald Dworkin (1985) argues that the fine arts equip us with a rich, complex, and deep "cultural structure"—a cultural vocabulary—to pass on to future generations. Thomas Scanlon (1985) proposes that the fine arts help us to reflect on what we want and value in our lives. Wollheim (1985) offers that they benefit us by showing us how pleasure can be obtained in ways we would not have imagined, encouraging us to form new conceptions of personal happiness. These might be perfectly good rationales in favour of state support of the fine arts, but one might challenge the implicit assumption that specifically aesthetic benefits are not weighty enough to warrant policies of generic entanglement.

Being for Beauty closes with an appeal to a policy of generic entanglement with specifically aesthetic benefits (Lopes 2018: ch. 12; see also Beardsley 1970, Beardsley 1973). Aesthetic profiles overlap, as can be seen in the fact that individuals can learn the profiles of nearby cultures more

150 AESTHETIC INJUSTICE

easily than they can learn the profiles of faraway ones (see Chapter 3). A French chef can more easily transition to cooking Italian than Chinese. Possibly, some aesthetic cultures are hubs with spokes connecting them to many nearby cultures. Training in Euro classical music might be a good example, since it ensures competence in the musical fundamentals of many genres in the tradition. If so, then an aesthetic education in the hubs might provide enough competence in a broad swath of nearby aesthetic culture. As long as the fine arts are the hubs, then state-funded arts education affords a degree of generic entanglement.

While this proposal might benefit some aesthetic cultures associated with minority identities, it does not go far enough. Fine arts education is unlikely to provide sufficiently broad generic entanglement to support the cultural associates of all minority identities. Aesthetic profiles are the formats, in Patten's sense, of aesthetic cultures, and the aesthetic cultures associated with minority identities are likely to be sufficiently distinctive in their aesthetic profiles for generic entanglement to fail. An education in Euro classical music might not do enough for those whose musical traditions centre on drumming, throat singing, or microtonal nuance. In general, minority-associated aesthetic cultures tend to differ far more from majority-associated aesthetic cultures than majority-associated aesthetic cultures differ from each other. The size of the difference is likely to be greater when a minority group is made up of immigrants, those who have endured segregation or unjust discrimination, or people equipped with minority bodies. Tactile images are a case in point, potentially differing vastly more in aesthetic profile from other image genres than other image genres differ from each other. Surely the same goes for signed Deaf poetry and wheelchair dance.

Patten's policy of customized accommodation applies to support for aesthetic culture when two conditions are met. First, policies of privatization and generic entanglement fail. We have just seen that this condition is sometimes met. Second, the aesthetic cultures to be accommodated are minority identity associates whose decline is highly consequential for those who identify with them.

Affiliation with aesthetic culture is a surprisingly powerful dimension of identity for anyone. In one study, subjects were presented with scenarios featuring a radical change in aesthetic engagement, religious

IDENTITY AESTHETICS 151

conviction, political stance, recreational activity, employment, or place of domicile (Fingerhut et al. 2021). Here is one prompt:

> Suppose your taste in music changed dramatically. For example, if you enjoy only classical music, imagine you grew to like listening to only pop music.

Subjects were then asked where they would regard themselves as the same person. The size of the effect in the aesthetic scenarios was as large as for religion and political stance, the three leading the other scenarios. Moreover, there is no reason to think that the phenomenon is less strong in minority identity groups. On the contrary, the decline of identity-associated aesthetic culture tends to be highly consequential precisely when it comes to members of minority identity groups. Valuing its associated aesthetic culture looms large as one identifies as a member of a minority identity group. Desi inhabitants of Mississippi cling more avidly to chaat aesthetic values than do South Asians in Mangalore.

As powerful as the case for robust liberal policies of customized accommodation may be, they have a limit. Customized accommodation allocates resources pro rata, based on existing preferences, assuming that the preferences are not distorted by discrimination or any other factor that the standard liberal package should eliminate. Nat and his peers might not have a preference for making tactile images. Given their preferences and the principle of allocating resources in proportion to preferences, tactile imaging will merit little or no support.

True, the preferences of Nat and his peers might be a product of the kind of discrimination that the standard liberal package disallows (Chapter 7). However, it does not follow from the policy of customized accommodations that the response to the history of discrimination should be to support tactile image-making. Consider a principle to the effect that resources should be allocated to aesthetic cultures so as to bring the preferences of minority group members closer to what they would have preferred were the discrimination not to have occurred. That is, allocations should remediate unjust preference formation by reversing it. The principle is too strong. A history of discrimination against a group can be a source for its aesthetic culture (Glasgow et al. 2019: ch. 2). For example, a long history of racism caused a preference for the blues among

152 AESTHETIC INJUSTICE

black people in the United States, but the remedy for the discrimination might be to support more blues, not to divest from the blues and invest in Schubert or polka.

Policies of customized accommodations have their place alongside policies of privatization and generic entanglement, but none of them warrant nurturing the growth of new aesthetic cultures around tactile images. None warrant incentives for aesthetic cultures that might potentially serve well as associates of minority identities.

Cosmopolitan Accommodations

Policies of cosmopolitan accommodations go further than policies of customized accommodations. They allocate resources, above the pro rata baseline, to nurture new or declining aesthetic cultures that could be associated with minority identities. Their aim is, roughly put, to nudge preferences towards minority identity associated aesthetic cultures. Put as baldly as that, they might seem illiberal as well as patronizing to members of minority groups. The next section replies to the concern. This section characterizes cosmopolitan accommodations and the conditions where they are warranted.

Before proceeding, it is worth observing that it is not unusual for states to allocate resources above the pro rata baseline to some cultures, incentivizing new preferences. Here are two non-aesthetic examples.

The Paralympics primed a pump. At a time when there was only modest interest among disabled people in Paralympic sports, the Paralympics piggybacked on the Olympics' prestige and worldwide audience to boost interest in Paralympic events. The result has been a remarkably broad and rapid expansion of the roster of athletic events. That the new sports could be cultural associates of disabled identity explains, at least in part, both why the expenditure was justified but also why it met with such success.

To take another example, programs to revive endangered languages also incentivize preferences. BBC Gàidhlig creates radio and television programming in order to drive new interest in the language, which is taking root among those who identify as Scottish. Scotland has legislation, five-year strategic plans, and a bureaucracy, the Bòrd na Gàidhlig,

IDENTITY AESTHETICS 153

aimed at reviving the language. Similar efforts, on a smaller scale, support Indigenous languages that are in danger of losing speakers. So, policies of cosmopolitan accommodation are not unprecedented; rather, the cosmopolitan theory gives them a new rationale.

Returning to aesthetic culture, what are the conditions where policies of cosmopolitan accommodation are warranted? First, policies of privatization, generic entanglement, and customized accommodation must fail. The previous section concluded that this condition is sometimes met. Second, the aesthetic cultures to be accommodated must be especially well suited to serve as minority identity associates of considerable consequence for those in the relevant identity groups. The concept of special suitability brings out how potential cultural associates of minority identities can come to be consequential.

Some aesthetic cultures are better suited or more apt than others for associating with a given identity. Which aesthetic cultures are suited to which identities is contingent, not implied by the nature of the identity group (hence talk of cultures as "associated" with identities). No doubt there are many dimensions of suitability, but three obvious ones are geography, tradition, and psychology. Inhabiting a place where spices grow makes chaat aesthetic culture apt to associate with being South Asian. Geography can make an aesthetic culture apt for association with an identity. So can tradition. Coming out of reggae, which was already beloved of West Indians, ska was apt to associate with being black in England in the 1980s. Rockabilly would have been less suitable. Finally, tactile images and signed poetry illustrate how psychological traits can determine suitability for identity association. Tactile images are apt to associate with being blind and signed poetry is apt to associate with being Deaf. The claim is not the patently false one that these formats are only accessible to blind or Deaf people. Suitability is not exclusivity.

Geography, tradition, and psychology do not suffice for suitability. Recall that to identify with being F is to value, endorse valuing, and commit to valuing the goods that come through its cultural associates. An aesthetic culture is hardly suited to be associated with an identity unless there is a fair chance that group members will indeed come to identify as members of the group by valuing, endorsing, and committing to value what the culture has to offer. (Policies must be effective.)

154 AESTHETIC INJUSTICE

Keeping this in mind, we can understand suitability by appeal to the lasting benefits that would accrue were an aesthetic culture to become associated with a minority identity. Members of minority identity groups seek ways to identify with being F that are suitable. Then, their having come to value, endorse, and commit to valuing what is good in a suitable aesthetic culture raises the probability that the culture will persist. After all, the cultural associates of being F are just the cultures whose goods are augmented when and because valuing them, endorsing valuing them, and committing to value them is a way to value being F. So, valuing the goods of a culture as an aspect of identifying with being F amplifies the goods of the culture. That gives identity group members further reason to participate in the culture. In this way, the fact that a culture is suited to be associated with a minority identity explains why the accommodation was warranted by explaining why the accommodation is likely to work. Finally, once members of a minority identity group are settled into an aesthetic culture, there is now a great deal at stake in its decline. The idea of special suitability brings out how the aesthetic cultures potentially associated with minority identities can come to be consequential.

This result suggest a rough guide to what cosmopolitan accommodations should look like. They allocate resources in proportion to expected benefits. Thus they are procedural, for they do not allocate resources to yield actual beneficial outcomes. Whether the benefits accrue is partly up to those who are expected to benefit. If, in fact, a culture of making and appreciating tactile images would be a highly consequential associate of blind identity, then the expected benefits are high and considerable allocations of resources would be warranted. Needless to say, allocations need not be or need not stop at funding. They might include revised curricula for art education, invitations to exhibit and compete, and attention from the press, just for a start.

Procedural Fairness and Deference

Unlike policies of customized accommodation, which satisfy preferences pro rata, policies of cosmopolitan accommodation seek to nudge preferences, within the bounds of the standard liberal package. With this we come to the concerns voiced at the beginning of the previous section. Are policies of cosmopolitan accommodation illiberal? And is it not patronizing to members of minority groups for anyone to presume to nudge their preferences in their own interest? To answer these concerns, we need to dwell a little more on the interests attributed by the cosmopolitan theory.

The first concern, that policies of cosmopolitan accommodation are illiberal, can be understood in two different ways.

On one understanding, the concern is that policies of cosmopolitan accommodation are incompatible with basic liberalism. Basic liberals hold that treatment of a minority group is just if the group enjoys the standard liberal package—Rawls's basic liberties, freedom from discrimination in the economy and civil society, a minimum with respect to income and essential goods, and policies to secure equality of opportunity. Nothing more is required. The state's role ends with ensuring the basic liberal package.

Clearly, policies of cosmopolitan accommodation are incompatible with basic liberalism, for they require that the state take on more than ensuring the basic liberal package. The argument against basic liberalism is the one given by Patten, namely that the basic liberal package and its policies of privatization and generic entanglement are not enough to protect minority identity groups from assimilation. Those unconvinced that the prospect of assimilation is the business of the state are liable to reject Patten's scheme of customized accommodations and also the scheme, proposed here, of cosmopolitan accommodations. This is not the place to debate basic liberals. Policies of cosmopolitan accommodations are intended to appeal to those already onside with Patten's robust liberalism. They extend robust liberalism.

On another understanding, the concern about illiberalism is that policies of cosmopolitan accommodation are incompatible with the basic liberal package. Basic liberalism is not equivalent to a commitment to the basic liberal package. Patten is committed to the basic liberal package, and policies of cosmopolitan accommodations have also been advertised as constrained by the basic liberal package. Nonetheless, one might think that the basic liberal package rules out policies of cosmopolitan accommodations. Here is why.

Patten argues that policies of customized accommodation are compatible with the basic liberal package because they treat everyone equally.

156 AESTHETIC INJUSTICE

They allocate resources in proportion to preferences, where all preferences are given equal weight. State subsidies of a Klezmer ensemble might have otherwise gone to support an Afro-Cuban jazz band. The correct response to complaints from fans of Afro-Cuban jazz is that the share of support for each genre corresponds with preferences for it in the population as a whole. All preferences are given equal weight.

The objection to policies of cosmopolitan accommodation is that they are not fair by the same reasoning. They allocate resources to new or declining aesthetic cultures that few or none prefer. Suppose that state subsidies of tactile imaging culture might have otherwise gone to poetry readings. The correct response to complaints from poetry fans cannot be that all preferences are given equal weight in allocating resources pro rata. Their preferences are discounted in order to support an aesthetic culture that, by hypothesis, few or no people prefer.

One reply is to appeal to an interest in remedying weaponized aesthetics. As Chapter 7 showed, the neglect of tactile images both stems from and compounds unjust treatment of blind people. Perhaps a remedy is in order. The trouble is that, as Chapter 7 concluded, the remedy need not be to allocate resources to fostering aesthetic cultures around tactile imaging. The remedy might be to allocate resources to blind people in accordance with their preferences.

A better reply appeals to cosmopolitan interests in the value diversity and social autonomy of aesthetic cultures. According to the cosmopolitan theory, an aesthetic injustice is a relatively large-scale social arrangement that subverts one or both of these interests by harming people in their capacities as aesthetic agents. A case has now been made that the theory earns its keep because it pinpoints interests that we have. We have the interests because the existence of aesthetic injustice is needed to make full sense of weaponized aesthetics.

The diversity interest is an interest in there being diverse cultures of aesthetic value. Aesthetic profiles are abstracta, so there are countless aesthetic profiles, but an aesthetic culture is a social reality, a pattern of behaviour in a group of people who actually coordinate their activities around the aesthetic profile. The interest is in there being diverse socially real groups like that. Such an interest is served by allocating resources to foster the capacities that make possible the coordinated activities of groups of aesthetic agents.

IDENTITY AESTHETICS 157

Yet an interest in the value diversity of aesthetic cultures hardly suffices to justify allocations in support of arbitrarily any new or threatened aesthetic culture. There are at least as many potential aesthetic cultures as there are aesthetic profiles, and there are indefinitely many aesthetic profiles, for aesthetic profiles are abstracta. Countless aesthetic cultures never attain social reality. Many simply fade from social reality, becoming mere heritage, vestiges of a prior social presence. In practice, our interest is an interest in viable aesthetic cultures.

Here the interest in the social autonomy of aesthetic cultures enters the picture. This is an interest in participants in an aesthetic culture having the destiny of the culture in their own hands. Specifically, and literally, it is an interest in their own acts of engagement playing a large enough role in determining the culture's aesthetic profile. The interest does not encourage putting weak cultures on protracted life support; it is an interest in priming a pump.

We have seen that, as a rule, minority identity groups can be expected to benefit from cosmopolitan accommodations in support of their aesthetic cultural associates. Aesthetic cultures associated with majority identities thrive on the open market and through policies of generic entanglement: they need no accommodation. Markets are likely to fail for aesthetic cultures associated with minority identities. Nevertheless, those aesthetic cultures can be highly consequential for members of minority identity group. After all, the goods of the cultures are amplified when valuing them is a way of valuing being F. Hence, members of minority identity groups have exceptionally strong reason participate in identity-associated aesthetic cultures. Once up and running, the cultures are apt to thrive. As it turns out, policies of cosmopolitan accommodation of the aesthetic cultural associates of minority identities tend to be effective in satisfying interests in the value diversity and social autonomy of aesthetic cultures.

A final claim completes the reply to the objection that policies of cosmopolitan accommodation are illiberal. Granting that policies of cosmopolitan accommodation do not weigh all preferences equally, they do give equal weight to the cosmopolitan interests of all. Anyone engaged in some local aesthetic culture thereby has the interests (Chapter 4). Granted, people might not know that they have the interests, but we often fail to recognize what is in our interest. The correct response to

158 AESTHETIC INJUSTICE

complaints from poetry fans who lose resources to a project to foster tactile imaging culture is that all relevant interests are given equal weight. If (big "if") it is in fact in the interest of blind people to adopt aesthetic cultures around tactile imagining, then that interest generates reasons for others, who have the cosmopolitan interests, to adopt policies in support of those cultures.

Just as testimony is a mechanism that makes my evidence your evidence, cosmopolitan interests are a mechanism that makes their interests our interests.

That is the reply to the concern that policies of cosmopolitan accommodation are illiberal—that is, incompatible with the basic liberal package. A second concern was that the policies are patronizing. Indeed, this second concern might seem more pressing in light of the reply just given to the concern about illiberalism.

What is certainly patronizing is for anyone to presume to know what is in the interest of others, especially members of minority groups. The problem is the presumption. Sometimes insiders are not in good a position to accurately assess their interests. All the same, the safe bet is to begin by listening to insiders, while keeping in mind that all parties to social injustice typically internalize ideologies that distort their perceptions of their own and others' interests. To listen with humility, it helps to remember how hard it is to predict how consequential any aesthetic culture will be as an associate of a minority identity. Cosmopolitan accommodations are not measured by their outcomes; the outcome is going to hang on what insiders ultimately decide is in their interest.

Moreover, except in the most entrenched and poisonous circumstances of social injustice, minority identity groups are likely to have intellectual leaders—perhaps nascent ones—who can speak for the group's interests—even if imperfectly. The pages of this book name or allude to examples: Bill Reid, Michael Yahgulanaas, and their peers; the thinkers of the Haarlem Renaissance, Toni Morrison, and feminist intellectuals; advocates of ASL poetry and storytelling. Needless to say, sometimes the task is to find and cultivate voices such as these. That also follows from having interests in the social autonomy and value diversity of aesthetic cultures.

This chapter has attempted, rather ambitiously, to place some of the responsibility for these matters with the state. If it has failed in its ambition,

IDENTITY AESTHETICS   159

then the attempt can help us to think through the considerations that nevertheless inform policies across civil society—from educational and arts institutions, to media, to companies, clubs, and associations. These are also important sites of cosmopolitan accommodations. Basic liberals should also support cosmopolitan accommodations in those sites.

Policies of cosmopolitan accommodation meet Silvers's call for justice for talent, and they prescribe a far more robust response to an Anishinaabe woman's indifference to Anishinaabeg culture than to a French emigrant's indifference to French culture. That countless possible aesthetic cultures never achieve social reality implies that we squander countless possible talents that might have flourished. The prospect is sad to contemplate. Still, it is not as sad as contemplating all the talents that might easily have flourished, including those that might easily have flourished because they gave people a way of valuing who they are. Indeed, because they did this for those who otherwise find it hard to value being who they are.

Afterword

Our cosmopolitan interests are ones that we have just because we engage in local arenas of aesthetic life. They are grounded neither in universal principles, reasons, or values nor in features of our common humanity. Some are suspicious of appeals to common humanity and universal principles, reasons, and values either in general or when it comes to aesthetics. Others fear the spectre of relativism that might arise but for such appeals. The suspicious should rest assured, and nobody need fear that the cosmopolitan theory raises the spectre of relativism.

Pluralism is the middle path. The network theory implies, as we saw in Chapter 3, that the aesthetic field subdivides into plural cultures of value. Their aesthetic value profiles are different yet all valid, but also incommensurable, compatible with one another, and to some degree mutually comprehensible. Being plural, they open a door to rooted and routed respect. Those who inhabit any aesthetic culture can discern how the values in nearby cultures give their neighbours reasons to act, or they can see that there is a route through the neighbourhoods that could lead them to a point where they would discern the normativity of values in faraway cultures. Thus respect is not a confidence in something transcending difference, with a promise to take the edge off difference. On the contrary, respect needs difference.

Relativism can worry the soul. In a world as small as ours, we must confront difference. But if others have their own values and reasons, and we are on a par with them, then our values and reasons are just values and reasons among many others. Waning confidence in the old certainties threatens a choice between a paralyzingly loss of meaning and a desperate search for commonality.

Worse, relativism is a practical worry too. Suppose that we are different and neither rooted nor routed respect is possible. Chances are the result will be conflict and the need for protocols of conflict management. They do not work perfectly well. Martha Minow famously pointed out a dilemma. When it comes to social injustice, both policies of

162 AFTERWORD

special treatment and policies of equal treatment can make things worse. She asked, "when does treating people differently emphasize their differences and stigmatize or hinder them on that basis? And when does treating people the same become insensitive to their difference and likely to stigmatize or hinder them on that basis?" (1991: 40; see also Silvers 2009: 167–169). If Minnow is left of centre, Brian Barry expresses similar misgivings from the centre-right: "a situation in which groups live in parallel universes is not one well calculated to advance mutual understanding or encourage the cultivation of habits of cooperation and sentiments of trust" (2001: 88).

Weaponized aesthetics operates partly by obscuring the pluralism of aesthetic culture and hence the prospect of rooted and routed respect. It transforms the field of aesthetic cultures into a conflict zone. This is a final plank in the error theory that explains why we have overlooked the reality of aesthetic injustice. Chapter 1 pointed out that we have often overlooked injustice and that aesthetic injustice stems from and compounds weaponized aesthetics, which grabs attention as the more urgent problem. Chapter 3 added that aesthetic hedonism, for a long time the default theory of aesthetic value, was never going to spotlight our cosmopolitan interests. Having attended, in Part II, to the details of how aesthetic injustice and weaponized aesthetics are in cahoots with one another, it should come as no surprise that we have been led to think about aesthetic engagement in ways that distract us from our true interests. Aesthetic injustice operates, through weaponized aesthetics, at least in part by harming us in our capacities for rooted and routed respect.

That the aesthetic field is not by nature a conflict zone is something to treasure. Contact with aesthetic others can model how to welcome difference through mutual understanding and without feeling vulnerable to a loss of meaning. That aesthetic cultures other than yours stand on their own normative buckets speaks not one bit against the reasons you have in your cultures. Any impression to the contrary is a symptom of aesthetics weaponized by ideologies of aesthetic universalism that are always ultimately parochial.

Clifford Geertz thought that ethnocentrism is the common destiny of universalism and relativism alike, and "the trouble with ethnocentrism is that it impedes us from discovering at what sort of angle … we stand to the world" (1985: 261). In living our aesthetic lives, personally and collectively, we have an opportunity to discover the angle at which we stand to the world. We can discover our place in the world as one among many places that together make up a world in which we are all at home.

References

Alcoff, Linda Martín. 1995. Mestizo Identity, *American Mixed Race: The Culture of Microdiversity*, ed. Naomi Zack. Rowman and Littlefield, pp. 257–278.

Appiah, Kwame Anthony. 1994. Race, Culture, Identity: Misunderstood Connections, *The Tanner Lectures on Human Values*. University of Utah, pp. 53–136.

Appiah, Kwame Anthony. 2005. *The Ethics of Identity*. Princeton University Press.

Appiah, Kwame Anthony. 2007. *Cosmopolitanism: Ethics in a World of Strangers*. W. W. Norton.

Appiah, Kwame Anthony. 2018. *The Lies That Bind: Rethinking Identity*. W. W. Norton.

Archer, Alfred and Benjamin Matheson. forthcoming. Emotional Imperialism, *Philosophical Topics*.

Archer, Alfred and Lauren Ware. 2018. Beyond the Call of Beauty: Everyday Aesthetic Demands under Patriarchy, *Monist* 101: 114–127.

Arina, Pismenny, Eickers Gen, and Jesse Prinz. 2024. Emotional Injustice, *Ergo* 11.6: 150–176.

Arneil, Barbara. 2006. Cultural Protections vs. Cultural Justice: Post-Colonialism, Agonistic Justice, and the Limitations of Liberal Theory, *Sexual Justice / Cultural Justice: Critical Perspectives in Political Theory and Practice*, ed. Barbara Arneil, Monique Deveaux, Rita Dhamoon, and Avigail Eisenberg. Routledge, pp. 50–68.

Arnold, Matthew. 1891. *Celtic Literature*. London.

Axel, Elisabeth Salzhauer and Nina Levent, eds. 2002. *Art Beyond Sight: A Resource Guide to Art, Creativity, and Visual Impairment*. American Foundation for the Blind Press.

Baldwin, John R., Sandra L. Faulkner, Michael L. Hecht, and Sheryl L. Lindsey. 2006. *Redefining Culture: Perspectives Across the Disciplines*. Routledge.

Barnes, Elizabeth. 2016. *The Minority Body: A Theory of Disability*. Oxford University Press.

Barry, Brian. 2001. *Culture and Equality: An Egalitarian Critique of Multiculturalism*. Harvard University Press.

Bartky, Sandra Lee. 1990. *Femininity and Domination: Studies in the Phenomenology of Oppression*. Routledge.

Beardsley, Monroe C. 1970. Aesthetic Welfare, *Journal of Aesthetic Education* 4.4: 9–20.

Beardsley, Monroe C. 1973. Aesthetic Welfare, Aesthetic Justice, and Educational Policy, *Journal of Aesthetic Education* 7.4: 49–61.

Benhabib, Seyla. 2002. *The Claims of Culture: Equality and Diversity in the Global Era*. Princeton University Press.

Berlin, Isaiah. 1997 [1958]. Two Concepts of Liberty, *The Proper Study of Mankind*. Farrar, Straus, and Giroux, pp. 191–240.

Berlin, Isaiah. 1997 [1979]. Nationalism: Past Neglect and Present Power, *The Proper Study of Mankind*. Farrar, Straus, and Giroux, pp. 581–602.

Bhattacharyya, K. C. 2011 [1930]. The Concept of *Rasa*, *Indian Philosophy in English: From Renaissance to Independence*, ed. Nalini Bhushan and Jay L. Garfield. Oxford University Press, pp. 195–206.

Bhattacharyya, K. C. 2011 [1954]. *Svaraj* in Ideas, *Indian Philosophy in English: From Renaissance to Independence*, ed. Nalini Bhushan and Jay L. Garfield. Oxford University Press, pp. 101–112.

166 REFERENCES

Bicchieri, Cristina. 2006. *The Grammar of Society: The Nature and Dynamics of Social Norms.* Cambridge University Press.

Bickenbach, Jerome. 1993. *Physical Disability and Social Policy.* University of Toronto Press.

Bilgrami, Akeel. 2015. Identity and Identification, *International Encyclopedia of the Social and Behavioral Sciences*, 2nd ed., ed. Neil J. Smelser and Paul B. Baltes. Elsevier, vol. 11, pp. 521–525.

Bolzano, Bernard. 2007 [1834]. Treatise of the Science of Religion, *Selected Writings on Ethics and Politics*, ed. and trans. Paul Rusnock and Rolf George. Rodopi, pp. 171–229.

Bolzano, Bernard. 2023 [1843 + 1849]. *Essays on Beauty and the Arts*, ed. Dominic McIver Lopes, trans. Adam Bresnahan. Hackett.

Bourcier, Benjamin. 2020. Jeremy Bentham's Principle of Utility and Taste: An Alternative Approach to Aesthetics in Two Stages, *Bentham and the Arts*, ed. Anthony Julius, Malcolm Quinn, and Philip Schofield. UCL Press. pp. 227–243.

Bourdieu, Pierre. 1984. *Distinction: A Social Critique of the Judgement of Taste*, trans. Richard Nice. Harvard University Press.

Bourdieu, Pierre. 1990. *Photography: A Middle-Brow Art*, trans. Shaun Whiteside. Stanford University Press.

Bradford, Gwen. 2015. *Achievement.* Oxford University Press.

Brand, Peggy Zeglin and Carolyn Korsmeyer, eds. 1995. *Feminism and Tradition in Aesthetics.* Penn State Press.

Brook, Timothy. 2008. *Vermeer's Hat: The Seventeenth Century and the Dawn of the Global World.* Viking.

Brosnan, Sarah F. and Frans B. M. de Waal. 2014. Evolution of Responses to (Un)fairness, *Science* 346.6207: 314 and 1251776-1–1251776-7.

Brown, Michael F. 1998. Can Culture Be Copyrighted? *Current Anthropology* 39.2: 193–222.

Brown, Michael F. 2009. Exhibiting Indigenous Heritage in the Age of Cultural Property, *Whose Culture? The Promise of Museums and the Debate over Antiquities*, ed. James Cuno. Princeton University Press, pp. 145–164.

Burnham, Douglas and Ole Martin Skilleås. 2012. *The Aesthetics of Wine.* Wiley.

Cahill, Ann J. 2003. Feminist Pleasure and Feminine Beautification, *Hypatia* 18.4: 42–64.

Camp, Elisabeth. 2017. Why Metaphors Make Good Insults: Perspectives, Presupposition, and Pragmatics, *Philosophical Studies* 174.1: 47–64.

Carroll, Noël. 1986. Art and Interaction, *Journal of Aesthetics and Art Criticism* 45.1: 57–68.

Carroll, Noël. 1990. The Image of Women in Film: A Defense of a Paradigm, *Journal of Aesthetics and Art Criticism* 48.4: 349–360.

Chakrabarti, Arindam, ed. 2016. *Bloomsbury Research Handbook of Indian Aesthetics and the Philosophy of Art.* Bloomsbury.

Chambers, Claire. 2008. *Sex, Culture, and Justice: The Limits of Choice.* Oxford University Press.

Clavel-Vazquez, Adriana. 2023. Controlling (Mental) Images and the Aesthetic Perception of Racialized Bodies, *Ergo* 10.25: 710–725.

Clifford, James. 1988. *The Predicament of Culture: Twentieth-Century Ethnography, Literature, and Art.* Harvard University Press.

Coleman, Elizabeth Burns. 2004. Appreciating "Traditional" Aboriginal Painting Aesthetically, *Journal of Aesthetics and Art Criticism* 62.3: 235–247.

Coleman, Elizabeth Burns. 2005. *Aboriginal Art, Identity, and Appropriation.* Ashgate.

Coleman, Elizabeth Burns. 2018. Cross Cultural Aesthetics and Etiquette, *Social Aesthetics and Moral Judgment: Pleasure, Reflection, and Accountability*, ed. Jennifer A. McMahon. Routledge, pp. 180–195.

REFERENCES 167

Coleman, Elizabeth Burns, Rosemary J. Coombe, and Fiona MacArailt, 2009. A Broken Record: Subjecting "Music" to Cultural Rights, *The Ethics of Cultural Appropriation*, ed. James O. Young and Conrad Brunk. Wiley, pp. 173–210.

Collins, Patricia Hill. 2000. *Black Feminist Thought: Knowledge, Consciousness, and the Politics of Empowerment*, 2nd ed. Routledge.

Coombe, Rosemary J. 1993. The Properties of Culture and the Politics of Possessing Identity: Native Claims in the Cultural Appropriation Controversy, *Canadian Journal of Law and Jurisprudence* 6.2: 249–285.

Coulmas, Peter. 1995. *Les Citoyens du Monde: Histoire du Cosmopolitisme*. Éditions Albin Michel.

Crow, Thomas, 1996. *Modern Art in the Common Culture*. Yale University Press.

Daniels, Norman. 1985. *Justice and Health Care*. Cambridge University Press.

Danto, Arthur C. 1964. The Artworld, *Journal of Philosophy* 61.19: 571–584.

Danto, Arthur C. 2003. *The Abuse of Beauty: Aesthetics and the Concept of Art*. Open Court.

Davies, Stephen. 1991. *Definitions of Art*. Cornell University Press.

Davies, Stephen. 2017. Bali and the Management of Culture, *Unsettled Boundaries: Philosophy, Art, Ethics East/West*, ed. Curtis Carter. Marquette University Press, pp. 141–153.

Davies, Stephen. 2020. *Adornment: What Self-Decoration Tells Us about Who We Are*. Bloomsbury.

de Beauvoir, Simone. 1953 [1949]. *The Second Sex*, trans. Howard M. Parshley. Jonathan Cape.

De Clercq, Rafaël. 2002. The Concept of an Aesthetic Property, *Journal of Aesthetics and Art Criticism* 60.2: 167–176.

De Clercq, Rafaël. 2008. The Structure of Aesthetic Properties, *Philosophy Compass* 3.5: 894–909.

De Clercq, Rafaël. 2019. Aesthetic Pleasure Explained, *Journal of Aesthetics and Art Criticism* 77.2: 121–132.

de Sousa, Ronald. 1987. *The Rationality of the Emotions*. MIT Press.

Dickie, George. 1984. *The Art Circle*. Haven.

Dotson, Kristie. 2011. Tracking Epistemic Violence, Tracking Patterns of Silencing, *Hypatia* 26.2: 236–257.

Driver, Julia. 2021. Expertise and Evaluation, *Philosophy and Phenomenological Research* 102.1: 220–226.

Dutton Denis. 1993. Tribal Art and Artifact, *Journal of Aesthetics and Art Criticism* 51.1: 13–21.

Dworkin, Ronald. 1985. Can a Liberal State Support Art? *A Matter of Principle*. Harvard University Press, pp. 221–233.

Dworkin, Ronald. 2013. *Justice for Hedgehogs*. Harvard University Press.

Eagleton, Terry. 2000. *The Idea of Culture*. Blackwell.

Eaton, Anne. 2003. Where Ethics and Aesthetics Meet: Titian's *Rape of Europa*, *Hypatia* 18.4: 159–188.

Eaton, Anne. 2016. Taste in Bodies and Fat Oppression, *Body Aesthetics*, ed. Sherri Irvin. Oxford University Press, pp. 37–59.

Eaton, Anne and Ivan Gaskell. 2009. Do Subaltern Artifacts Belong in Art Museums? *The Ethics of Cultural Appropriation*, ed. James O. Young and Conrad G. Brunk. Wiley, pp. 235–267.

Egan, Andy. 2010. Disputing about Taste, *Disagreement*, ed. Richard Feldman and Ted A. Warfield. Oxford University Press, pp. 247–292.

Epstein, Brian. 2015. *The Ant Trap: Rebuilding the Foundations of the Social Sciences*. Oxford University Press.

168   REFERENCES

Ewing, Alfred C. 1939. A Suggested Non-Naturalistic Analysis of Good, *Mind* 48.189: 1–22.

Falk, Richard. 1988. The Rights of Peoples (In Particular, Indigenous Peoples), *The Rights of Peoples*, ed. James Crawford. Oxford University Press, pp. 17–37.

Fanon, Frantz. 1963. On National Culture, *The Wretched of the Earth*, trans. Constance Farrington. Grove Press, pp. 206–249.

Fanon, Frantz. 2008 [1952]. *Black Skin, White Masks*, trans. Charles Lam Markmann. Pluto.

Feagin, Susan. 1995. Feminist Art History and De Facto Significance, *Feminism and Tradition in Aesthetics*, ed. Peggy Zeglin Brand and Carolyn Korsmeyer. Penn State Press, pp. 305–325.

Feinberg, Joel. 1985. *The Moral Limits of the Criminal Law: Offense to Others*. Oxford University Press.

Feld, Steven. 1996. Pygmy POP: A Genealogy of Schizophrenic Mimesis, *Yearbook for Traditional Music* 28: 1–36.

Fingerhut Joerg, Javier Gomez-Lavin, Claudia Winklmayr, and Jesse J. Prinz. 2021. The Aesthetic Self: The Importance of Aesthetic Taste in Music and Art for Our Perceived Identity, *Frontiers in Psychology* 11.577703: 1–18.

Francis, Leslie and Anita Silvers. 2016. Perspectives on the Meaning of "Disability," *American Medical Association Journal of Ethics* 18.10: 1025–1033.

Fraser, Rachel. forthcoming. Aesthetic Injustice, *Ethics*.

Frazier, Cheryl. 2023. Beauty Labor as a Tool to Resist Antifatness, *Hypatia* 38.2: 231–250.

Fricker, Miranda. 2007. *Epistemic Injustice: Power and the Ethics of Knowing*. Oxford University Press.

Galston, William A. 1995. Two Concepts of Liberalism, *Ethics* 105.3: 516–534.

Ganeri, Jonardon. 2017. Freedom in Thinking: The Immersive Cosmopolitanism of Krishnachandra Bhattacharyya, *Oxford Handbook of Indian Philosophy*, ed. Jonardon Ganeri. Oxford University Press, pp. 718–736.

Gaskell, Ivan. 2018. Aesthetic Judgment and the Transcultural Apprehension of Material Things, *Social Aesthetics and Moral Judgment: Pleasure, Reflection, and Accountability*, ed. Jennifer A. McMahon. Routledge, pp. 161–179.

Gaus, Gerald. 2016. *The Tyranny of the Ideal: Justice in a Diverse Society*. Princeton University Press.

Geertz, Clifford. 1985. The Uses of Diversity, *The Tanner Lectures on Human Values*. University of Utah, pp. 253–275.

Glasgow, Joshua, Sally Haslanger, Chike Jeffers, Quayshawn Spencer. 2019. *What Is Race? Four Philosophical Views*. Oxford University Press.

Glover, Jonathan. 1997. Nations, Identity, and Conflict, *Morality of Nationalism*, ed. Robert McKim and Jeff McMahan. Oxford University Press, pp. 11–30.

Gorodeisky, Keren. 2021. On Liking Aesthetic Value, *Philosophy and Phenomenological Research* 102.2: 261–280.

Gorodeisky, Keren and Eric Marcus. 2018. Aesthetic Rationality, *Journal of Philosophy* 15.3: 113–140.

Grant, James. 2022. A Sensible Experientialism? *Philosophy and Phenomenological Research* 107.1: 53–79.

Guala, Francesco. 2016. *Understanding Institutions: The Science and Philosophy of Living Together*. Princeton University Press.

Hamermesh, Daniel S. 2011. *Beauty Pays: Why Attractive People Are More Successful*. Princeton University Press.

Handler, Richard. 1985. On Having a Culture: Nationalism and the Preservation of Quebec's *Patrimoine*, *Objects and Others: Essays on Museums and Material Culture*. University of Wisconsin Press, pp. 192–217.

REFERENCES 169

Hannerz, Ulf. 1990. Cosmopolitans and Locals in World Culture, *Theory, Culture, and Society* 7.2–3: 237–251.

Hardimon, Michael. 2003. The Ordinary Concept of Race, *Journal of Philosophy* 100.9: 437–455.

Harding, Sarah. 1999. Value, Obligation, and Cultural Heritage, *Arizona State Law Journal* 31: 291–354.

Harold, James. 2006. On Judging the Moral Value of Narrative Artworks, *Journal of Aesthetics and Art Criticism* 64.2: 259–70.

Harold, James. 2016. On the Ancient Idea that Music Shapes Character, *Dao* 15.3: 341–354.

Hart, Herbert L. A. 1994 [1961]. *The Concept of Law*, 2nd ed, ed. Penelope A. Bulloch and Joseph Raz. Oxford University Press.

Haslanger, Sally. 2000. Gender and Race: (What) Are They? (What) Do We Want Them to Be? *Noûs* 34.1 31–55.

Haslanger, Sally. 2012. On Being Objective and Being Objectified, *Resisting Reality: Social Construction and Social Critique*. Oxford University Press, pp. 35–82.

Haslanger, Sally. 2017. Culture and Critique, *Aristotelian Society Supplementary Volume* 91.1: 149–173.

Hein, Hilde and Carolyn Korsmeyer, eds. 1993. *Aesthetics in Feminist Perspective*. Indiana University Press.

Herman, Barbara. 1997. A Cosmopolitan Kingdom of Ends, *Reclaiming the History of Ethics: Essays for John Rawls*, ed. Andrews Reath, Barbara Herman, Christine M. Korsgaard, and John Rawls. Cambridge University Press, pp. 187–213.

Herrington, Susan and Jamie Nicholls. 2007. Outdoor Play Spaces in Canada: The Safety Dance of Standards as Policy, *Critical Social Policy* 27.1: 128–138.

Heyd, Thomas. 2007. Cross-Cultural Contact, Etiquette, and Rock Art, *Rock Art Research* 24.2: 191–197.

Heyes, Cressida J. 2007. *Self-Transformations: Foucault, Ethics, and Normalized Bodies*. Oxford University Press.

Higgins, Kathleen Marie. 2007. An Alchemy of Emotion: Rasa and Aesthetic Breakthroughs, *Journal of Aesthetics and Art Criticism* 65.1: 43–54.

Higgins, Kathleen Marie. 2017. Global Aesthetics—What Can We Do? *Journal of Aesthetics and Art Criticism* 75.4: 339–349.

Hobbes, Thomas. 1983 [1651]. *De Cive*, ed. Howard Warrander. Oxford University Press.

Hopkins, Robert. 2000. Touching Pictures, *British Journal of Aesthetics* 40.1: 149–67.

Howard, Dana and Sean Aas. 2018. On Valuing Impairment, *Philosophical Studies* 175.5: 1113–1133.

Hume, David. 1777. Of the Standard of Taste, *Four Dissertations*. London, pp. 227–249.

Hutcheson, Francis. 1738. *An Inquiry into the Original of Our Ideas of Beauty and Virtue*, 4th ed. London.

Hutton, Eric L. and James Harold. 2016. Xunzi on Music, *Dao Companion to the Philosophy of Xunzi*, ed. Eric L. Hutton. Springer, pp. 269–289.

Hutton, Eric L. 2023. Ethics and the Arts in Early China, *Oxford Handbook of Ethics and Art*, ed. James Harold. Oxford University Press, pp. 15–30.

Irvin, Sherri. 2014. Is Aesthetic Experience Possible? *Aesthetics and the Sciences of Mind*, ed. Greg Currie, Matthew Kieran, Aaron Meskin, and Jon Robson. Oxford University Press. pp. 37–56.

Irvin, Sherri. 2016. Introduction: Why Body Aesthetics? *Body Aesthetics*, ed. Sherri Irvin. Oxford University Press, pp. 1–11.

Irvin, Sherri. 2017. Resisting Body Oppression: An Aesthetic Approach, *Feminist Philosophy Quarterly* 3.4: 1–25.

170 REFERENCES

Ivanhoe, Philip J. 2014. Confucian Cosmopolitanism, *Journal of Religious Ethics* 42.1: 22–44.

James, Robin. 2013. Oppression, Privilege, and Aesthetics: The Use of the Aesthetic in Theories of Race, Gender, and Sexuality, and the Role of Race, Gender, and Sexuality in Philosophical Aesthetics, *Philosophy Compass* 8.2: 101–116.

Jeffers, Chike. 2015. The Ethics and Politics of Cultural Preservation, *Journal of Value Inquiry* 49.1–2: 205–220.

Jeffreys, Sheila. 2005. *Beauty and Misogyny: Harmful Cultural Practices in the West.* Routledge.

Jenkins, Katharine and Aness Webster. 2020. Disability, Impairment, and Marginalised Functioning, *Australasian Journal of Philosophy* 99.4: 1–18.

John, Eileen. 2012. Beauty, Interest, and Autonomy, *Journal of Aesthetics and Art Criticism* 70.2: 194–202.

Jones, Douglas A. 2014. *The Captive Stage: Performance and the Proslavery Imagination of the Antebellum North.* University of Michigan Press.

Kahane, Guy and Julian Savulescu. 2009. The Welfarist Account of Disability, *Disability and Disadvantage*, ed. Kimberley Brownlee and Adam Cureton. Oxford University Press, pp. 14–53.

Kant, Immanuel. 2000 [1790]. *Critique of the Power of Judgement*, trans. Paul Guyer and Eric Matthews. Cambridge University Press.

Kant, Immanuel. 2006 [1795]. Toward Perpetual Peace: A Philosophical Sketch, *Toward Perpetual Peace and Other Writings on Politics, Peace, and History*, trans. David L. Colclasure, ed. Pauline Kleingeld. Yale University Press, pp. 67–109.

Karp, Ivan. 1991. How Museums Define Other Cultures, *American Art* 5.1–2: 10–15.

Keene, Adrienne. 2014. Dear Christina Fallin, *Native Appropriations.* <https://nativeapp ropriations.com/2014/03/dear-christina-fallin.html>.

Kennedy, John M. 1993. *Drawing and the Blind: Pictures to Touch.* Yale University Press.

Kilani, Mondher. 2019. Culture, *Anthropen.org.* Éditions des Archives Contemporaines.

Kim-Prieto, Chu, Lizabeth A. Goldstein, Sumie Okazaki, and Blake Kirschner. 2010. Effect of Exposure to an American Indian Mascot on the Tendency to Stereotype a Different Minority Group, *Journal of Applied Social Psychology* 40.3: 534–553.

Kleingeld, Pauline, 1999. Six Varieties of Cosmopolitanism in Late Eighteenth-Century Germany, *Journal of the History of Ideas* 60.3: 505–524.

Kleingeld, Pauline and Eric Brown. 2019. Cosmopolitanism, *Stanford Encyclopedia of Philosophy*, ed. Edward N. Zalta. <https://plato.stanford.edu/archives/win2019/entr ies/cosmopolitanism/>.

Kölbel, Max. 2016. Aesthetic Judge-Dependence and Expertise, *Inquiry* 59.6: 589–617.

Konstan, David. 2014. *Beauty: The Fortunes of an Ancient Greek Idea.* Oxford University Press.

Korsmeyer, Carolyn. 2016. Real Old Things, *British Journal of Aesthetics* 56.3: 219–231.

Kubala, Robbie. 2021. Aesthetic Practices and Normativity, *Philosophy and Phenomenological Research* 103.2: 408–425.

Kubala, Robbie. forthcoming. Non-Monotonic Theories of Aesthetic Value, *Australasian Journal of Philosophy.*

Kuper, Adam. 1999. *Culture: The Anthropologists' Account.* Harvard University Press.

Kymlicka, Will. 1995. *Multicultural Citizenship.* Oxford University Press.

Kymlicka, Will. 2001a. From Enlightenment Cosmopolitanism to Liberal Nationalism, *Politics in the Vernacular: Nationalism, Multiculturalism, and Citizenship.* Oxford University Press, pp. 203–20.

REFERENCES 171

Kymlicka, Will. 2001b. Liberal Culturalism: An Emerging Consensus? *Politics in the Vernacular: Nationalism, Multiculturalism, and Citizenship*. Oxford University Press, pp. 39–48.

Kymlicka, Will and Kathryn Walker. 2012. Rooted Cosmopolitanism: Canada and the World, *Rooted Cosmopolitanism: Canada and the World*, ed. Will Kymlicka and Kathryn Walker. UBC Press, pp. 1–27.

Langford, Roslyn. 1983. Our Heritage—Your Playground, *Australian Archaeology* 16: 1–6.

Langlois, Judith H. and Lori A. Roggman. 1990. Attractive Faces Are Only Average, *Psychological Science* 1.2: 115–121.

Lawson, Emily and Dominic McIver Lopes. in press. Courageous Love: K. C. Bhattacharyya on the Puzzle of Painful Beauty, *Journal of the American Philosophical Association*.

Layton, Robert. 2012. Aesthetics: The Approach from Social Anthropology, *The Aesthetic Mind: Philosophy and Psychology*, ed. Elisabeth Schellekens and Peter Goldie. Oxford University Press, pp. 208–222.

Lena, Jennifer C. 2019. *Entitled: Discriminating Tastes and the Expansion of the Arts*. Princeton University Press.

Lenard, Patti Tamara and Peter Balint. 2020. What Is (the Wrong of) Cultural Appropriation? *Ethnicities* 20.2: 331–352.

Levinson, Jerrold. 2002. Hume's Standard of Taste: The Real Problem, *Journal of Aesthetics and Art Criticism* 60.3: 227–238.

Levinson, Jerrold. 2010. Artistic Worth and Personal Taste, *Journal of Aesthetics and Art Criticism* 68.3: 225–233.

Liao, Shen-Yi. 2018. Is Cultural Appropriation Ever Okay? *Aesthetics for Birds*. <https://aestheticsforbirds.com>.

Lopes, Dominic McIver. 1997. Art Media and the Sense Modalities: Tactile Pictures, *Philosophical Quarterly* 47.189: 425–440.

Lopes, Dominic McIver. 2002. Vision, Touch, and the Value of Pictures, *British Journal of Aesthetics* 42.2: 191–201.

Lopes, Dominic McIver. 2014. *Beyond Art*. Oxford University Press.

Lopes, Dominic McIver. 2018a. *Aesthetics on the Edge: Where Philosophy Meets the Human Sciences*. Oxford University Press.

Lopes, Dominic McIver. 2018b. *Being for Beauty: Aesthetic Agency and Value*. Oxford University Press.

Lopes, Dominic McIver. 2019. Feeling for Freedom: K. C. Bhattacharyya on *Rasa*, *British Journal of Aesthetics* 59.4: 465–477.

Lopes, Dominic McIver. 2021a. Beyond the Pleasure Principle: A Kantian Aesthetics of Autonomy, *Estetika: The European Journal of Aesthetics* 57.1: 1–18.

Lopes, Dominic McIver. 2021b. Normativity, Agency, and Value: A View from Aesthetics, *Philosophy and Phenomenological Research* 102.1: 232–242.

Lopes, Dominic McIver. 2021c. Two Dogmas of Aesthetic Empiricism, *Metaphilosophy* 52.5: 583–592.

Lopes, Dominic McIver. 2023a. Big Tent Aesthetics, *Journal of Aesthetics and Art Criticism* 81.1: 87–88.

Lopes, Dominic McIver. 2023b. Pleasure, Desire, and Value, *Disinterested Pleasure and Beauty: Perspectives from Kantian and Contemporary Aesthetics*, ed. Larissa Berger. De Gruyter, pp. 233–256.

Lopes, Dominic McIver. 2024a. Bolzano on Aesthetic Normativity, *British Journal of Aesthetics* 64.2: 143–156

172 REFERENCES

Lopes, Dominic McIver. 2024b. Experts in Aesthetic Value Practices, *Expertise: Philosophical Perspectives*, ed. Mirko Farina, Andrea Lavazza, and Duncan Pritchard. Oxford University Press.

Lopes, Dominic McIver, Samantha Matherne, Mohan Matthen, and Bence Nanay. 2024. *The Geography of Taste*. Oxford University Press.

Lopes, Dominic McIver, Bence Nanay, and Nick Riggle. 2022. *Aesthetic Life and Why It Matters*. Oxford University Press.

Lopes, Dominic McIver and Davide Zappulli. MS. The Beauty of Grimacing Xishi: Aesthetic Agency and Value in the *Zhuangzi*.

MacIntyre, Alasdair. 1981. *After Virtue: A Study in Moral Theory*. University of Notre Dame Press.

Mackenzie, Catriona. 2014. Three Dimensions of Autonomy: A Relational Analysis, *Autonomy, Oppression, and Gender*, ed. Andrea Veltman and Mark Piper. Oxford University Press, pp. 15–41.

MacKinnon, Catharine A. 1987. *Feminism Unmodified: Discourses on Life and Law*. Harvard University Press.

Manne, Kate. 2018. *Down Girl: The Logic of Misogyny*. Oxford University Press.

Margalit, Avishai and Moshe Halbertal. 1994. Liberalism and the Right to Culture, *Social Research* 61.3: 491–510.

Margalit, Avishai and Joseph Raz. 1990. National Self-Determination, *Journal of Philosophy* 87.9: 439–461.

Martin-Seaver, Madeline. 2023. Personal Beauty and Personal Agency, *Philosophy Compass* 18.12: 1–12.

Mason, Andrew. 1993. Liberalism and the Value of Community, *Canadian Journal of Philosophy* 23.2: 215–239.

Mason, Andrew. 2004. *Community, Solidarity, and Belonging: Levels of Community and Their Normative Significance*. Cambridge University Press.

Mason, Andrew. 2021. What's Wrong with Everyday Lookism? *Politics, Philosophy, and Economics* 20.3: 315–335.

Matherne, Samantha. 2021. Aesthetic Learners and Underachievers, *Philosophy and Phenomenological Research* 102.1: 227–231.

Matthen, Mohan. 2017. The Pleasure of Art, *Australasian Philosophical Review* 1.1: 6–28.

Matthen, Mohan. 2018a. Art, Pleasure, Value: Reframing the Questions, *Philosophic Exchange* 47.1: 1–16.

Matthen, Mohan. 2018b. New Prospects for Aesthetic Hedonism, *Social Aesthetics and Moral Judgment: Pleasure, Reflection, and Accountability*, ed. Jennifer A. McMahon. Routledge, pp. 13–33.

Matthes, Erich Hatala. 2015. Impersonal Value, Universal Value, and the Scope of Cultural Heritage, *Ethics* 125.4: 999–1027.

Matthes, Erich Hatala. 2016. Cultural Appropriation Without Cultural Essentialism? *Social Theory and Practice* 42.2: 343–366.

Matthes, Erich Hatala. 2019. Cultural Appropriation and Oppression, *Philosophical Studies* 176: 1003–1013.

Mehta, Pratap Bhanu. 2000 Cosmopolitanism and the Circle of Reason, *Political Theory* 28.5: 619–639.

Mejía Chaves, Andrea and Sondra Bacharach. 2021. Hair Oppression and Appropriation, *British Journal of Aesthetics* 61.3: 335–352.

Melchionne, Kevin. 1998. Living in Glass Houses: Domesticity, Interior Decoration, and Environmental Aesthetics, *Journal of Aesthetics and Art Criticism* 56.2: 191–200.

Melchionne, Kevin. 2007. Acquired Taste, *Contemporary Aesthetics* 5.

REFERENCES 173

Melchionne, Kevin. 2010. On the Old Saw, "I Know Nothing about Art but I Know What I Like," *Journal of Aesthetics and Art Criticism* 68.2: 131–141.

Melchionne, Kevin. 2015. Norms of Cultivation, *Contemporary Aesthetics* 13.

Merryman, John Henry. 1986. Two Ways of Thinking about Cultural Property, *American Journal of International Law* 80.4: 831–853.

Mezey, Naomi. 2007. The Paradoxes of Cultural Property, *Columbia Law Review* 107.8: 2004–2046.

Mill, John Stuart. 1859. *On Liberty*. London.

Mills, Charles W. 1997. *The Racial Contract*. Cornell University Press.

Minow, Martha. 1991. *Making All the Difference: Inclusion, Exclusion, and American Law*. Cornell University Press.

Mitchell, David T. and Sharon L. Snyder, eds. 1997. *The Body and Physical Difference: Discourses of Disability*. University of Michigan Press.

Morphy, Howard. 1996. Aesthetics Is a Cross-Cultural Category, *Key Debates in Anthropology*, ed. Tim Ingold. Routledge, pp. 206–209.

Mothersill, Mary. 1984. *Beauty Restored*. Oxford University Press.

Mothersill, Mary. 1989. Hume and the Paradox of Taste, *Aesthetics: A Critical Anthology*, ed. George Dickie, Richard Sclafani, and Ronald Roblin. St Martin's, pp. 269–286.

Morrison, Toni. 1970. *The Bluest Eye*. Random House.

Moustakas, John. 1989. Group Rights in Cultural Property: Justifying Strict Inalienability, *Cornell Law Review* 74.6: 1179–1227.

Muldoon, Ryan. 2016. *Social Contract Theory for a Diverse World: Beyond Tolerance*. Routledge.

Mulvey, Laura. 1989. Visual Pleasure and Narrative Cinema, *Visual Pleasure and Other Pleasures*. Indiana University Press, pp. 14–26.

Nandy, Ashis. 1988. *The Intimate Enemy: Loss and Recovery of Self under Colonialism*. Oxford University Press.

Nandy, Ashis. 2000. Time Travel to a Possible Self: Searching for the Alternative Cosmopolitanism of Cochin, *Japanese Journal of Political Science* 1.2: 295–327.

Nehamas, Alexander. 2007. *Only a Promise of Happiness: The Place of Beauty in a World of Art*. Princeton University Press.

Nguyen, C. Thi. 2020a. Autonomy and Aesthetic Engagement, *Mind* 129.516: 1127–1156.

Nguyen, C. Thi. 2020b. The Arts of Action, *Philosophers' Imprint* 20.14: 1–27.

Nguyen, C. Thi and Matthew Strohl. 2019. Cultural Appropriation and the Intimacy of Groups, *Philosophical Studies* 176.4: 981–1002.

Nicholas, George P. and Alison Wylie. 2012. "Do Not Do unto Others …": Cultural Misrecognition and the Harms of Appropriation in an Open-Source World, *Appropriating the Past: Philosophical Perspectives on the Practice of Archaeology*, ed. Geoffrey Scarre and Robin Coningham. Cambridge University Press, pp. 195–221.

Nieguth, Tim and Tracey Rainey. 2017. Nation-Building and Canada's National Symbolic Order, 1993–2015, *Nations and Nationalism* 23.1: 87–108.

Nowak, Ethan. 2019. Multiculturalism, Autonomy, and Language Preservation, *Ergo* 6.11: 303–333.

Nowak, Ethan. 2020. Language Loss and Illocutionary Silencing, *Mind* 129.515: 831–865.

Nussbaum, Martha C. 1996. Patriotism and Cosmopolitanism, *For Love of Country: Debating the Limits of Patriotism*. Beacon Press, pp. 2–20.

Nussbaum, Martha C. 1997. Kant and Stoic Cosmopolitanism, *Journal of Political Philosophy* 5.1: 1–25.

Nussbaum, Martha C. 2001. *Upheavals of Thought: The Intelligence of Emotions*. Cambridge University Press.

174 REFERENCES

Nussbaum, Martha C. 2003. Capabilities as Fundamental Entitlements: Sen and Social Justice, *Feminist Economics* 9.2–3: 33–59.

Nussbaum, Martha C. 2006. *Frontiers of Justice: Disability, Nationality, Species Membership*. Harvard University Press.

Nussbaum, Martha C. 2019. *The Cosmopolitan Tradition: A Noble but Flawed Ideal*. Harvard University Press.

O'Neill, Onora. 2012. *Towards Justice and Virtue: A Constructive Account of Practical Reasoning*. Cambridge University Press.

Page, Scott E. 2007. *The Difference*. Princeton University Press.

Pankratz, David B. 1983. Aesthetic Welfare, Government, and Educational Policy, *Journal of Aesthetic Education* 17.2: 97–110.

Parfit, Derek. 1984. *Reasons and Persons*. Oxford University Press.

Parsons, Glenn. 2016. The Merrickites, *Body Aesthetics*, ed. Sherri Irvin. Oxford University Press, pp. 110–126.

Patten, Alan. 2014. *Equal Recognition: The Moral Foundations of Minority Rights*. Princeton University Press.

Pearson, Phyllis. 2021. Cultural Appropriation and Aesthetic Normativity, *Philosophical Studies* 178.4: 1285–1299.

Phillips, Anne. 2006. What Is "Culture"? *Sexual Justice / Cultural Justice: Critical Perspectives in Political Theory and Practice*, ed. Barbara Arneil, Monique Deveaux, Rita Dhamoon, and Avigail Eisenberg. Routledge, pp. 15–29.

Pollock, Sheldon. 2000. Cosmopolitan and Vernacular in History, *Public Culture* 12.3: 591–625.

Protasi, Sara. 2017. The Perfect Bikini Body: Can We All Really Have It? Loving Gaze as an Antioppressive Beauty Ideal, *Thought* 6.2: 93–101.

Ransom, Madeleine. 2020a. Attentional Weighting in Perceptual Learning, *Journal of Consciousness Studies* 27.7–8: 236–248.

Ransom, Madeleine. 2020b. Expert Knowledge by Perception, *Philosophy* 95.3: 309–335.

Ransom, Madeleine. 2020c. Waltonian Perceptualism, *Journal of Aesthetics and Art Criticism* 78.1: 66–70.

Ravasio, Matteo. 2023. Engineering Human Beauty, *Australasian Journal of Philosophy* 101.4: 998–1011.

Rawls, John. 1971. *A Theory of Justice*. Harvard University Press.

Rawls, John. 1993. *Political Liberalism*. Columbia University Press.

Raz, Joseph. 1986. *The Morality of Freedom*. Oxford University Press.

Raz, Joseph. 1994. Multiculturalism: A Liberal Perspective, *Ethics in the Public Domain*. Oxford University Press, pp. 171–191.

Raz, Joseph. 2004. *Value, Respect, and Attachment*. Cambridge University Press.

Reid, Bill. 1992. *Gallant Beasts and Monsters*. Vancouver: Buschlen Mowatt.

Rhode, Deborah L. 2010. *The Beauty Bias: The Injustice of Appearance in Life and Law*. Oxford University Press.

Rhode, Deborah L. 2016. Appearance as a Feminist Issue, *Body Aesthetics*, ed. Sherri Irvin. Oxford University Press, pp. 81–93.

Richerson, Peter J. and Richard Boyd. 2005. *Not by Genes Alone: How Culture Transformed Human Evolution*. University of Chicago Press.

Riggle, Nick. 2013. Levinson on the Aesthetic Ideal, *Journal of Aesthetics and Art Criticism* 71.3: 277–281.

Riggle, Nick. 2016. On the Interest in Beauty and Disinterest, *Philosophers' Imprint* 16.9: 1–14.

Riggle, Nick. 2022. Toward a Communitarian Theory of Aesthetic Value, *Journal of Aesthetics and Art Criticism* 80.1: 16–30.

REFERENCES 175

Rings, Michael. 2019. Aesthetic Cosmopolitanism and the Challenge of the Exotic, *British Journal of Aesthetics* 59.2: 161–178.

Rogers, Richard A. 2006. From Cultural Exchange to Transculturation: A Review and Reconceptualization of Cultural Appropriation, *Communication Theory* 16.4: 474–503.

Rosenkoetter, Timothy. 2014. Kant, Bolzano, and Moore on the Value of Good Willing, *New Anti-Kant*, ed. Sandra Lapointe and Clinton Tolley. Palgrave Macmillan, pp. 235–271.

Rushdie, Salman. 1991. *Imaginary Homelands: Essays and Criticism, 1981–1991*. Penguin.

Saito, Yuriko. 2008. *Everyday Aesthetics*. Oxford University Press.

Sandel, Michael J. 1998. *Liberalism and the Limits of Justice*, 2nd ed. Cambridge University Press.

Santayana, George. 1896. *The Sense of Beauty*. Scribner's.

Scanlon, Timothy M. 1985. Public Support for the Arts, *Columbia Journal of Art and the Law* 9.208: 167–171.

Scanlon, Timothy M. 1998. *What We Owe to Each Other*. Harvard University Press.

Scheffler, Samuel. 1999. Conceptions of Cosmopolitanism, *Utilitas* 11.3: 255–276.

Scheffler, Samuel. 2007. Immigration and the Significance of Culture, *Philosophy and Public Affairs* 35.2: 93–125.

Sewell, William H., Jr. 1999. The Concept(s) of Culture, *Beyond the Cultural Turn: New Directions in the Study of Society and Culture*, ed. Victoria Bonnell and Lynn Hunt. University of California Press, pp. 35–61.

Shelby, Tommie. 2003. Ideology, Racism, and Critical Social Theory, *Philosophical Forum* 34.2: 153–188.

Shelby, Tommie. 2005. *We Who Are Dark: The Philosophical Foundations of Black Solidarity*. Harvard University Press.

Shelley, James. 2010. Against Value Empiricism in Aesthetics, *Australasian Journal of Philosophy* 88.4: 707–720.

Shelley, James. 2011. Hume and the Value of the Beautiful, *British Journal of Aesthetics* 51.2: 213–222.

Shelley, James. 2019. The Default Theory of Aesthetic Value, *British Journal of Aesthetics* 59.1: 1–12.

Shelley, James. 2021. Punting on the Aesthetic Question, *Philosophy and Phenomenological Research* 102.1: 214–219.

Shelley, James. 2023a. Beyond Hedonism about Aesthetic Value, *Disinterested Pleasure and Beauty: Perspectives from Kantian and Contemporary Aesthetics*, ed. Larissa Berger. De Gruyter, pp. 257–273.

Shelley, James. 2023b. Simple Theory of Aesthetic Value, *Journal of Aesthetics and Art Criticism* 81.1: 98–100.

Shim, Joy. 2021. Literary Racial Impersonation, *Ergo* 8.31: 219–245.

Shiner, Larry. 1994. "Primitive Fakes," "Tourist Art," and the Ideology of Authenticity, *Journal of Aesthetics and Art Criticism* 52.2: 225–334.

Shiner, Larry. 2001. *The Invention of Art: A Cultural History*. University of Chicago Press.

Sibley, Frank. 1959. Aesthetic Concepts, *Philosophical Review* 68.4: 421–450.

Siebers, Tobin. 2006. Disability Aesthetics, *Journal for Cultural and Religious Theory* 7.2: 63–73.

Silvers, Anita. 1998. Formal Justice, *Disability, Difference, Discrimination: Perspectives on Justice in Bioethics and Public Policy*, ed. Anita Silvers, David Wasserman, and Mary B. Mahowald. Rowman and Littlefield, pp. 13–145.

Silvers, Anita. 2002. The Crooked Timber of Humanity: Disability, Ideology, and the Aesthetic, *Disability/Postmodernity: Embodying Disability Theory*, ed. Mairian Corker and Tom Shakespeare. Continuum, pp. 228–244.

176 REFERENCES

Silvers, Anita. 2003. On the Possibility and Desirability of Constructing a Neutral Conception of Disability, *Theoretical Medicine and Bioethics* 24.6: 471–487.

Silvers, Anita. 2009. No Talent? Beyond the Worst Off! A Diverse Theory of Justice for Disability, *Disability and Disadvantage*, ed. Kimberlee Brownlee and Adam Cureton. Oxford University Press, pp. 163–199.

Silvers, Anita. 2010. An Essay on Modeling: The Social Model of Disability, *Philosophical Reflections on Disability*, ed. D. Christopher Ralston and Justin Ho. Springer, pp. 19–36.

Silvers, Anita. 2016. Philosophy and Disability: What Should Philosophy Do? *Res Philosophica* 93.4: 843–863.

Smith, Ralph A. 1975. Cultural Services, the Aesthetic Welfare, and Educational Research, *Studies in Art Education* 16.2: 5–11.

Soucek, Brian. 2017. Aesthetic Judgment in Law, *Alabama Law Review* 69.381: 382–467.

Soucek, Brian. 2019. Regulating for Beauty, *Studi di Estetica* 47.4: 286–292.

Steinberg, Leo. 1972. Jasper Johns: The First Seven Years of His Art, *Other Criteria: Confrontations with Twentieth-Century Art*. Oxford University Press, pp. 17–91.

Stock, Kathleen. 2015. Sexual Objectification, *Analysis* 75.2: 191–195.

Stokes, Dustin. 2014. Cognitive Penetration and the Perception of Art, *Dialectica* 68.1: 1–34.

Stokes, Dustin. 2018. Rich Perceptual Content and Aesthetic Properties, *Evaluative Perception*, ed. Anna Bergqvist and Robert Cowan. Oxford University Press, pp. 19–41.

Strohl, Matthew. 2022. *Why It's OK to Love Bad Movies*. Routledge.

Sundell, Timothy. 2011. Disagreements about Taste, *Philosophical Studies* 155.2: 267–288.

Sundell, Timothy. 2017. Aesthetic Negotiation, *Semantics of Aesthetic Judgement*, ed. James O. Young. Oxford University Press, pp. 82–105.

Sunstein, Cass R. 1994. The Anticaste Principle, *Michigan Law Review* 92.8: 2410–2455.

Swidler, Ann. 1986. Culture in Action: Symbols and Strategies, *American Sociological Review* 51.2: 273–286.

Tagore, Saranindranath. 2008. Tagore's Conception of Cosmopolitanism: A Reconstruction, *University of Toronto Quarterly* 77.4: 1070–1084.

Tappolet, Christine. 2016. *Emotions, Value, and Agency*. Oxford University Press.

Taylor, Charles. 1991. *The Ethics of Authenticity*. Harvard University Press.

Taylor, Charles. 1994. The Politics of Recognition, *Multiculturalism: Examining the Politics of Recognition*, ed. Amy Gutman. Princeton University Press, pp. 25–73.

Taylor, Paul C. 1999. Malcolm's Conk and Danto's Colors; Or, Four Logical Petitions Concerning Race, Beauty, and Aesthetics, *Journal of Aesthetics and Art Criticism* 57.1: 16–20.

Taylor, Paul C. 2016. *Black Is Beautiful: A Philosophy of Black Aesthetics*. Wiley.

Thompson, Janna. 2003. Cultural Property, Restitution, and Value, *Journal of Applied Philosophy* 203: 251–262.

Thompson, Janna. 2004. Art, Property Rights, and the Interests of Humanity, *Journal of Value Inquiry* 38.4: 545–560.

Thompson, Janna. 2012. The Ethics of Repatriation, *Appropriating the Past: Philosophical Perspectives on the Practice of Archaeology*, ed. Geoffrey Scarre and Robin Coningham. Cambridge University Press, pp. 82–97.

Thompson, Robert F. 1983. *Flash of the Spirit*. Random House.

Thomson, Rosemary Garland. 1997. *Extraordinary Bodies: Figuring Physical Disability in American Culture and Literature*. Columbia University Press.

Todd, Loretta. 1990. Notes on Appropriation, *Parallelogramme* 16.1: 24–33.

Tully, James. 1995. *Strange Multiplicity: Constitutionalism in an Age of Diversity*. Cambridge University Press.

REFERENCES 177

Turino, Thomas. 2008. *Music as Social Life: The Politics of Participation*. University of Chicago Press.

Tuvel, Rebecca. 2021. Putting the Appropriator Back in Cultural Appropriation, *British Journal of Aesthetics* 61.3: 353–372.

Tylor, Edward B. 1871. *Primitive Culture: Researches into the Development of Mythology, Philosophy, Religion, Art, and Custom*. London.

Van der Berg, Servaas. 2020. Aesthetic Hedonism and Its Critics, *Philosophy Compass* 15.1: 1–15.

Walden, Kenny. 2023. Legislating Taste, *Philosophical Quarterly* 73.4:1256–1280.

Waldron, Jeremy. 1995. Minority Cultures and the Cosmopolitan Alternative, *University of Michigan Journal of Law Reform* 25.4: 751–793.

Waldron, Jeremy. 2000. What Is Cosmopolitan? *Journal of Political Philosophy* 8.2: 227–243.

Waldron, Jeremy. 2003. Teaching Cosmopolitan Right, *Citizenship and Education in Liberal–Democratic Societies: Teaching for Cosmopolitan Values and Collective Identities*, ed. Kevin McDonough and Walter Feinberg. Oxford University Press, pp. 23–55.

Waldron, Jeremy. 2020. Property and Ownership, *Stanford Encyclopedia of Philosophy*, ed. Edward N. Zalta. <https://plato.stanford.edu/archives/sum2020/entries/property/>.

Walker-Andrews, Arlene S., Lorraine E. Bahrick, Stacy S. Raglioni, and Isabel Diaz. 1991. Infants' Bimodal Perception of Gender, *Ecological Psychology* 3.2: 55–75.

Walton, Kendall. 1970. Categories of Art, *Philosophical Review* 79.3: 334–367.

Watkins, Michael and James Shelley. 2012. Response-Dependence about Aesthetic Value, *Pacific Philosophical Quarterly* 93.3: 338–352.

Weiser, Peg Brand and Edward B. Weiser. 2016. Misleading Aesthetic Norms of Beauty: Perceptual Sexism in Elite Women's Sports, *Body Aesthetics*, ed. Sherri Irvin. Oxford University Press, pp. 192–221.

Whitman, Walt. 1871. *Democratic Vistas*. Washington, DC.

Widdows, Heather. 2017. The Neglected Harms of Beauty: Beyond Engaging Individuals, *Journal of Practical Ethics* 5.2: 1–29.

Widdows, Heather. 2018. *Perfect Me: Beauty as an Ethical Ideal*. Princeton University Press.

Widdows, Heather. 2022. No Duty to Resist: Why Individual Resistance Is an Ineffective Response to Dominant Beauty Ideals, *Proceedings of the Aristotelian Society* 122.1: 28–46.

Williams, Bernard. 1985. *Ethics and the Limits of Philosophy*. Harvard University Press.

Williams, Raymond. 1961. *The Long Revolution*. Chatto and Windus.

Wolf, Naomi. 1990. *The Beauty Myth: How Images of Beauty Are Used Against Women*. Random House.

Wolf, Susan. 2011. Good-for-Nothings, *Proceedings and Addresses of the American Philosophical Association* 85.2: 47–64.

Wollheim, Richard. 1985. Public Support for the Arts, *Columbia Journal of Art and the Law* 9.208: 179–186.

Wolterstorff, Nicholas. 2015. *Art Rethought: The Social Practices of Art*. Oxford University Press.

Yahgulanaas, Michael Nicholl. 2008. *Flight of the Hummingbird: A Parable for the Environment*. Vancouver: Greystone Books.

Young, Iris Marion. 1990. *Justice and the Politics of Difference*. Princeton University Press.

Young, James O. 2008. *Cultural Appropriation and the Arts*. Wiley.

Young, James O. 2012. The Values of the Past, *Appropriating the Past: Philosophical Perspectives on the Practice of Archaeology*, ed. Geoffrey Scarre and Robin Coningham. Cambridge University Press, pp. 25–41.

178 REFERENCES

Young, James O. 2021. New Objections to Cultural Appropriation in the Arts, *British Journal of Aesthetics* 61.3: 307–316.

Ypi, Lea. 2017. Structural Injustice and the Place of Attachment, *Journal of Practical Ethics* 5.1: 1–21.

Zheng, Robin and Nils-Hennes Stear. 2023 Imagining in Oppressive Contexts, or What's Wrong with Blackface? *Ethics* 133.3: 381–414.

Zuckert, Rachel. 2010. *Kant on Beauty and Biology: An Interpretation of the* Critique of Judgment. Cambridge University Press.

Zuckert, Rachel. 2019. *Herder's Naturalist Aesthetics.* Cambridge University Press.

Index

For the benefit of digital users, indexed terms that span two pages (e.g., 52–53) may, on occasion, appear on only one of those pages.

achievement 47, 54
acts, aesthetic 4–5, 35; *see also* engagement
aesthetic hedonism 37–44, 162
  basic 40
  and diversity 41–44
  standardized 40–41
aesthetic profiles 47, 96–97
affect 34–35, 104–5, 110, 114, 115–16, 123, 131
agency 63, 70; *see also* acts, aesthetic; capabilities; capacities, aesthetic; expertise; talent
Appiah, Kwame Anthony 16, 27, 59–60, 73, 143
appropriation 16–17, 81, 83–84
  aesthetically unjust 96–99
  assimilative 93–96
  and dispossession 84–85, 86–88
  disrespectful 92–93
  and law 84–85
  and misrepresentation 88–90
  offensive 91–92
  and weaponized aesthetics 84
Archer, Alfred 123
art 30, 31–33
Assu, Billy 86, 94
authenticity 62–63
autonomy 62, 63, 69–72; *see also* social autonomy

Barnes, Elizabeth 125–26, 127–28, 129, 137–38, 141
Barry, Brian 161–62
beauty ideals 13–14, 106–8
  and adornment 107–8
  aesthetically unjust 116–22
  discriminatory 111–14
  and gender 108–10

objectifying 108–11
and race 114–16
recent 119–21
and weaponized
  aesthetics 108, 131–32
Berlin, Isaiah 26–27
Bickenbach, Jerome 126
Bilgrami, Akeel 140–41, 142
Black Canoe, see Reid, Bill
blindness 128–29, 135; *see also* disability; pictures, tactile
Bluest Eye, see Morrison, Toni
Bolzano, Bernard 37, 38
Bourdieu, Pierre 33
Brook, Timothy 82
Bulun Bulun, John 93–94

capabilities 74, 145–46
capacities, aesthetic 4–5, 11, 47, 74–75, 97; *see also* capabilities; expertise; talent
Carroll, Noël 104
Coleman, Elizabeth 93–95
Collins, Patricia Hill 9
commitment 140–41
communitarianism 61–64
conflict 35, 59–61, 63–64, 65–66, 162
  compatibility 60, 65
  competitive 59–60
  comprehensibility 60, 65
  demanding 60–61
Coombe, Rosemary 90
cosmopolitanism 23–27
  cultural 24, 26–27, 42–44
  and diversity 27
  history of 23–24
  normative 26–27, 142–43
  rooted 25, 26, 49, 74–75, 161
  and sociality 26

180 INDEX

Crow, Thomas 69
cultures
  adaptive 29
  aesthetic 5, 30–33, 47–48
  contact between 5, 57–58, 81–83
  elite 28
  identity-suited 153–54
  indifference to 139, 151–52
  material 30
  migration between 53–55, 149–50
  minimal 29–30, 58, 141
  national 29, 58
  normativity of 26–27, 142–43
  organic 28–29, 58, 63–64, 65
  resources of 83
  as social practices 94–95
  societal 29, 59
  see also diversity; identity; property,
    cultural

Davies, Stephen 100, 107
de Beauvoir, Simone 103
de Sousa, Ronald 104–5
dignity 62–63
disability 18–19
  and aesthetic injustice 135–36
  evaluative theories of 125–27
  non-evaluative theories of 125–26, 127–30
  and weaponized aesthetics 130–32
  see also blindness
disagreement 71–72, 98
diversity
  aesthetic 5, 6, 27, 30, 41–44, 48–49, 75–76
  finally good 68–69
  interest in 6, 66–68, 72–73, 118–19, 121–
    22, 123–24, 136–38, 156–57
  and network theory 44–46, 48–49
Dotson, Kristie 101
Dworkin, Ronald 149

Eaton, Anne 104
emotion, *see* affect
engagement 51–52, 74
error theory 21–22, 44, 162
ethics, *see* morality
ethnocentrism 162–63
evaluation, aesthetic 34–35; *see also* ideals
expertise 44, 97, 101–2

Fanon, Frantz 93, 116
Feinberg, Joel 91

Feld, Steven 89
Forster, Georg 29
Franklin, Benjamin 13, 115
Fricker, Miranda 101, 102, 139–40

gamelan 100
Gaskell, Ivan 83
Geertz, Clifford 162–63

Hamermesh, Daniel 111
Hannerz, Ulf 24
harm 6, 7–8, 10, 11
Hart, Herbert L. A. 112–13
Haslanger, Sally 104, 105, 108–10, 126–27
Herder, Johann Gottfried 29
Hobbes, Thomas 64
Hopkins, Robert 134
Hume, David 40, 41
Hutcheson, Francis 32, 38

ideals 106–7, 130–31; *see also* beauty ideals;
    evaluation, aesthetic
identity 140–41
  accommodations for 147–48, 157–58
  aesthetic 150–51
  cultural associates of 142–43
  and culture 28, 141–42, 153–54
  minority 140, 143–44
  prejudice 139–40
  and value 141, 142–44
ideology 103–6
  defects of 106
  impact of 105
  scope of 104
  sources of 104–5
  vehicles of 104
injustice 3, 8, 56–57
  aesthetic 3–4, 6, 19–22
  affective 8
  epistemic 34, 101–2, 135–36
  social 7–10
  see also appropriation; beauty ideals;
    disability; ideology; identity;
    weaponized aesthetics
insignia 94–95
Irvin, Sherri 111

Jeffers, Chike 139
Jefferson, Thomas 115

Kennedy, John 17–18

INDEX 181

Kymlicka, Will 29, 59, 62, 68–69

Langford, Roslyn 87
language 67, 152–53
Lena, Jennifer 32
Levinson, Jerrold 41
Lévi-Strauss, Claude 31–32
liberalism 61, 63, 68–69, 73
  basic 155
  essential entitlements of 144, 155–56, 157–58
  procedural 144–45, 146–47
  robust 144
  see also policies, of cosmopolitan
    accommodation; policies, of customized
    accommodation

MacIntyre, Alasdair 61–62
Mackenzie, Catriona 69–70
MacKinnon, Catharine 108–10
Mason, Andrew 143
Matthes, Erich 83–84
Medusa syndrome 16, 81, 98, 99, 102
Melchionne, Kevin 32
Minnow, Martha 161–62
morality 7–8, 10, 11, 24–25, 120–21, 123
Morrison, Toni 12–14, 114, 116, 117–18, 158
Mothersill, Mary 38, 41
Muldoon, Ryan 69
multiculturalism 15–16, 58; *see also*
  identity; policies, of cosmopolitan
  accommodation; policies, of customized
  accommodation

Nanay, Bence 123
Nehamas, Alexander 64–65
network theory 44, 46–47, 96–97, 121–22
  and derived aesthetic reasons 54
  and diversity 44–46, 48–49
  and practice-internal reasons 49–50
Nguyen, Thi 95–96
Nussbaum, Martha 74, 145

O'Neill, Onora 60, 61–62

Paralympics 152
Patten, Alan 68, 144–45, 146–48, 150, 155
pictures, tactile 17–18, 133–34
Plato 38
pluralism, aesthetic 50–51, 52, 161–62
  awareness of 74–75
  and commensurability 50–51

  and compatibility 51
  and comprehensibility 51, 53
policies
  and aesthetic injustice 75–77, 100–
    1, 122–24
  of cosmopolitan
    accommodation 144, 152–54
  of customized accommodation 148–52, 155
  generic entanglement 144–45,
    147, 149–55
  privatization 65, 144–45, 147, 149, 153
  statutory 84–85, 122–23
  see also communitarianism; liberalism;
    social arrangements
property 85
  cultural 84–86, 101

Rawls, John 56–57, 63, 64–65, 155
Raz, Joseph 51–52, 74–75
reasons, aesthetic 35–37, 49–50, 54, 121–22
recognition 62–63
Reid, Bill 15–17, 81, 96, 101–2, 158
relativism 161
respect 52, 74, 162
  rooted 52–53
  routed 53
Rhode, Deborah 111–12, 113, 122–23
Rings, Michael 25, 26
Rubin, William 89–90

Sandel, Michael 63
Scanlon, Thomas 149
Shelby, Tommie 87, 103–6, 124
Shiner, Larry 90
Sibley, Frank 37
Silvers, Anita 125, 128–29, 131–32, 136,
  141, 146
social arrangements 4, 10, 56–57
social autonomy 6, 69, 70–73, 98, 101–
  2, 157–58
social positions 8, 9
Sontag, Susan 111–12
Soucek, Brian 77
Spirit of Haida Gwaii: Black Canoe, see
  Reid, Bill
Steinberg, Leo 133–34
stereotypes, *see* social positions
Stock, Kathleen 108–9
Strohl, Matthew 95–96

talent 18, 129–30, 135, 136, 137–38, 146–47

182 INDEX

Taylor, Charles 62–63
Taylor, Paul 108, 114, 117–18
Thomson, Rosemary Garland 131
Todd, Loretta 98–99, 101
Tully, James 15–16
Tylor, Edward Burnett 28–29

value
  aesthetic 31, 35, 37
  dimensional 128
  and identity 141, 142–44
  intrinsic 128
  see also aesthetic hedonism, network theory
Van der Berg, Servaas 41

Waldron, Jeremy 26, 58

Ware, Lauren 123
weaponized aesthetics 7, 9–12, 65–66, 156, 162
Whitman, Walt 28
Widdows, Heather 13, 103, 119–21, 122–23, 132
Wieland, Christoph Martin 27
Williams, Bernard 40
Wolf, Naomi 103
Wollheim, Richard 69, 149

Yahgulanaas, Michael Nicoll 16–17, 96, 98, 158
Young, Iris Marion 25, 105
Young, James O. 85–86, 105